W9-CFN-258

THAT
WE
MIGHT
LIVE

ABOUT THE AUTHOR

GRACE C. NASH, violinist, teacher and established author of twenty books that use music, language and movement to foster child development, is an internationally known educator with a spine-tingling past that is now revealed in a highly personal account of her imprisonment by the Japanese during World War II in the Philippines.

"It is a story you won't believe," says the author, "but it had to be told."

Mrs. Nash resides in Scottsdale, Arizona with her husband, Ralph.

THAT WE MIGHT LIVE

By

GRACE C. NASH

SHANO
Publishers

Scottsdale, Arizona

Published by:
SHANO PUBLISHERS
Post Office Box 1753-N
Scottsdale, AZ 85252

Produced by Lewis Associates, Phoenix, AZ
Cover illustration by Desert Sky Art & Graphics, Phoenix, AZ

Table of Contents

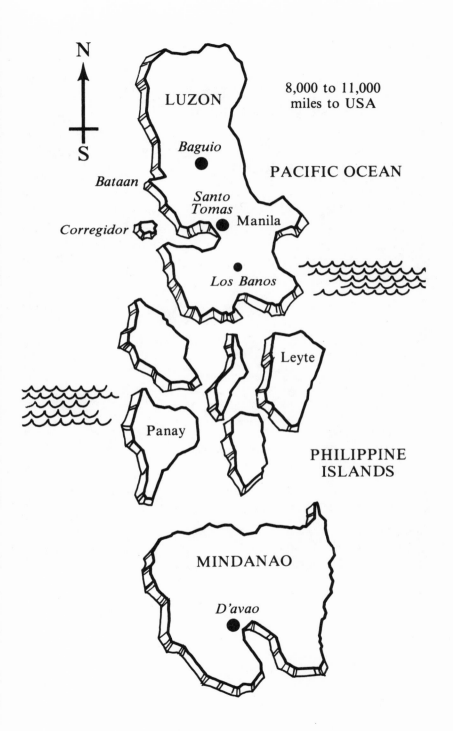

The Nash Family, 1945

DEDICATION

A Letter To Our Sons

Dear Stan, Gale and Roy,

This book is the story of our experiences in World War II in the Philippines. You are the main characters. You gave us the strength and commitment to survive, and although you were too young then to realize or remember what took place, we want you and your families to have this true account of our imprisonment by the Japanese.

We want you to know about the fleeting moments of joy, fun and food during the long periods of our separation, hunger and fear; to know how courageous and great you were as small children — and you still are; how you shared and cared for each other in your distinctly different ways.

I believe you will agree that these experiences, sordid as they were, have been an unconscious part of your growing up — contributing factors in your present sense of values beyond the material, in your various commitments and belief in yourself, in your care and concern for others.

We were not alone. Many people of different nationalities were involved in our survival. They gave that we might live — even to the enemy.

With love,

Mother and Dad

FOREWORD

A personal experience account is for the general reader only as good as the writing of it. That is to say, the selection of concrete detail, the characters, the scenes and the themes are combined in a dramatic presentation.

"That We Might Live" reads for this retired English teacher like good fiction, with its suspense, its dramatized themes of war, loss, death and survival. It has been said that truth is stranger than fiction. That is not so, of course. What is so, however, is that true experiences have rarely been written with the compelling intensity of art. Grace Nash has accomplished this feat.

I don't think I have ever read anything in fiction or biography that portrays any better the determination and will power of a mother to keep life going in those about her.

William Parquette, fellow survivor and
former Reporter with the Boston Globe

Prologue

HOW IT HAPPENED /
THE VIOLIN

In 1936 I boarded a ship for Manila to become the bride of a man I had met nine months before — on a train going to Chicago. It was a storybook romance between an American engineer home on leave from the Philippines and a music teacher who was struggling to get a master's degree in violin and composition at Chicago Musical College. Ralph Nash, an engineer, had lived in the Orient for ten years — in Japan, Formosa, and then in the Philippines since 1930 — and was an experienced traveler and businessman. I had grown up on a farm in Ohio, attended small colleges and taught in public schools near Cleveland. My traveling had been with college choirs and a trip to Buffalo to visit my Great Aunt Lou. The worldly side of my education consisted of playing violin as a stroller in the Chicago Bar & Grille to help with my tuition and living costs in graduate school.

That train ride on January 1st, 1936 changed the entire course of my life, altering my perspectives, my sense of values and my understanding of people. As I think back it seems strange how many times a single event or incident has changed the focus of my life. It is curious too that many of these changes have occurred about ten years apart — except one, an acquisition which has followed and affected my life thereafter, even unto death!

How could one acquired possession — in this instance, a violin — hold such influence and control over its owner? It has no papers or proof of origin or maker and therefore is of limited commercial value, but it isn't just any violin, to be sure. It is Italian

1

in pattern and slightly smaller than usual.

My getting it was a mere happenstance. In 1928 I needed some violin strings before going back to college. The violin shop was upstairs in a back room on a side street in Akron, Ohio. As I walked in, Mr. Rellini looked up from his work bench with his usual greeting. "Hello, hello, Miss Chapman." He selected the strings I asked for. "Yes, business is bad," he said. "Everybody's poor, but some are desperate." He brought down a case from the shelf above. "See this?" he said, taking out a violin and bow. "The young lady who owns it needs money. Her father is in the hospital. She's a fine player, but she must have money." He put the instrument into my hands. "Try it."

The rest of my shopping was forgotten. With the violin case held tight against my body, I hurried back to my father's insurance office, the rich sound still singing in my ears. This violin felt so good under my fingers, its tone so mellow and warm, so responsive to the bow. I was excited. How would I approach Father, who professed to hate music? Mother would approve, I knew. "Yes, Grace, it's beautiful and it's time you had a good instrument." Her one year in Oberlin Conservatory had been cut short by her mother's untimely death and later, despite all the farm work and baby tending, she had managed to start the four of us on piano — all except Jim, the oldest and only son who would have nothing to do with "sissy music stuff."

I was the middle child; a tomboy who rode my pony bareback through fields and woods, hoed corn and picked potatoes. "Our second boy," Father often said, until the summer Aunt Mary stayed with us and gave me a few violin lessons, among other things. From then on my interests were divided.

Finally, with enthusiastic support from Mother, my three sisters, and even our own Dr. Miller who loved violin music so much, Father gave in and I took the check to the violin shop the following Monday.

"Wait," said Mr. Rellini, raising a forbidding hand. "There are two conditions that go with this instrument." I was holding the check in mid-air. "Before you take ownership you must promise me two things," he said.

"Yes, yes, Mr. Rellini. What are they?"

"First, that you will never part with this violin." He waited for my response.

"Of course, I intend to keep it," I said, "Forever!"

"Second," He paused and cleared his throat. "That you will never tell what you paid for it."

"I agree," I said, repeating his statement verbatim. He accepted the check and as we shook hands he said, "Guard it always, won't you?"

He saw the question in my eyes and following me to the door, he said softly, "Someday you will know."

Although my high elation was tinged with sadness when I thought about the owner, the fact of my having this violin brought a surge of confidence and urgency to become a fine player.

From the beginning of college my heart was set on performance — playing in a symphony orchestra or a traveling group of some sort. Teaching was the last thing I wanted to do. Maybe, I might accept a college position. However, to be prepared, I finished my AB degree with a double major in music, a major in French, and two minors, Education and English.

It was 1930. The Depression was in full swing. There were no openings in symphony orchestras, and very few orchestras! I must deal with reality. I'd better teach and get it over with first, I said, adding my name and credentials to the list of thirty-five applicants for an opening in a public school in Ohio. It would be doing all the music from first grade through high school, plus junior high English. But the need to get a job, and the competition involved, pushed me on. When the number of applicants had been narrowed to five, I took my violin along to the interview. Out of curiosity or kindness, the Principal asked me to play. "I'll do just a fun piece," I said lightly, and played 'Fiddlin' the Fiddle' for him. Afterwards we both laughed and I got the job.

For five years I continued teaching, my violin always in hand to accompany younger voices, to lead the orchestra in the upper school, and once a year to give an evening recital. But it was far from satisfying. My small salary of $1,200 for the school year was used up for continuing lessons in Cleveland, and Education courses in summer school. Finally I took a chance and tried out for a scholarship in Chicago . . . and made it!

3

After two successive summer scholarships studying violin with Max Fischel at Chicago Musical College, I resigned from teaching that fall in favor of a Bachelor of Music degree — providing I could win a scholarship for tuition and get a playing job to pay for my board and room. It worked! I landed two playing jobs, one during the noon hour at the YMCA; the other at night where I had played as a strolling musician that summer. Neither job paid very much but, with the scholarship and the $200 savings I had extracted from the Ohio Teachers' Retirement Fund I could manage. What I hadn't counted on was Elmer's cunning!

Elmer had come into my life that summer during his frequent nightly visits to the Bar & Grille where I played. He was tall, sleek and handsome to behold — as long as he remained silent. Elmer talked through his nose (sinus trouble, he explained). However I managed to overlook his nasal tones and irregularities in his "early-farm-intermixed-with-Chicago-street-talk" when he escorted me to various night clubs after-hours so I could hear Horace Heidt and other Big Bands. Although he was a reluctant dancer (feet problems, he said) and a very light drinker (just a beer or two), I always felt safe in his car and appreciated his interest, which seemed more father-figure than suitor-like — until at the end of the summer when he offered to drive me back to Ohio. "It's ogay," he said through his nose, "to taghe tibe off. I hab fibe days cubbig to be."

I still couldn't understand just what his business was but his offer meant no train fare and no luggage problem, so I brushed aside any thoughts of my family's reactions to Elmer, and accepted. We drove all night, arriving just in time for Sunday dinner — chicken, biscuits and gravy, etc. — into which Elmer dove without reservations!

Mother was understanding and gentle. Father looked on in awe, clearing his throat every now and then, but my sisters who, after my phone call about driving home with Elmer, had made a special effort to be on hand, stifled their giggles between their off-side remarks at the table. After Elmer's third complete helping, Mother's strawberry shortcake was served and dinner was finished. We showed Elmer to his room where he lapsed into resounding snores for several hours. Over the dishwashing, I tried to answer their questions without success. My sisters never stopped laughing during their nasal imitations of Elmer . . . and I despaired over my unwise acceptance of Elmer's offer.

By the third day it was evident that Elmer was in no hurry to leave. Between meals he strolled over our two acres and shook our favorite sugar-pear tree bare of fruit. He investigated the town, end to end, and "Is didder reddy?" became his favorite sentence. A week went by before he finally responded to my urging and said goodbye. It took two starts to get him on his way and I fully realized that his intent had become serious; I would have to come to grips with the problem when I returned to Chicago, later. Right now we all heaved great sighs of relief as his car gunned out of the driveway.

My first night back in Chicago, Elmer appeared at the Bar & Grille, delighted to see me despite his somewhat subdued countenance. I told him about my scholarship and the $200 Retirement refund. "I can't stay long," he said. "I'll see you tomorrow."

It was a week later before he returned, looking depressed and downcast. He had lost his job, he said, because of too much time in Ohio. "I'm broke," he added. I should never have let him drive me home — famous last words I had said to myself a thousand times before, now repeated with real remorse and feelings of guilt added. I offered my sympathy to the fullest. He brightened with, "My brudder says he'll hab a job for be in a weeg or so ... but could you possibly lend be sub cash for dow? Two hudred dollars would do it," he said, "and I'll hab it back to you in two weegs."

Two weeks, three, four and more went by with no word, no Elmer, and no response from the one phone number he had given me. His disappearance in gangland fashion was a bitter experience. I had paid dearly for that ride to Ohio. There would be no further entanglements with the opposite sex. I was through with men!

Over the next few weeks and months I studied all the harder, practiced more and often went without breakfast for lack of funds. Further declaration of my resolve about "men" came during Christmas vacation at home when by choice, I refused a New Year's Eve invitation from an old flame, preferring to stay at home with my parents over a glass of ginger ale!

Although my classes would not be starting until January 8th, I was returning to Chicago on New Year's Day to keep my playing jobs — noontimes at the YMCA and dinner hours at the Bar and

Grille just below the college location.

Florence, my youngest sister, and Frank, her fiance were driving me to Cleveland to board the train. We were ready to leave when Father spoke. "Grace, I don't want you riding the Coach to Chicago," he said, pressing a bill into my hand. "I want you to have a Pullman seat."

I argued, pushing the bill away. My sense of independence bristled under adversity. He handed the bill to Frank. "See that Grace has a Pullman ticket, Frank, and thank you."

At the Cleveland Station, amid jokes and laughter, Frank got the ticket and handed over my ten pieces of luggage to the Porter. *"I'm* carrying my violin, Frank. It stays with me!" I said.

"Magazines," called Florence, pulling me toward the newsstand. By the time I got on the train my luggage was spread over the car seat and I was trying to decide which pieces to put in the overhead rack — my saxophone, clarinet and radio, or suitcases and boxes.

"Let me help you," a masculine voice said. I turned to see a well dressed businessman, smiling.

The train ride to Chicago was followed by a late dinner at the College Inn. He was on leave from Manila, an American engineer and head of an office branch there. His descriptions of life and travel in the Orient were intriguing. "I'll have a few days in Chicago," he said. "What should I see?" He wrote down my suggestions of shows, concerts and places I had also wanted to take in. "These sound wonderful," he said, "if you will go, too." "You must be a serious musician," he added. "I practically grew up with my brother's practicing, and my ex-wife (we are separated)," he continued, "is a radio and concert pianist."

The next day while I was playing for the "Blue Plate Special" at the YMCA, I glanced down from the small podium — straight into his eyes. My bow skittered across the strings and my face colored to match the piece I was playing, "Red Sails in the Sunset." At intermission I gained composure and went over to his table.

"Your music —" he said, standing, "you must never let anything take you away from it. Please sit down." After a few words of greeting, he said casually, "I have two tickets for 'The Great Waltz' tomorrow evening. Could I persuade you to go with me?"

6

"I would love to," I responded enthusiastically. (I was dying to see it!) — "if I can finish my playing early from the dinner hour."

"The Chicago Bar & Grille, isn't it? I'll be there to hear you and then we'll go to the theater." He finished his cherry pie and left for a business appointment.

After "The Great Waltz," we used up the rest of the week taking in the Art Museum, a symphony concert and several night clubs, followed by late evening strolls along Michigan Avenue, sharing our thoughts, family histories and our hopes. On Friday, January 6th, his last day in Chicago, we met for breakfast. Over coffee his conversation became serious. His plans were confirmed, he said quietly. He would see his parents in California, then go to Seattle, the Home Office, and while there see his wife and arrange for a long delayed divorce. Then, would I come to Manila in the fall and marry him? "You'll be able to continue your music there," he had added. "Opportunities are unlimited — and our servants will do the housework."

I heard my voice answer him quite calmly, "Yes, I will come." It was January 6th, a date that was to have special significance in the years ahead.

That same night I had finished playing at the Bar & Grille and was changing from evening dress in my dormitory room when I was called to the phone.

"Grace, dear, this is your Cousin Grace from New York. I am in Chicago for a few days. Couldn't you join me for dinner here at the Drake Hotel? I do want to hear about your music and what you are doing."

I was more than surprised. "Yes, I certainly can, Cousin Grace. It will be wonderful to see you."

"My chauffeur, John, will call for you — in half an hour?"

"Fine, I'll be at the doorway of the college." I put down the phone. Cousin Grace was Mother's cousin who lived in The Plaza Hotel in New York City. I was her namesake which made me feel very special, but in her presence we each felt blessed — especially at Christmas time when her huge box of personally wrapped gifts arrived in the mail. We were in awe of her wealth and marveled at her zest for life, and her genuine interest in our pursuits and accomplishments. And tonight I was bursting with desire to tell her about Ralph, as well as my now completed Bachelor of Music degree and beginning of a Masters.

Three days later in the Registrar's office with Cousin Grace, arrangements for my enrollment in doubled courses for an M.M. degree were finalized. I was one semester ahead in violin credits, therefore I could TRY double courses in counterpoint and composition, they said, and write my thesis during the summer, before leaving for Manila. "Grace dear, since this is your last opportunity for study, why not give up all those restaurant engagements and devote full time to your work? Let this be my wedding present to you and Ralph," she said, making out one check to Chicago Musical College and another to me for living expenses. "It will make me so happy," she finished.

Could all this be real? For many days afterwards, I kept pinching myself just to make sure. I wrote to my parents in Florida with a glowing report about Ralph Nash, engineer, and my hopes to earn a Master's degree through Cousin Grace's enormous gift.

I had been known to brag about my ability to go without sleep, but now with double sessions and preparations under two terrifying artist-composers, my nights dissolved into dawns, sometimes without removing my clothes. Other times I would sleep from 2 to 5 am, arise to finish an assignment for my 9 o'clock class and continue. Meanwhile the subject and outline for my thesis had been approved for writing in the summer. I could put that out of my mind for now, but somehow the thought of not receiving my degree with the other six graduates in June really bothered me. Six weeks to go. I started writing and writing.

Exams were finished. The violin recital I had given the previous summer counted for my Master's requirement, so I had two days left before Commencement. I began typing the manuscript at 7 pm the next night. Mother was arriving at noon on the following day, even though she knew I wouldn't be receiving my degree at the evening exercises. What a surprise awaited her — IF I could make it. With cokes and coffee, I continued on through the night.

I rolled the last sheet into the typewriter at 7 am . . . It was done! After a cold shower, more mouth wash and fresh coffee, I hurried to the Registrar's office, folder in hand. "For Max Fischel, my Advisor, Mrs. Farquar," I said. "The committee agreed to accept his judgment on my thesis if I delivered it this morning," I explained.

"Yes, Grace, I know. Mr. Fischel is coming at 9 o'clock." She seemed to be staring at me. "Grace, are you all right? Your skin looks yellow."

At one o'clock when I returned from the train station with Mother, there was a note on my door from the Registrar's office. "Be on stage at 7 tonight," it said, "to receive your degree." I shouted my exuberance, twirled my diamond ring three times in the June sunlight, and danced my mother around the room. It was all too wonderful.

After the graduation and concert, we had hot fudge sundaes at Schraffts and then we talked until dawn. "I do love Ralph so very much," I said, "and if father hadn't insisted on that Pullman ticket, I never would have met him." We talked about my violin, too. "It seems as if so many wonderful things have happened to me, Mother, since getting this instrument."

My skin that had turned yellow from lack of sleep finally normalized. There was long overdue dental work to attend to, shopping, passport forms, etc. and many trips into Akron. Margaret, my older sister who lived nearby, took charge of dress alterations, measurements and reduction of my weight. I must lose seven pounds! So I went from dental sessions to Turkish baths and melba toast. One afternoon, however, instead of the Turkish bath, I went directly from the dentist to the passport photographer, forgetting that novocain shots affect one's facial expression. The results were horrendous — one half of my face looked frozen, embalmed, while the other side folded into a lopsided smile!

Letters were coming regularly from Manila, filled with plans and loving thoughts; several were addressed to my parents, reassuring them, and one letter was Ralph's reply to my sister Florence's "confidential" report on the idiosyncracies and strange eating habits of his future bride! True, I did have a healthy appetite, and sometimes I even relished the taste of mashed potatoes or celery — after my dessert.

Neighbors and former classmates stopped in. They couldn't imagine my going so far away. "You'll get so homesick, Grace. How can you do it?" But I had never experienced homesickness, maybe lonesomeness a few times for my pony, or just the 'feel' of home and the smell of warm crusts of bread spread with butter and brown sugar, or chocolate cake. But not real homesickness. There were too many other things, and never enough time for my practicing.

At last my trunk was packed, every garment measured to match my exact weight, 116 pounds. I would take the train to California to meet Ralph's parents who would then drive me to Seattle to meet his one sister and family before boarding the S.S. Jefferson for Manila in late September.

After a farewell dinner of fried chicken and strawberry shortcake, much visiting and laughter, Father called me into the bedroom. He had arranged for the midnight train to be flagged down at our small station and he seemed quite resigned to my leaving, contrary to his usual objections-on-principle to our requests. "I have something to show you, Grace." He brought out a typewritten letter. "You don't think, do you, that I'd be letting you go off to the other side of the world and marry a man we know very little about?"

"But, Father," —

Interrupting, he handed me the letter. "Here is a report," he said.

It was a copy of a letter addressed to Uncle John Chapman, Father's older brother in the Cleveland office of their insurance company — a confidential resume of Ralph's character, integrity, solvency and business record. He had been given a straight "A."

I looked up from the letter as Father spoke. "You're marrying a fine man, Grace, and I know you'll be a good wife to Ralph. You have our blessing."

The tears I had held back with jokes and laughter now spilled down my cheeks. Father dabbed them away with his handkerchief, and I hugged him tightly.

Chapter One

MANILA WEDDING /
A NEW LIFE
(1936 - 1941)

After twenty-one days of seasickness, with port stops in Yokohama, Kobe, Shanghai and Hongkong that were scarcely long enough to regain my land legs, I disembarked at Pier 7, Manila, on October 20th, 8 am. Grasping the folds of my skirt band with one hand, my violin and purse in the other, I started down the gangplank. If only Margaret could see me now, I thought. Thinner than a fence post! I'd have to eat bushels to grow back into my trousseau. I ran into Ralph's arms. With his party of friends at the Pier, we were escorted to the Bayview Hotel for refreshments and good wishes. I wanted so much to make a good impression, but I couldn't seem to drink beer at this hour in the morning, on top of my 'mal-de-mer' hangover! My corsage of gardenias was wilting fast in the steaming heat, and I could hardly breathe. The air was so soft I had no sensation of inhaling or exhaling. But I smiled a lot and tried to make light conversation.

With shopping for furniture, Ralph's work at the office, cocktail and dinner parties, wedding arrangements, the next four days went very fast. I chose our wedding music, to be played by Ernesto Vallejo, who was known as the "Heifetz of the Far East," and Spanish pianist, Julio Esteban-Anguita, both esteemed friends and soon to become my colleagues and partners in music making.

At the Ellinwood Church, before going down the aisle, I listened intently to their music — *Bach's Air* for the G String, *Romance* from the Wieniawski violin concerto — wishing my family could be there. After the ceremony we went to the Oak Room of the Manila Hotel for the reception and buffet, the only

11

air-conditioned room in the city, other than theaters. Then, in Ralph's light blue Nash car we drove to Baguio Mountains Resort, 350 kilometers away, for our honeymoon.

Ralph's quiet disposition, his genuine concern, and his calm but authoritative manner in stores and restaurants gave me a secure feeling. He was a person of few words most of the time and when he smiled an aura of joy radiated around him. It was a wonderful week. We took morning walks around the Country Club, breathing in the brisk mountain air and fragrance of flowers more brilliant than I'd ever seen. During rainy afternoons we sat by a blazing fire in our honeymoon cottage. Baguio was almost a temperate climate in comparison to the equatorial heat of Manila.

We had been married only two months when Dr. Lippay, Vienese conductor of the Manila Symphony asked me to play solo with the orchestra. The January concert was three weeks away. With Turkish towels around my neck to absorb perspiration, I plunged into practicing. The high humidity and temperature were enervating; my violin lacked resonance. "That's to be expected," Dr. Lippay said. But I was worried. I had never played it in a large theater with a full orchestra. In solos with piano or organ, in string quartets it projected well.

The final rehearsal in the empty theater gave forth too many echoes to judge either balance or projection. Ralph had seen to the stage lights and had helped select a royal blue gown embroidered with rhinestone butterflies. That evening with butterflies also in my stomach and apprehensive fingers, I walked on to the stage. With those first solo strains of the Bruch Concerto, I gained confidence. I could feel and hear the clear, resonant tones of my violin over the orchestra. There came a long ovation from the audience, then Ralph's wholehearted response. He was now my most dependable critic. "Your role in the musical life of Manila is launched," he said (and it would spread into many areas before January 6, 1942).

THE PHILIPPINES HERALD
January 20, 1937
MRS. R. NASH RECEIVES PROLONGED
OVATION AS SOLOIST IN SYMPHONY
CONCERT AT METROPOLITAN
Mrs. Ralph Nash, violinist, scored a definite
triumph when she made her first appearance before

12

*a Manila audience as soloist of the symphony
concert given in the Metropolitan Theatre under
the direction of Alexander Lippay. Mrs. Nash
played the solo part of Bruch's Concerto in G minor,
Op. 26. She displayed excellent technique and rich
tone quality which evoked an unusually enthusiastic
response from the audience. Mrs. Nash was given
an overwhelming ovation.*

Our first son, Ralph Stanley Nash was born in late October, 1937. Gale, our second son arrived thirteen months later. Meanwhile I had played one season with the symphony, seated beside Ernesto Vallejo, as assistant concert master. I was the only woman, and only American in the orchestra. It was a challenge to keep up with them. I also belonged to a Chamber Music group which met each week and presented a series of radio concerts.

In September, 1939, three years after my departure from Ohio, I sailed for the States with Stan and Gale to see our families in California and Ohio. Ralph would join us in time for Thanksgiving. Without our accustomed amahs to look after Stan and Gale, and with my continuous sea sickness, the voyage was a nightmare. Our return trip with Ralph along would be much easier. In the States we had glorious reunions with both families and friends from coast to coast. Our tow-headed tots made lasting impressions on their grandparents, aunts and uncles. As for Ralph, his reserved manner may have surprised some, but his warm smile and forthrightness won him respect wherever we went.

In late February we said goodbye and traveled by train to Los Angeles where we boarded the S.S. Hoover for Manila. Ralph was looking forward to our scheduled port stops in Japan. It would be good to see Tokyo and Kobe again. He had spent a year in Japan before taking over the Manila office in 1930.

Upon reaching Yokohama, Port of Tokyo, passengers were asked to submit stool specimens and fill out numerous forms giving itinerary, destination, family names, etc., all of which we made light of — and then complied. Japanese police lined the Pier. "No cameras ashore, and no more than twenty cigarettes," they said. With other passengers from the ship we climbed into their charcoal-fueled bus and headed for the Imperial Hotel in Tokyo.

13

After my usual bout of sea sickness I was glad to be on land, even though Japan was extremely cold in both weather and attitude. In the hotel, Ralph's one time headquarters, he spied his former room boy. "Boisan, Komo," he called, hurrying across the Lobby to greet him. Komo stood there expressionless, looking blankly over Ralph's head. He then turned and walked away. This was the first of many shocks. Another was to see two such booming cities — Tokyo and then Kobe — in the throes of austerity, with no heat in their hotels or shops and few people on the streets. In the shops, clerks turned their backs to avoid serving us. We were like enemies in their sight. Why this change in attitude? Japan must be on her last legs economically — on the verge of collapse unless she could make peace with China, were our immediate reactions. Her war with China had been going on since 1937!

Our group of eight planned to have a sukiyaki dinner before going back to the ship but we couldn't get served. Only through contact with the American Embassy did we finally have dinner. By this time we also realized that we had been followed most of the day, and our cabins had been searched! We were baffled by this change in Japan. Only later would we learn about their rapid indoctrination of white race hatred under a military regime.

Our ship continued on its way, by-passing Shanghai. Spring in Hongkong was a welcome change. After shopping and sightseeing, we enjoyed an all-Chinese dinner on the roof terrace of the Hongkong Hotel overlooking this city-of-lights in the Far East.

Then Manila once again, with its soft tropical breeze, warm sunshine, highly colored flowers, the same servants to greet us — Sofronio and Tonia, our cook and housegirl, Peen our Chauffeur, and Ah Kwai San, our beloved amah. Stan and Gale, once more under her watchful eyes, thrived on their daily sunbaths and swimming at the Polo Club pool. Ralph was again in his routine of diesels, castings and engineering, and weekly meetings as secretary of the Rotary Club. I was practicing daily, before the schools opened in June, 1940.

All too soon my projects and obligations increased. The Children's Art Center, begun the year before by several colleagues and myself, was attracting more and more children and parents. Besides concert playing, I was asked to teach the music classes at the American School, and in addition to directing the all-city

14

Junior Orchestra, I became Music Critic of the *Manila Daily Bulletin* newspaper.

Refugees from war-torn China began pouring into Manila, bringing first-hand reports about the "Rape of Nanking," bombings of Shanghai and Hongkong. I played in numerous benefit concerts for them. How much longer could Japan continue this cruel war? What we had seen in Tokyo so recently indicated her resources were practically exhausted. Could we have been wrong? A growing concern over the imminence of war infiltrated cocktail and dinner parties, civic meetings and newspapers. No one wanted to admit such possibilities — even after the Navy and army wives were sent home. People said what they wanted to hear from others: "There's nothing to worry about. Japan can't touch us; she'd be wiped out! And she knows it!"

I was in the minority; almost an outcast in these conversations. I had a gut feeling, without any facts, figures or geographical knowledge to back it up. I just felt that war was coming; that the Islands were defenseless. Like most Americans in business in Manila, Ralph's company was doing very well. He was involved with new engineering projects for the government. This was not the time to pick up and leave, he said.

We had had few arguments in our marriage; very few in fact, because Ralph refused to argue. There were times, however, when his actions would reveal a change of heart. Now the subject of war was to become a sore point between us. The first time I brought up my concern and each time thereafter, his response was unchanged: "I'll get you the tickets. You and the boys go home but I can't leave." My answer was repeated each time with variations: "I don't want to leave without you." Then, "I won't leave without you," and finally, "No, I refuse to go home without you." Yet the dark feeling of war never left me. I knew it was coming . . . so why couldn't I bring myself to leave?

If I had analyzed the reasons for my insistent refusals to take the children and go home, the truth might have shamed me into leaving at once or have made me even more determined to stay. Either way I presume that I couldn't or didn't wish to face the truth: that Ralph was more married to his work and his company than to me! His good friend, Bill Chittick had warned me several times. "Don't let Ralph bring his office work home, Grace. He's been married to his job too long. He needs to learn how to play."

More and more I had seen how Ralph loved his work — not only the creative engineering but all aspects of it — and his was a unique position. Not only was he Number "1" American in the Manila branch, he was the *only* American. His staff was all-Filipino, loyal and able. He had taken over the Manila assignment when embezzlement by a former manager had bankrupted the firm. It had taken dedication far beyond a 40-hour week to bring it to the present prospering and respected company. And now as vice president of the Seattle Home Office he had every reason to be proud of his business and engineering acumen, as well as his recent yearly bonuses.

There was no doubt in my mind that he loved us, yet the strong dedication, concern and responsibility that he felt toward his company had become more evident of late. Perhaps my own self-esteem and pride together with a questioning that kept edging into my thoughts prevented me from admitting to myself that we, his wife and sons, were not as important at this crucial time as his work for the company and/or his financial success.

Mixed with these denials and questions were my distraught feelings of guilt over the thought of leaving him to face destruction and even death without us. I couldn't bring myself to leave. And so our hectic pace continued, with more projects and activities filling the days and nights. There were social functions, despedida parties, teaching and ever more concerts that had to be reviewed.

Our usual custom after the Friday night symphony concerts was to meet with friends in the Palm Garden of the Manila Hotel for refreshments and relaxed conversation. On this particular Friday evening, December 5th, 1941, a Navy Captain had joined our party. We were sipping drinks, gazing up at the star-filled sky and nearly full moon when someone said, quietly, "What a perfect night for a surprise bombing!"

The Captain to my right spoke out quickly. "Don't be foolish! Why, we could finish off their navy over the weekend!"

With such authoritative words, everyone settled back comfortably in their rattan chairs. It was such a beautiful night and in a few minutes we said our goodnights to the group. It was time to write my review for Monday morning's newspaper.

16

Chapter Two

WAR STRIKES THE PHILIPPINES
(December 8, 1941)

s Peen, our driver took us home that night, I kept thinking what that Navy Captain had said. I wanted so much to believe him. My hand closed over Ralph's and I edged closer to him. "If the captain's right," I said softly, "there's really no need to worry about a war with Japan." Ralph didn't answer. He leaned over and kissed me lightly.

"Besides," I continued, "isn't Kurusu in Washington right now, conferring with Secretary Hull? The way he rushed into and out of Manila indicates the Japanese government is worried — they're scared yellow," I chuckled, and then recalled that it was Mr. Kurusu who had ruined our dinner party the week before when he had arrived in Manila unannounced, without any diplomatic papers or visa — essentials for his immediate departure to Washington. It had fallen to Jack from the High Commissioner's office to supply these papers. "It will take hours," explained his wife in her frantic phone call just ten minutes before the scheduled hour of our dinner. "Please forgive us . . ." And *they* were our designated guests of honor!

Writing the concert review that night took more time than usual. Between the Captain's words about finishing off the Japanese Navy over the weekend and trying to find understanding words about the concert coming at full moon time — with its ill-effects on the musicians — made this review difficult. The saying "Only mad dogs and Englishmen go out in the noonday sun" had a parallel appropriate in the islands: "When Filipinos and baying dogs stay out (all night) in full moon's light — disaster reigns on concert night!''

Ralph was sleeping soundly when I climbed under the mosquito net at 2 am. My thoughts and fears had eased and I soon closed my eyes against the silver shaft of moonlight that played back and forth on our bedroom wall through the swaying curtains.

I awoke at 7:30 with a faint dream-memory of distant planes in formation. Stan and Gale were eating breakfast and Ralph had already left for the office. No school today but many other things to do, yet I felt quite relaxed and equal to the day's schedule. After typing my review for messenger delivery to the newspaper office, I played outside with the boys and then made several phone calls confirming our reservation for a holiday cottage at Tagaytay Ridge the week after Christmas. It was to be a perfect vacation place for all of us after our heavy schedules, programs and festivities during the next three weeks. Tagaytay was only forty kilometers from Manila, and cooler than the city. With no phone or radio we could relax and enjoy our boys together.

Ralph came home for lunch but had to return to the office. Peen would be back to drive Ah Kwai and the boys to Donny's birthday party at 3 pm . . . and I must leave for orchestra practice. Putting my baton inside the violin case, I hurried to the American School two blocks away.

This would be the final rehearsal for my junior orchestra before their many Christmas appearances. With several players leaving for the States, we'd have some rearranging to do but these young people could meet the challenge, I knew. They were real pioneers, proud and determined about their achievement — the first youth orchestra in Manila, with many nationalities among their forty-five members. The city had responded with applause, editorials and invitations. Nineteen Christmas programs had been scheduled.

Before the last piece that afternoon, Burt Fonger, their elected president and drummer-timpanist of the orchestra, gave out the program schedule and reminded them that "professionals play and *act* like professionals." The orchestra was sounding better and better, I thought. How exciting it was to work with such kids. Where else could one find such rewards? Manila was an open door of opportunities. You could turn your hand to any task and get results . . . and there were so many areas to choose from.

At home Ralph and I listened to birthday party reports from Stan and Gale over their scarcely touched supper. "The ice cream and cake were so-o good," they explained. "There were clowns and balloons, too. When can *we* have a party?" Gale's third birthday was scarcely a week away, December 15th — just too close to Christmas, was my parental excuse, but we would certainly have a birthday cake and candles — and presents, too, I assured him.

This was our first Saturday evening at home in some time. We sat outside on the screened porch and talked about Christmas, our vacation plans. Our gifts and greeting cards had been mailed six weeks before and should be arriving in the States in another two weeks. (None of those packages or cards ever reached the States; and none of our families' gifts ever reached us.)

It was ten o'clock and time for the news. We listened to Don Bell, our Manila newscaster. "Hitler's armies are advancing through blizzards into the outskirts of Moscow." Would this mean the fall of Russia? A frightening situation, I thought. "In Washington D.C., two Japanese diplomats are still conferring with Secretary Hull," Bell continued. "There is no report as yet." With no further news on war threats in the Pacific, we turned off the radio and went to bed.

Unknown to us, at that moment Japanese guns were pointed at the Philippines from all four directions.* Huge convoys had been sighted in the South China seas by our merchant ships and our P-40's. Peace talks between Secretary Hull and Japanese envoys had reached a stalemate. On November 24th, nearly two weeks earlier, our Pacific commanders had been radioed that a "surprise aggressive movement in any direction" — even the Philippines or Guam — was a possibility.

On November 27th, three days later, warnings of war had been sent to General MacArthur, High Commissioner Sayre, and Admiral Hart. However, MacArthur believed an attack would not be launched before April of '42. Later he changed his mind to a January date. Meanwhile, a task force was steaming toward Pearl Harbor. In Manila, President Quezon strongly advocated neutrality for the islands — like Switzerland. He sincerely believed such a neutrality would be honored by the Japanese, even if war were declared.

Some of the long-promised B-17 Flying Fortresses and P-40

fighter planes had arrived at Clark Field from Hawaii, where they remained wing to wing, carefully guarded against sabotage by soldiers. More planes, tanks and men would be coming soon on ～U.S. ships. On this Saturday night, December 6th, 1941, the 27th Bombardment Group of 1200 airmen had taken over the Manila Hotel Ballroom for a celebration party honoring their Major General Lewis H. Brereton. The party continued into Sunday's dawn.*

On Sunday we put aside our usual work and took the boys to the Polo Club for swimming, Ralph's softball game and an early lunch. The usual Sunday crowd had dwindled but there was still plenty of laughter, as well as cheers and boos during the ballgame that covered any war talk and current rumors. So far no word had come from the High Commissioner's office advising Americans to return to the States, so why should we think of leaving, was the reasoning. The fact that there might not be ships or planes available to take us home wasn't mentioned.

Sunday afternoon I wrote up my class plans and rehearsal schedule for the coming week while Ralph and the boys took their siestas. Later I practiced violin for my part in the coming Benefit Concert on Friday, but my mind wandered far from the composition at hand. I was thinking about my family in the States, what each of them might be doing: Florence in Boston, newly married to Dr. Robert Pearson, surgeon; Mabel, married to Jack, a lawyer in Cleveland; Margaret and her husband, John in Akron at the Radio Station; Jim, Helen and family also in Akron; and Mother and Father in Florida, catching blue gills and worrying about each of us. (I wouldn't know for a long, long time that within the month, Florence's husband would be on his way to Europe as surgeon in the Armed Forces; Margaret would have joined the USO, entertaining our troops and teaching Morse Code to 1200 sailors in Boot camp while John would be in Radar for the Navy; and Father fighting cancer.)

The Sunday evening news brought no further word on Japanese peace talks in Washington, so we went to bed. Mornings, we left so early we seldom turned on the radio for news. Ralph was at his office at 7 am, and I had to be at the American School at 7:30

_____

*Information drawn from the book *American Caesar* by WM Manchester © 1978, Little Brown & Company.

am classes — except on Mondays, my free day. On this particular Monday, Peen was driving Ralph to his office and promptly returning to take me into the city for Christmas shopping.

With shopping list in hand, I put on my sun glasses and hat, ready to go. As I stepped into the car I heard the phone ringing. Sofronio or Ah Kwai would take the message, I said, so we drove on. The stores opened at 7:30 am. Going over my shopping list, I scarcely noticed that groups of people were congregated along Dewey Boulevard; but into the Escolta main street downtown, in front of a Japanese Bazaar, variety store, I saw two policemen rounding up clerks. Why? "Is there a burglary going on, Peen?" "I don't know, ma'am," he answered. As we continued through traffic, there seemed to be more confusion and many people on the streets. Peen let me out at the first store on my list. "Meet me in one hour, Peen, here at this corner. I looked at my watch. "That will be at 8:45, Peen." "Yes, ma'am," he called, driving on.

I hurried into the Hamilton-Brown Department Store and into the elevator. The toy section was on the second floor. In the moving elevator I heard the news: "Pearl Harbor bombed! President Roosevelt has declared war! We're at war with Japan!" "War! War! It's here!"

The elevator had already reached the fourth floor and was starting down. My lips tightened over clenched teeth. I wasn't numb, I was befuddled and angry. Why had I believed that Navy Captain's foolish words? I knew war would come . . . and now it has come! I pushed my way out of the elevator and headed for the toy section. War or not, Stan and Gale were going to have their Christmas presents!

Selecting toys was not as difficult as getting a clerk to wait on me. Clustered with friends, they were panic stricken and didn't want to break away from each other. Most of the clerks had come to work that morning without knowledge of Pearl Harbor or declaration of war.

Outside the streets were filled with people and cars, all pushing their way through traffic against honking horns and shouts of paper boys. Crossing off the rest of my shopping list, I bought a paper and waited on the corner for Peen. We went straight home to find Sofronio and Ah Kwai holding things together. Sofronio had already boxed his few belongings. "I want to go to my family in the provinces," he said. "Yes, Sofronio, I understand." I paid him the next week's wages and wished him well as he mounted his bicycle to ride the sixty kilometers north.

Ah Kwai had not told Stan and Gale about the war. They were playing outside. I put away my packages and went out to them, giving each a big long hug. "We're okey-dokey, Mommie." said Stan, scooping up another shovel of sand into a bucket. "Me, too," added Gale, smiling up at me.

There were messages by the phone: Ralph had called about the news. He wouldn't be home for lunch. Stan's Nursery School had closed until further notice. The Benefit Concert had been canceled.

I must get a notice off to orchestra members about cancellation of our Christmas programs. Many of them attended the American School so I hurried over to the building. It was locked and a small notice on the door said, "Closed indefinitely." Decisions had been made fast. Everyone would know there would be no concerts.

The Philippines were closer to Japan than to Pearl Harbor, so we could expect bombs any time now and any place. I turned on the radio for information: "All schools and colleges had closed; meetings, concerts canceled; stores and offices would close at 4:30 daily so that people could reach home before 6 o'clock curfew and the enforced blackout." With the reports of death and destruction at Pearl Harbor, I shuddered, acutely aware of what could happen here at any minute.

By the time Ralph arrived home at 4:30, news was broadcast that both Clark Field, approximately eighty kilometers north of Manila, and Camp John Hay in Baguio had been bombed! Would Nichols Field be next? We were living in the Pasay residential section of the city, hardly five miles from this well known U.S. Army Air Base.

While Ah Kwai was getting the boys ready for bed, I told them about the blackout, recalling the practice-blackout we'd had a month before. We boosted them up on the window ledge to see the moon and stars and the rooftops of darkened houses along the street. Gazing out, Stan said, "Look, Mommie, they forgot to turn off the moon and stars! What'll we do?"

I thought of the revealing Pasig River that ran through the

city. What chance did we have? Now it would be survival! Trying to stay alive from one raid to the next. No more challenging pleasurable living, nor even comfortable dying in the wake of an enemy known for its inhuman atrocities. What would become of our children? How could we protect them tonight and the days and nights that lay ahead?

With Ralph's help we brought their mattresses downstairs and placed them on the floor close to the inside wall of the livingroom. Like everyone else, we had no air raid shelter, but the thick walls of concrete would offer fair protection.

With darkened windows and only candlelight we retired early but sleep was not within reach for me. In trying to look ahead I took a panoramic view of the past months . . . How many things we were involved in! Had all of our work ended overnight? And what would I do if the enemy tried to rape me? Answers would not come; only anger and tears.

JAPANESE BOMB MANILA
(December 8, 1941)

Nichols Field was bombed! We had expected it, yet the fright that comes with those first bombs is indescribable. I heard a distant drone of planes, but no warning siren. Without waking Ralph, I made my way to the stairs. Halfway down, the house shook with such a jolt that I made the rest of the steps in one leap, landing crumpled on the rug, but Stan and Gale were safe. They scarcely roused.

We must leave Pasay. Go anywhere; away from another bombing so close. Ralph went to the office, showing more calmness than I could pretend to have. I spent the day going from room to room, nervously checking food supplies, our clothes, and putting away letters; I listened to radio news and answered the phone. Everyone was frantic about what to do or where to go. Was there any place that would be safe? And where were our American planes?

When Ralph returned at five o'clock we hurriedly packed the

car with food and a small mattress. Kwai San stayed with us as we headed toward San Juan where we had formerly lived, a few miles north of the city. Mr. and Mrs. Evans, our former San Juan neighbors, offered us shelter for the night together with several other families. We slept on mattresses on the floor. There was only one air raid during the night. Pasay was not bombed.

On Wednesday morning we found a small bungalow in this northern sector of the city. After writing a check for two months rent, we left Kwai San with Stan and Gale at the Evans's while we went back to our Pasay home to gather up more mattresses, mosquito nets, kitchenware, food and a one-burner stove, and of course, my violin.

We reached our newly rented bungalow just before noon and began to unload the car. The sound of enemy planes, followed by a screaming siren, warned us. We raced over to the Evans' house where the children had gone for lunch. We found them with young Georgie Evans squatting inside a freshly dug trench in the front garden. It was only deep enough to protect them from flying shrapnel if they kept their heads between their knees.

Along with the rising drone of planes and thunderous bombs hitting their targets, there was an aerial dogfight going on high overhead between a lone American plane — the only U.S. plane we would see for three years — and two or three Jap planes. From their cramped positions in the trench, Stan and George were still trying to watch the sky, and I could hear George yelling, "Duck, Stan, here comes a plane!" "Where's the duck, George? I don't see it!" shouted Stan, peering upright into the sky. Gale, after keeping his head down for too long, added his voice to the din, "Duck!" "Me duck no more. Me see no duck!" He raised his tired head in defiance of the dangers above.

This raid, aimed at Cavite Navy Yard approximately twenty miles south of Manila, Nichols Field, Pasay and the Polo Club, lasted two hours. It was a tremendous success for the enemy. They had wiped out valuable installations, churches and homes, and killed hundreds of civilians as well as army and navy personnel.

Who would be next? With each successive raid spent in the basement shelter of the Walker family across the street, I went through the same mental horrors, picturing the great numbers killed and injured. The bombings affected Stan and Gale quite

24

differently. Gale would clutch my shaking knees with all his strength, then bury his face in my skirt during those tense moments that would stretch into hours. For Stan, it was excitement. He wanted to go outside and watch the planes, to see the action.

The fear I experienced now was physically exhausting, yet with so many air raids coming during the day, I dared not let the boys out of sight. Each meal, each bath, had to be hurried before another raid would come. In the back of my mind there was increasing anxiety over Ralph who went into the city each day.

Tension increases hunger, yet I couldn't eat. I couldn't sleep. Planes might be upon us before I could get the children over to the shelter. We were defenseless. The islands were defenseless — no possible escape. And what would come with invasion by the enemy? The first hand accounts of the Rape of Nanking and the China massacres that we had heard two months before became more vivid in our minds.

One of the regular noon raids was directed with intensity on the Port area where both Mr. Walker and Ralph had their offices. Each day we expected their section to be bombed. Mrs. Walker and I worried together. At last the "All Clear" sounded. We waited anxiously for a call to know if they were still alive. Finally the phone rang. It was Mr. Walker. I stood by listening to the conversation. "You're all right, Johnnie?" "Oh, no, you're kidding." "I don't believe it!" "What happened?" . . . "Come home, please, right away!" She hung up the phone and paced the floor hysterically. "Grace, a bomb hit in the middle of his office! But he said he is all right! The two men with him weren't hit either, but there's nothing left of the place — except the telephone that he called me on!"

Ralph and his Filipino staff were just across the street from Johnnie Walker's office. With trembling fingers, I dialed his number. Mr. Garcia, one of his salesmen, answered. "No, Mr. Nash is not here," he said. "He was out on a call at the time of the raid. We haven't heard from him yet, but we were not hit. The building across the street was a direct hit!" I put down the phone and waited, praying that Ralph was still alive.

An hour later he drove into the yard. After hugging the boys and sending them out to play, he quietly told me that when the air raid alarm sounded he was on his way to one of the government buildings in the area. He had started for the nearest shelter — the Bureau of Printing Building. On seeing it jammed with office workers, he dodged into a ditch nearby. A few minutes later the Bureau of Printing building was hit! People were blown to bits. "One Filipino, still alive, got up from the debris," he said, "and walked out. The force of the bomb had torn every stitch of clothes from his body, plus several layers of skin!"

Mr. Walker arrived home about four o'clock that afternoon. He described his narrow escape over a double scotch and soda. "I was thrown into the air, back onto the floor, then bounced in the air again, and, thud, to the floor." His calmness after such an experience was unbelievable. He seemed remarkably steady, but two hours later he collapsed from nervous exhaustion. For two days he walked like a drunken man. His hands shook, he couldn't even hold a spoon.

One family from Cavite gave us great concern during the first days of the bombings. The Fennels lived just outside the Cavite Navy Yard and, as meteorologist with Pan American Airways, Les worked closely with the Navy. Jeanette, his wife, was one of my dearest friends, and John, their four-year-old "block-buster," was one of Stan's playmates. Now we couldn't locate them! After the first bombing I had tried to call. No answer. After several days we learned from their Manila office that they had fled to Baguio, 160 miles north of Manila, on December 8th, but Mr. Fennel would be bringing them back to Manila, according to orders.

At least they were still alive. Two days passed before I reached them by phone. They were at the Manila Hotel, but Jeanette's voice told me that all was not well. She was reluctant to talk. Impetuous and high strung, she went on nervous energy much of the time. Her fate was a more bitter one than ours because she and young John were to have left for the States on the last Pan Am Clipper — which had never arrived from the States. Throughout the succeeding 38 months, the thought pursued her, "If only . . ."

The next afternoon between air raids Ralph and I drove to the Hotel to see the Fennels. Jeanette met us in the lobby and poured out the story of their horrendous experiences since December 8th. "At four o'clock on Monday morning, one hour after the Pearl Harbor attack, a naval officer phoned us. 'Get your family out of here, Les. No time to lose. We expect to be bombed any time.' By five o'clock we were on our way to the Baguio Mountains. We arrived at noon and drove to the gate of Camp John Hay. It was heavily guarded and we asked for Mrs. Dudley, the friend who would share her quarters with us. 'Do you know Mrs. Dudley?' the guard asked. 'Yes, of course,' I said, 'we are to be her guests.' 'That's too bad,' he said, 'because she and her baby are casualties of the bombing.' 'What bombing?' I shrieked. 'Where is she?' I still didn't realize that the Japs had hit Baguio while we were driving up those mountain roads.

"Mrs. Dudley and the baby were in the hospital, but no civilians could be housed there; so Les took us over to the Pines Hotel and he waited for darkness before driving back to Manila alone. Driving without lights down the mountain trails took him thirteen hours (the normal driving time was four to five hours.) Blackouts are enforced, even on those mountain roads! His appointment in the Pan American office in Manila the next morning saved him from sure death in the Cavite raid that very day!"

Jeanette continued her story. "Officials advised Les to bring us back to Manila, so on Friday night he drove to Baguio again in the blackout." (I thought of the suspense and nervous tension that Les must have endured, with the greatest strain on the last trip when any misjudgment along those narrow trails would have taken three lives instead of one.) "We were totally exhausted when we entered the Manila Hotel to occupy one of the Pan American rooms there," she said. "A suite of two singles with adjoining bath, and one of those singles was for us. Without a second thought we turned the key. The room was occupied by an unmarried couple in bed! How I have struggled to guard young John's innocence," she went on. "Imagine, adultery and intrigue at a time like this!"

At first the Fennels were hesitant about accepting our invitation to share our bungalow, but with a little more urging they said yes and moved in with us the next day. Thereafter we laughed and cried, consoled and cajoled each other during the long days and nights. Many nights after our children and husbands had retired, Jeanette and I sat outside on the steps discussing the meanings of latest reports from headquarters and exploring every possibility of escape from the inevitable. What might befall us in the hands of the Japanese? We rehearsed these forebodings until mosquitoes had bitten every inch of our exposed flesh and our eyelids were too heavy to linger any longer.

OPEN CITY AND
INVASION BY THE JAPANESE
(January 1, 1942)

The day before Christmas I went into the city to buy food. A young army recruit, surely no more than eighteen, gave me a lift. He was on his way to get his uniforms and baggage in preparation for departure. "Manila is being declared an 'Open City,'" he said. "Our troops are leaving for the north tonight." His remarks made me sick at heart as I thought of the fate that awaited him. "I'm going out," he said, "but I hope to God I get ten of them before they get me."

The wailing of an air raid siren late that Christmas Eve hurried us from our beds to the garage shelter across the street, where we had to remain for three hours while mosquitoes chewed our legs, arms and faces. How ironic, I thought, after the Christmas cards we had mailed to the States a month before. I had written the verses in September, long before even a suggestion of "blackouts" was made. What a sad Christmas this one, with Santa Claus trying to get through between raids. "Will he make it, Mom?" was Stan's question, over and over.

* * * * * * * * * *

'Twas the night before Christmas
And all thru the villa,
Few creatures were stirring,
A Blackout in Manila.

Some stockings were hung
In the darkness with care,
In hopes that St. Nick
Would somehow get there.

The children were hurried to bed very early
To be safe when the siren screamed "Lights out in a hurry";
And I in shinelas and Ralph in his shorts
Were stumbling and groping over parcels, all sorts

When high overhead there arose such a drone
We tho't many bombers attacking our zone.
We rushed to the windows to watch the bombs fall;
But lo, and behold — no bombs came at all.

28

In a matter of few seconds tho', a thud hit our roof —
All we could think of — was parachute troops!
We felt ourselves quaking, awaiting attack,
But would you believe, I had just turned my back

When out on the roof, there arose such a clatter
Ralph turned on his flashlight — to see what was the matter
When what to our wondering eyes should appear
But Santa himself — And nothing to fear.

Attached by a cord tied round his belly
Was a very large parachute — and they both shook like jelly.
A 'chute full of toys loomed up in the shadow,
(Tell me what word now will rhyme right with shadow?)

His eyes how they watered! His dimples, how wary!
His cheeks were like roses — but not from some sherry;
His droll little mouth was drawn up in a tension
With his chafed grizzly chin adding greater dimension.

No stub of Corona could be seen from his "lowers"
But instead he clinched hard to hang on to his molars;
All this resulted from his quick voyage down.
He might even be called — a "Stratosphere Clown."

He spoke not a word but went straight to his work
And filled all the stockings by a fifth column approach
Then quick as a flash he tied on his chute
And threw up a flare from the top of our roof.

Before we could thank him he was lost to our sight,
Swooped up by his plane — in the black of the night;
But we tho't he exclaimed 'ere his 'chute got too tight
"Merry Christmas to all — And to all a Goodnight."

A note he had penned — which we found in due time;
Its contents requested to please drop him a line
As to what plans he should make and how next he should
    come
As we write on our card, next year, how it's done.

— G.C.N.

* * * * * * * * *

The declaration of 'Open City' made no difference to the Japanese. Their raids continued and we spent half of our days and nights in the shelter; always fearful, always worrying over our husbands who still made their daily trips to their offices.

Demolitions had started on oil and fuel dumps around the city. We were told that within a few days Manila would be filled with Japanese officers and troops. We knew well about the "Rape of Nanking" from former evacuees. Now we awaited out fate as if it were a death sentence. Rumors, questions and suggestions were rampant. Should we flee to the hills? Should we congregate in large groups according to nationalities in different sections of the city? Or, should we remain quietly in our respective homes?

The first idea of fleeing to the hills was out. No gasoline was available, and little chance of escape. Were there any hills *not* infested with Japanese? They were invading our island, Luzon, from all sides, it was reported.

On the last day of December we decided to return to our residence in Pasay. The Fennels had been instructed to join their Pan American group to await the incoming troops, so we said goodbye. With our car filled with luggage and family, we drove across town through black smoke and fire to our desolate house in Pasay.

It was New Year's Eve but there was no gaiety as we listened over the radio to Claude Buss of the High Commissioner's Office telling us to dispose of all liquor, to remain in our homes and await whatever was to come. With several friends we talked quietly about the past and the future as we drained the contents of the few bottles of liquor left in the house.

The first day of 1942 dawned grey and overcast, symbolic of the years ahead. Oily raindrops drizzled over the houses and streets. We stayed inside most of the day without any news. The radio was silent — that had been destroyed, too. Rumors came only by telephone. The suspense and strain were too much. Finally I crept out of the house and over to Taft Avenue two blocks away, to witness Japanese forces entering Manila. They were cheered on by earlier interned Japanese civilians who were crowding the *sawali* fences and waving their "rising sun" flags, shouting, "Banzai, Banzai!" The first Japanese troops came riding on bicycles. They were followed by cavalry . . . large horses carrying midgets in sloppy khaki uniforms whose bayonets dangled over their horses' midriffs. The thought of enemy occupation of our beloved city sickened me. I turned away and hurried home to my children.

We had been advised against wearing nail polish or make-up and to avoid any likeness to the Japanese geisha girls. I had removed my engagement and wedding rings and hidden them. They were never to be found. The next days were nightmares of waiting, with reports by phone that Americans were being picked up off the streets and not being heard from again. We kept the boys in the house behind locked doors. The suspense from one hour to the next, not knowing what would happen to us, keyed out nerves to a high pitch. We had been told that a packed bag should be kept ready with enough food and clothing for three days. Each day we packed and repacked, trying not to show fear before Stan and Gale.

Gale, just three years old, developed a fever that rose steadily. We suspected it was Dengue fever and hoped that it was not more serious. Dengue fever, carried by mosquitoes, runs through three cycles of fever, followed by a measle-like rash. Although a common ailment in the tropics, it could be most uncomfortable with its flu-like body aches, chills and fever. In the midst of trying to comfort Gale, the ever-ringing telephone jangled our nerves. A discreet voice would disclose that another family had been taken. "They're beginning on the Pasay section. Perhaps you — tomorrow!" We all knew the wires were being tapped by the Japanese. To avoid revealing anyone's identity no names were given on the telephone, no revealing conversations. We ate all of our meals early in anticipation of their arrival. With Sofronio gone, Ah Kwai San had become our cook. Somehow she remained calm, just as she had during the bombings. But how often I heard her whispering to herself, "Those awful Japs! Rats they are! I no like them! Too bad, too bad! I want to see them die! Here all the same as China now." She sponged Gale's feverish body and sang to him to soothe his aches and pains.

IMPRISONMENT BEGINS
(January 6, 1942)

On the afternoon of January sixth, two of Ralph's Filipino

office staff came by and offered to remove our car to their residence to keep it out of enemy hands. American and British cars, as well as people were being collected, they told us. Ralph backed our nearly new silver-grey Ambassador out of the garage while they watched the roads for enemy soldiers. At six o'clock they drove it away and we went inside to dinner. We tried to eat, but the food stuck in our throats. Would this be our last meal at home?

Ah Kwai and I were putting the boys to bed. It was almost seven o'clock. Supposedly the Japanese stopped their collecting about six each evening. "One more night at home!" I said, taking out a few essentials from our packed bag. I started down the stairs. Just as I reached the midway landing, my heart jumped to my throat. Two Japanese soldiers were clumping up to our front door! It was dusk. All the more reason to fear the consequences. I managed a weak call to Ralph and leaped back to the top of the stairs, out of sight. "Ah Kwai, dress the boys and get out of sight!" I whispered.

Just then a bayonet clanked against our door. I rushed downstairs as Ralph opened the door. The soldiers pushed inside. "Amelicans here?"

"Yes," Ralph replied.

"How many?" They were looking over our furniture and peering into the other rooms.

"Two children, two adults," Ralph said calmly.

"Three minutes, get out," ordered this burly soldier.

"Children in bed, little one sick," Ralph said quietly.

"Get up, come. Have car?"

"There is no car," was Ralph's careful reply. One soldier muttered something to the other and stalked out the door.

I rushed upstairs to Stan and Gale. Holding them tightly, I whispered to them, "Never say a word!" Ah Kwai had disappeared by this time, and we heard the guard clanking up the stairs to have a look for himself.

Ralph followed the guard upstairs to our bedroom where I was stuffing things into our bag. The soldier looked at the boys and asked their ages as he poked through the contents of our bag with

32

his bayonet. Gale was clinging to my knee, sick with fear as well as fever.

Ralph picked up two mosquito nets and blankets but the guard grunted, "No can take. Go *now!*"

We started down the stairs behind him. I clutched Gale with one hand and picked up my violin. This, I take, I thought to myself. Ralph followed with Stan and our one piece of luggage. As we made ready to file out, the Jap spied my violin. "No take!" he commanded, pushing us on.

I stood my ground, refusing to move on. "Must have!" I replied. I heard the violin maker's words in my ear, "...and never part with it." I bent down and opened the case to show that it was not a gun or weapon, strumming the strings softly.

"No take!" he grunted, shuffling his boots.

"Only violin," I said, still not moving. "It must go with me! Must have!" I said as clearly as I could. Tears filled my eyes. This display of emotion proved to be a more persuasive argument. In desperation to get us out of our house before darkness closed in, the soldier finally nodded and pushed us on.

This was our goodbye to our home and material possessions. We were shoved into a car driven by an American. At least we would be safely chauffeured, I thought, but we were driven only two blocks away to the Rizal Stadium, the huge municipal stadium where I had played violin solos accompanied by Colonel Loving and the Philippine Constabulary Symphonic Band — less than a year ago. It was a gala concert celebrating the Commonwealth Anniversary . . . 5,000 people!

We were ordered out of the car. I held onto my violin. In the half darkness we could see clusters of people waiting to be registered but my thoughts centered on Gale. What would this do to his fever? We stood waiting for an hour to give our names and answers to their detailed questions. Finally, loaded into another car, a Japanese soldier took the wheel. Trucks and cars ahead and behind us pulled away while our driver stomped, grunted, sucked in his breath, and shouted. He couldn't start this newly acquired model. He kicked the starter, choked and flooded the carburetor, tried all the knobs and buttons, his anger increasing. Finally, several other soldiers began pushing it and we jerked down the road.

The drive across Manila was more than we wanted. Stan, bouncing in the seat, shouted, "Daddy, you drive! You know better!" Ralph quickly clamped his hand over Stan's mouth to muffle those words. He did not intend to reveal his engineering skills and be forced to work for the Japanese. It was a wild and reckless ride, dodging telephone poles, pony carts and speeding army trucks. With each near collision, Gale clung to me harder. His fever was rising. At last we were unloaded in front of the main building of Santo Tomas University — the last family to be delivered that night — at 9:30 p.m. There were several thousand other frantic people besides ourselves, of many nationalities, colors and ages, all milling through the buildings.

Gale clutched my hand with all his strength. It felt so hot. We must find a space for him and Stan somewhere. Several friends who had arrived earlier rushed forward to help us. Men were hurrying back and forth, carrying strings of chairs out of the rooms to give more floor space for sleeping. The classrooms were filthy. As I looked around, I saw that many had mosquito nets and blankets which we had been forbidden to bring. I kept dreading the hours ahead. What could we do for Gale? He couldn't lie down on the filthy stone floor and fight mosquitoes all night. Mrs. Toyne, one of my fellow teachers at the American School, came to our rescue. She insisted that Stan and Gale share a net and blanket with her small daughter, Mary Helen. How grateful I felt as we squeezed these three pathetic tots under a single sized net. After we were established, Ralph hurried on to the men's section which was in the Education Building next to this one, to get at least a foothold, a place to stand or sit for the night.

Many of us were too distraught to attempt sleep that first night. We whispered back and forth, sharing our experiences and what we knew of others . . . what mistreatments, lootings and assaults by the Japanese had taken place so far. We speculated about the next few days. We all seemed to have come with the same meager provisions: food and clothing for only three days. Surely we would be allowed to return to our homes after they had collected everyone and given us their orders.

Our bags were being searched. Any firearms, flashlights, scissors, knives, and cameras were to be turned over to the Japanese at once. Every half hour guards stumped and shuffled through the corridors, gaped into the rooms, snorted and then moved on.

Some of the people had been here for three days already, but we still thought in terms of three days more. Mixed with these immediate concerns and fears were underlying thoughts about my repeated refusals to take the boys and go home. What a fool I had been, knowing so well that war was coming. Yet somehow I couldn't . . . and wouldn't. I knew that Ralph must be thinking about it, too, but there would be no point in mentioning it — and we didn't . . . ever again. Whatever was to come, we were in it together.

Chapter Three

FORCED SEPARATION
(January 12, 1942)

ur problems mounted. As bedbugs streamed out of the walls of the old Spanish university, we awoke each morning to feel a swatch of burning, itching welts around our midriffs — their favorite area of attack. We were bitten other places, too; a nightly torture that went on throughout internment.

On each floor of the Main building there were two lavatories. Now heavily overtaxed and with scores of people waiting in line, the pipes often clogged. Similarly with the two newly installed water spigots-for-showers; but somehow the next night I managed to get a partial shower. I was about to leave when the door was swung open by three Jap guards. Pushing me aside, they clumped angrily into our crowded shower space. I swore mightily to myself and ran to my room. No sense of decency, dignity or privacy! Less than a week later, *all doors* were removed from the internment quarters by order of the Commandant. There were to be no doors, no privacy ANYPLACE!

In the morning, Gale's fever had diminished, but he was fretful and weary and a slight rash was showing. We stood in line two hours for the boys to receive their portions of hot oatmeal and cocoa being served from a small canteen set up by the Red Cross — welcome nourishment for the five hundred children now imprisoned. Then I hurried to the Red Cross Clinic — a desk and chair set up in the main corridor — to report Gale's condition. The doctor made application for hospitalization and release from camp. "It might be measles," he said.

As more truckloads of people poured in, more buildings had to be cleared of desks and debris. Thirty to forty persons in each classroom was the present arrangement. Near the Main Building was an Annex which had housed the Home Economics and Elementary Education Departments of the University. Here was a kitchen with stoves, sinks and cupboards — just what was needed for a children's kitchen. The small canteen was no longer feasible. But the kitchen was being used by a small group of Britishers who prepared food for themselves — no intruders permitted. Children's needs were primary, however, and when Jim Cullens, a Red Cross official, suggested the Annex kitchen to our newly formed Internee Council, they agreed.

Their request to the Britishers was rudely refused, however. After several days of attempted persuasion failed, the Internee Council physically removed them. This noticeable aloofness and unconcern for the needs of others on the part of some of the British in camp brought disdain and made them the butt of many camp jokes throughout our imprisonment.

Any such friction between allied nationals within the camp delighted our captors, who played it up with front page coverage in their newspapers. Further disagreements between Americans and British, or other nationals, would have to be hushed up immediately. These daily papers, edited by the Japanese military, gave progress reports on their Co-Prosperity Sphere of "Asia for the Asiatics" and the "New Order in East Asia" — which Filipinos quickly renamed, "The New Odor," which became more offensive, they said, as the days wore on.

Filipinos knew that the Japanese were not providing food for the camp. Each morning they came by the hundreds, lining the street outside the camp gate, their arms loaded with food and supplies for their friends inside. On the third day, we hurried to the gate, hoping to communicate with someone from Ralph's office staff. We hoped they would manage to get us bedding and mosquito nets and perhaps some bananas and bread. Our three tins of food were gone.

We peered and searched through the crowds of people who were shouting back and forth. Filipinos had climbed the trees and wire fences across the street, trying to make contact with their "masters" and good friends. Some were crying as they pitched their bundles over the high *sawali* fence. Suddenly we spied Mr. Fabian, Ralph's accountant. He was unusually tall, but before we could get his attention, Jap guards began knocking the Filipinos off the fences. Striking them with bayonets, they forced them to withdraw.

Finally, through diplomacy by our Internee Council, permission was granted for food and supplies to be left at the gate for internees. No verbal contact was allowed. Filipinos had to sign their names and addresses. Later, after inspection by the guards, internees could claim the packages. The next afternoon we received two mattresses, nets and sheets, and some fresh fruit. Despite the risk involved, Filipinos continued to come with unselfish and lasting loyalty, causing no small sacrifices in the months ahead — even to loss of life for some.

Some months later, when the Japanese decided to provide food for the camp, they allowed only half portions for children. According to our camp policy, the food was distributed differently: three meals a day for children, two for adults.

We began to think in terms of weeks now, and concern over food lessened our composure — evident in our lack of patience with our children. Stan found the camp a lark, a chance to play with the gang, picnic on the grass without an amah at his heels, and best of all, no need to wash up! There were only three outside water taps for the four thousand internees.

Parents were becoming irritable; scolding and shouting at their children. The children went merrily on, each group wilder than the other and more daring in the face of danger when the Japanese hell-drivers began practicing their limited skills on the front lawns, testing the speed of newly-commandeered cars in sharp turns across the grounds in front of the main building. They crashed into fences, concrete walls and other cars. Somehow we had to stay out of their paths, yet this was where the children played!

If these first days were adventure for Stan and many of the children, they were the opposite for Gale. He wanted quiet and home, his Chinese amah; not crowds of people and shouting soldiers at every turn. His security had vanished with that first bombing. Our hearts ached for him. Little did we know of the crises that lay ahead.

It was noon on the sixth day, a bright, hot Sunday. I had just put Gale down for a rest. Mrs. Toyne and I were the only ones in the room when a messenger appeared and handed me a note. "Come to the Main desk," was all it said. Helen Toyne remained with Gale as I hurried out. Earl Carrol, head of our Internee Council, was waiting for me. "You and Gale will be released in a half hour," he said, "because of Gale's Dengue fever. It is an order from the Commandant's office."

"Where will we go?" I said.

"That we don't know. Perhaps some hospital. They've ordered an ambulance."

"But I can't leave Stan, our four-year-old," I said. (Women and children together; men assigned to another building, were the rules.)

"We'll try to get the order changed for both children to go with you, Grace. Pack at once," he finished.

I ran to find Ralph. He was out somewhere doing camp work. It was taking all available manpower to transform these old buildings into housing for the thousands of civilians. The Japanese took no responsibility for providing livable quarters. Guided by our Council, the men went ahead installing sanitation facilities, water spigots and lights. Ralph was with them. An able engineer, he was equally skilled with his hands. He and his brothers had grown up that way, learning from their father how to build, repair and install — do whatever had to be done. Friends offered to look for him. He could be anywhere over the several acres of the university.

My fears over leaving camp without him blinded me. Yet the hope of finding a quieter place for Gale drove me to packing. Should I leave the mattress and mosquito nets for others and trust to outside accommodations? I had only two pesos in cash, but there were canned goods in our house in Pasay. Maybe I could get food and clothes for all of us . . . send things in to Ralph. I was putting our few things together when a messenger brought word from Mr. Carrol. "Yes, both boys are to go with you, Mrs. Nash." If only Ralph would come, I kept thinking.

Leaving the mattress and net behind, we lined up in the hot

sun with a dozen others to wait for the ambulance. Friends gathered around to say goodbye and wish us well. "Where is Daddy? Isn't he going to come?"

Pushing through the crowd and out of breath, Ralph finally appeared. The ambulance was pulling into the drive as he whispered instructions to me. "There's a cigarette carton with thirty pesos (approximately $15.00 U.S. dollars) hidden on the ledge over the sliding door to our bedroom. Contact one of the office men to get it. Take no chances yourself!" He knelt down and kissed Stan and Gale. "I know you'll be good boys," he said.

When would we be reunited? What might happen to us in this separation? Ralph put his hand on my shoulder. "No display of affection between sexes," was the order. He helped us into the ambulance. As we took our places, Stan and Gale edged closer to me, away from the soldier beside them. I had seen too many of these uniforms already. They sickened me. But what I had seen so far was nothing. Manila was overrun with soldiers of "The New Odor."

The ambulance made its last stop at Philippine General Hospital. The guard led us into the main office and presented our entrance card to the Filipino at the desk. As soon as he left, the nurses and doctors surrounded us with questions. They brought us cookies and juice. It was five o'clock. "You must be hungry," they said, scurrying off to get food. While the doctor examined Gale, I explained that I thought he was over most of the Dengue fever — only a trace of rash was still visible. "I know the hospital is overcrowded with bombing casualties," I said. "Perhaps we could find outside quarters."

"Yes," he answered, "let me try." He was calling the Assumption Convent, asking to speak with Mother Hope. A long conversation followed as he presented our case in English, then in Tagalog, asking over and over before she finally gave an acceptance. Meanwhile Stan and Gale were finishing their plates of rice and fish between answers given to the nurses' questions. There were oh's and ah's after every statement. The nurses patted them and tucked a sack of cookies into their pockets. Then, making sure no soldiers were in sight, they carried our luggage outside and quickly put us into a waiting ambulance.

41

ASSUMPTION CONVENT
(January - May, 1942)

In a few minutes we were at the gates of Assumption Convent located in the heart of the city. A tall Chinese-Filipino nun dressed in flowing maroon-colored robes unlocked the high iron gates. Her large hands moved fast as she directed the driver. Each finger fluttered wildly and independently as she spoke rapidly to him in Tagalog. We were whisked inside. She raced ahead of us, all ten fingers fluttering. I was impressed with her great stature and her efficiency as she spoke in rapid-fire English to me. An amazing person. We were running to keep from losing sight of her.

Finally, on the first landing of the wide Spanish stairs, she paused. Quickly she whispered to me, "Great difficulties here; so many to care for. British women and babies; fear of the Japs; little space left. You will share the large room with a Frenchman, his wife and son," she said, making little explanation about this man being in the Convent other than, "He serves as a protection for us in case of night inspection by the Japanese."

I asked no questions. My one request to call Mr. Garcia, a member of Ralph's staff, was reluctantly granted. "He might be able to bring a mattress and net for us," I explained. She stood at my elbow while I made the phone call.

Later that evening, after the curfew hour, Mr. Garcia arrived in a pony *caratela* with mattress and net. Mother Hope whisked him in, tugging at one end of the mattress, and after a quick thank you, rushed him out again. It was a single mattress and net, but so much better than the hard floor. What peace, I thought, as I crawled under the net beside Stan and Gale. Our quarters were at the opposite corner of the large classroom where the Frenchman and his family slept.

I lay awake most of the night, but Gale slept. For that I was thankful. Stan wanted to visit, to find out about our new quarters; about Mother Hope; about Daddy back in camp. I tried to whisper answers while mosquitoes bit my elbows, knees and toes through the net.

The next morning Mother Hope came in with some cracked wheat from Red Cross supplies. Mrs. Castleton from the next room shared her small hot plate with us. We cooked the delicious cereal for breakfast, while the French family prepared hot cakes, bacon and eggs over their utility stove. Stan and Gale stared wide-eyed at their plates.

After breakfast Mrs. Castleton beckoned me into her room and closed the door. "Be very careful what you say or do in front of Mr. De La Monte," she whispered. "He has a 'Number One'* Japanese Military Pass — a Vichy Frenchman," she added. "And he also holds the key to the stores of canned goods left here by the British community."

Later that morning she introduced me to the other British women living in the convent with their small babes. "They were all enroute to Australia from Shanghai and Hongkong," she explained, "when they were put off the ship in Manila at the outset of the war. Their ship departed for Australia during the night, leaving them stranded in Manila with little cash and only one suitcase. No food was supplied. Their respective husbands are in various ports, some with our forces," she said, "and some still in China and Hongkong as civilians." Her own situation was different, however. She and her two sons, aged two and one, had come from Australia to Manila to meet Mr. Castleton who was coming in from Hongkong. His scheduled Pan American flight had not materialized (the same clipper that Jeanette Fennel and her son had booked passage on to the States). "My last word from Mr. Castleton in Hongkong," she finished, "was, 'Have joined British Forces.' "

The next day Santiago, our former temporary cook-houseboy came to see me. "Mr. Garcia told me you were here," he explained, "when he got the mattress yesterday." Excitedly he told me that our neighbors, the Parquettes had moved most of our canned goods and our camphorwood chest to their apartment. It was located in the upstairs of a Swiss-owned house. "They haven't been picked up yet," he said. "They said I can bring you some of the cans and hot food, too, which I'll fix for you each day. Your house has not been sealed yet by the Military."

The Parquettes, Bill and Rosemary had come to Manila in

---

*Priority Status with Japanese Military Regime in their occupation of Manila.

June, 1941 for Bill's teaching assignment in the American School where I taught. They were newlyweds from Istanbul — Bill, one-time Harvard football star and English instructor at Robert College, and Rosemary, English, born and raised in Turkey where her father had been a Consultant to the Turkish government. With music, our common interest, Rosemary and I became good friends, often playing violin and piano sonatas together while Bill and Ralph shared their views on sports, business and whatever. Bill's dry humor and often cynical outlook, and Rosemary's warm affectionate nature that broke through her accustomed English modesty and reserve made them an interesting couple and stimulating company. What would happen to our friendship? Would we all survive?

While Santiago waited, I wrote a note to the Parquettes thanking them for their help, and a second note addressed to Mr. Garcia describing the location of the thirty pesos Ralph had hidden on the ledge in our house.

Meanwhile, the tension of keeping on good terms with my roommates, the De la Montes, increased. The aroma from their endless cooking of bounteous meals made us want to swoop down on the food, vulture style. I tried to keep Stan and Gale outside as much as possible for several reasons. Mr. D. was erratic and highstrung, deliberately mean to his Australian wife and her son by a former marriage. Yet each morning he opened the store room and generously doled out one can of meat or beans to each "inmate" who met with his favor. Somehow we managed to stay on his list. With the Red Cross supplies of cracked wheat and brown sugar, plus an almost daily can of "scrabble" or beans from Mr. De la Monte, we were managing pretty well. I had bought some bread and fresh vegetables which took most of the two pesos, but soon I would be getting the thirty pesos from our house, I thought.

The next afternoon Mr. Garcia met me in the convent garden. He looked sad and worried. "Mrs. Nash," he said, "I have looked everywhere in your house but there is no cigarette carton with thirty pesos."

"Perhaps Ah Kwai, our Chinese amah, would know," I said. I could not give up. He left immediately to find Ah Kwai.

Two days later Ah Kwai was waiting in the garden to tell me that she had walked to our house (more than three kilometers from her quarters) to search for the money. "No can find," she said in tears. "Parquettes, too, no can find." I thanked her and thought, I must see for myself.

The next afternoon while Mrs. Castleton took charge of the boys, I borrowed dark glasses and a large hat and started out on the long walk to Pasay. Moving around buildings and in and out of stores to keep out of sight of enemy soldiers, I reached our house at two o'clock. Making sure no soldiers were in sight, I walked to the back door. It was already open! Listening for any sounds, I hurried upstairs. That money *must* be somewhere. With a footstool, I peered over the door ledge. No sign of a cigarette carton here, or anywhere upstairs. It was gone . . . but there were clothes and other things to get.

Gathering clothes for each of us, I suddenly heard footsteps. Someone was downstairs . . . a soldier? Who? Terrifying thoughts raced through my mind. My heart pounding, slowly I crept out to the hall where I could peer over the railing. Steps were coming into the livingroom now, into my view. "Oh," I gasped, "Santiago! You frightened me. I thought . . ."

He stepped back and, looking up, was noticeably shaken. "Mrs. Nash, how did you come here?"

"I walked, Santiago." My voice was still trembling. "I'm here to get clothes and things. Will you help me?"

Together we packed several sacks of clothes, a few pots, plates and spoons, violin music, Stan's handmade quarter-size violin, baby books, my scrap book containing five years of concert programs, my reviews, our photograph album, and finally our wedding book with marriage license. Putting the last things into a sack, I asked Santiago to go to the street and hail a pony caratela. There was no time to lose. In my rush to get out of the house, I gave one last look at our comfortable, unpretentious home, the ivory painted rattan furniture with turquoise cushions, and the matching hooked rugs. I must not think back.

We loaded the rig and I climbed in. *"Sigena* (hurry), Assumption Convent," I said to the driver and we trotted off.

We reached the convent a few minutes before the six p.m. curfew hour. Mother Hope opened the gate and motioned us to hurry. After paying the driver I had ten centavos left. At top speed,

Mother Hope scooped up my bundles and we went inside. I must get them upstairs and hidden from the sight of Mr. De la Monte. "He's not back yet," she said, reading my thoughts. "But you shouldn't have taken such risk. Oh my! Oh my! It's not safe on the streets!" she scolded.

The following day word came that the Military Seal had been placed on our house.

Little by little, Santiago brought canned goods to us from the Parquettes' house. He also rode the office bike which Mr. Garcia had loaned him to take food and clothes to Santo Tomas for Ralph. This continued for a week. On the eighth day he did not appear, nor the next day. A note came from the Parquettes: "Where is Santiago?" The note went on to say, "We are turning ourselves in tomorrow, the last day for enemy aliens to register. Your Chinese chest and a few remaining tins of food are here. Our housegirl will keep them for you. Good luck, Rosemary and Bill."

What had happened to Santiago? He might be ill, I thought. Then Mr. Garcia and Mr. Camballa, two of Ralph's office staff, came to the convent to see me. They, too, were upset over his sudden disappearance. "He was using our only bicycle which we need badly and we had given him money for a new tire," they said. "Santiago was to have brought my sterling silverware and the rest of my music library the day he vanished," I added.

Then Mr. Garcia said quietly, "We must tell you, Mrs. Nash. There are Japanese people occupying your house now. We are sorry."

Santiago was never heard from again. Later on a partial answer to his disappearance came when I heard of my engraved Chantilly sterling being sold, piece by piece, in the marketplace with a "caller" advertising the ownership and taking bids!

Stan and Gale needed fruit and vegetables. The highly seasoned scrabble meat upset their stomachs. Gale was still stoo weak to climb the tall stairways to our quarters. He found little happiness in his play and cried for his Daddy. Stan was nervous and very restless in his sleep. They were both hungry and cross. Somehow I must get some money. One afternoon Stan came running in from outside. "Mommie, Trudl is in the garden. Come."

I hurried downstairs to meet my Viennese friend, Trudl

Dubsky. She and her husband, Herbert Zipper, had come to Manila before the war. Herbert directed the Manila Symphony Orchestra and Trudl was a ballet instructor and a beautiful dancer. Ralph and I knew that Herbert had spent many months in a German concentration camp but he had never talked about it until one evening in our home several months before Pearl Harbor. It came about because of a request by a certain Lt. Miles of Ft. McKinley whom I had met at a social function. "I understand you know Dr. Herbert Zipper," he began. "I want to meet him. Could you arrange it?" he asked. "My purpose is to get information on the organization and discipline in German camps. My assignment, in case of war, is Enemy Concentration Officer. I understand he was in Dachau and Buchenwald Concentration Camps." "Yes, Lieutenant."

The meeting between the Zippers and Lt. Miles was arranged that October. After a pleasant dinner, Sofronio cleared away the dishes and Herbert explained, with maps, layouts and words, the ruthless principles followed in German camps. He portrayed a vivid picture of the treatment and discipline. For days afterwards I was unable to eat or sleep. And now, less than three months later, we were in a prison camp!

"Grace, how are you?" were Trudl's first words. She was thinner and there were dark circles under her eyes. "I have come to see if I can help you."

"We're all right, Trudl; yes, all right. Where is Herbert?"

Trudl's eyes changed expression. "Herbert is in the University Concert Hall, now a military prison. They picked him up ten days ago; gave no reason."

My thoughts raced back to that evening with Lt. Miles. Could Herbert's pro-American activities be the reason? I tried to comfort Trudl, then told her of my despair. "I must find some means of support for the boys, Trudl, but whatever I do must be carried on by underground methods. The Japs must not know. I do have my violin," I said.

"Ah, perhaps I can get you a violin pupil, Grace. Could you go out to teach?"

"I have a medical pass from Santo Tomas Camp which allows outside trips for food and medicine. I'll manage somehow if there is a pupil."

"As soon as I have word, I'll return," she said, pressing something into my hand. "This will keep you until then. Goodbye."

Trudl had little for herself, yet she had given me a ten peso bill!

Mrs. Castleton and I shared our meals. Her funds were less than mine but she seldom complained. She carried her burden stoically and seldom spoke of her husband whom she might never see again. We discussed bits of news and rumors, and continued to wonder about our temperamental Frenchman, Mr. De la Monte, my roommate.

One means of keeping on good terms was playing bridge with him and his wife each evening. It was a strange foursome playing cards under the gruesome green light in the high ceiling above us. Saving on electricity was an important factor in the convent. Under the diffused green light all red cards showed black, so we continually mistook hearts for clubs, spades for hearts, and hearts for spades. At least once each night Mr. D. exploded in a stream of profanity against his wife, blaming her for his overbidding and/or missing game. He was indeed Latin in temper and emotions and his wife quite Australian. Mrs. Castleton was thoroughly English in her speech and restraint, and I simply rode along, struggling to keep my American sense of humor.

One of those evenings, however, is unforgettable. We had been playing about half an hour when suddenly our various accents were silenced in the heavy drone of an airplane diving low over the convent. "The Japs must be night-stunting. What next?" spoke Mrs. De la Monte. Almost instantly there came an ear-splitting burst of anti-aircraft guns.

We threw down our cards and rushed to the windows in a great surge of hope. But Mr. D.'s outburst of profane condemnation against American planes and his sudden fright revealed *his* status and sympathies instantly.

In spite of this enemy in our midst, we rejoiced. Our hopes were revived, even though some of the anti-aircraft guns were so close to our building that the fireworks came against our windows. Several heavy thuds caused by exploding bombs came next, and the whole convent shook. I ran to the boys, awakened by the noise. It was hard to control my excitement in the presence of Mr. D. who was whispering blasphemy against such a bombing. He had not planned on a return of our planes at all, at least not for years. In the darkness, Mrs. Castleton and I nudged each other, thankful that he could not see our expressions of delight. We felt confident that relief would come in a few weeks. This was January 26th, 1942.

Much later we learned that this raid had been carried out by a lone American plane, piloted by Jesus Villamor, a daring Filipino Ace.* Diving low over Japanese Military Plaza in the next block from us, he had terrorized them in this single mission. They began strengthening their defenses, pouring more troops into Luzon, troops intended for Australia. Our hopes had risen high, only to be crushed. This would happen again and again during the long months ahead.

Finally Stan, Gale and I were assigned a separate room in the convent. What a relief it was after the heavy dose of living with an enemy; having to dress and undress with only a mosquito net and floor space between us! What relief to get away from the tantalizing aroma of their huge meals. Sometimes it seemed as if their entire days were given over to cooking and eating food.

Trudl returned to the convent. "Good news," she said. "You have a violin pupil, Grace." Then she gave me the details. It was the son of Stella Brimo, concert pianist. Their home was in Pasay, more than a mile from the convent. "Two lessons a week, at their home," she said, handing me eight pesos, a half-month's payment in advance. "Herbert is still a prisoner," she finished and waved goodbye.

---

*See book THEY NEVER SURRENDERED, by Col. Jesus A. Villamor, copyright 1982.

Chapter Four

UNDERGROUND SCHOOL
(February, 1942)

usic had always played an important part in my life, but strangely perhaps, it was destined to play a leading role in our struggle with life and death under the Japanese.

Before the war, Manila had offered every opportunity for music development. The days were not long enough to carry out the various jobs I had assumed. One of the most difficult, yet challenging roles was that of music critic for the *Manila Daily Bulletin,* an American newspaper. Heretofore, the concerts had received little in the way of critical reviews. Instead, there were descriptions of the personages attending and the gowns worn. Filipinos, like everyone else, enjoyed praise, but criticism, constructive or otherwise, is never easily digested.

Florence, my violinist sister in Boston, had written an apt reply to my new assignment: "The title for your column, Grace, should be, 'How to Lose Friends and Alienate People!' " It was true, perhaps, that I had fewer speaking acquaintances at first. Yet the joys of reviewing one good concert made up for those which didn't satisfy. One such soloist who always brought excellence to her audience was Stella Goldenberg Brimo, Spanish pianist. It was her eight-year-old son, Rene', whom I would be teaching.

On February 1st, after putting the boys down for their naps, I donned dark glasses and large hat and started out with my violin. It was one o'clock, the hottest party of the day, but the problem of dodging enemy soldiers was a greater strain than the heat of tropical sun. I carried my medical pass and an old prescription in case I was challenged.

I gave Rene' his violin lesson. What a restful feeling to be in a private home again. Afterwards Stella served me cake and coffee and her husband joined us. He was connected with a Manila firm which carried medical and hospital supplies. "If you need anything, Mrs. Nash, just make out a list," he said. "Never mind the cash. You can pay me after the war."

I was indeed grateful. This day marked the beginning of my underground teaching and invaluable help from the Brimos; help that proved a salvation for us in the coming months. The delicious *"meriendas"* they served each lesson day became my main meal and often I carried extra cookies or a bag of candy back to Stan and Gale.

Gradually I got another pupil, then another. My elementary teaching certificate helped, too. I began tutoring children in grade school who came to the convent garden for their lessons; Swiss, Spanish, German refugees and Filipinos. Many of them were children of third party nationals who were not interned. Some paid, some could not, but with this small income I was able to buy native produce for Mrs. Castleton and her two boys as well as ourselves.

Every hour was filled with work, adding to the strain of guarding against Japanese interference which never lessened. The children understood. At the sight of a soldier entering the convent garden, or at a given signal from me they would quickly disperse, feigning play in far corners of the garden.

If days were difficult, the nights were horrible. We could certainly do without lights, put up with our hunger and the continuous artillery flashes in the distance, but hardest to bear were the ghastly sounds from across the street. One of the first changes to take place after the Japanese occupation of Manila was the conversion of many American hotels and homes into houses of prostitution. The Leonard Wood Hotel directly across from the Assumption Convent had been a beautiful residential hotel. Now in the hands of the Military, it was used for the troops who were brought in by truckloads each night, along with Filipino ballerinas collected for their use. Bloodcurdling screams and drunken brawls prevailed through most of the darkened hours.

Nurses and doctors in Philippine General Hospital told us of some of the sad cases they treated — young girls, their bodies lacerated and mangled, their breasts chewed off.

Like the Nazis, the Japanese openly advertised financial support fo Filipino women giving birth to Japanese-fathered babies. They guaranteed a certain amount for the mother's subsistence plus training and adoption of the child, if it was a boy! If the baby was a girl, no consideration would be shown.

Rape of white women was infrequent. Other than a few hazy incidents, I heard of only one account of extreme sexual abuse of an American woman. Mrs. L., an elderly business woman, was caught at the outbreak of war in the far northern mountains of Luzon on a business trip. She was captured by incoming troops and held prisoner in one of their guard houses. At every change of the guard she was raped by each soldier in turn. They urinated down her throat. Mutilated and hopelessly insane, she was too ill to be removed to a prison camp.

Japanese army training included instruction on the inferiority of the white woman, such as: "A Japanese should never degrade himself to such company." But we were warned against riding alone in a pony *caratela*. Conveyances with extra space were regularly stopped by soldiers who would climb in and take over! I dreaded my daily trips more and more. Sometimes I would take Stan with me for protection. Gale was not strong enough to walk very far.

Soon after I began teaching, Tonia, our former housegirl appeared. "Let me help you, Mrs. Nash."

"But, Tonia, I have no money for your services. I could scarcely give you food," I replied.

"That's all right, ma'am. I bring my own food. Never mind money. You have been good to me, now I help you," was her answer.

Tonia came two days a week. This eased my work considerably. She washed, took care of the boys, played with Gale. And as soon as my classes enlarged, I did what I could to remunerate her. Her faithfulness, in spite of her own hardships, was another example of Filipino courage and loyalty.

My classes, kindergarten through fifth grade with each pupil at a different level, were requiring much preparation. There were few textbooks or workbooks, so I had to prepare most of the study materials and seat work. Without night lights there was no chance to work after 8 p.m. I was giving violin, viola, cello, saxophone, and piano lessons also. My own playing was sketchy, other than a few request pieces for the British women and Maryknoll sisters during the darkened evenings.

Food prices were soaring now. Everything was at a premium. Mrs. Castleton and I searched the streets for canned goods, trying to invest wisely for rainy days ahead — rainy days that turned into stormy months more grim than we could imagine at this time.

Through the underground network, I sent notes to Ralph, and he smuggled notes to me. His words were always morale-boosters. He had designed a wire clothespin, he said, and was spending every spare minute making them for the camp hospital. His camp work was kitchen cleanup. From 5 o'clock to ten or eleven at night, he washed heavy cauldrons. Bill Parquette and Les Fennel were working with him. "Don't send me any more canned goods. Keep them for the boys," he added.

For the men in camp the loss of their businesses and their office routines was a severe shock. Adjustments were more difficult for them than for the women. Like Ralph, some were doing more than the assigned two hours of camp work. Others organized classes and gave lectures in their special fields. For recreation they formed softball teams and played volleyball. There were bridge tournaments, and a few men took up knitting.

Ralph had an eye for spotting anything that needed correcting or fixing. Looking across the compound one day, he noticed bed sheets from the Infirmary laundry being blown off the clothesline. "We have no clothespins," the nurses explained. Maybe he could do something about it, he told them. From somewhere he got a coil of soft wire, a thick board, nails and hammer and began experimenting. Finally he developed a technique for winding the wire around nails driven into the board to make a workable clothespin. The nurses were delighted and soon the hospital staff procured more coils of wire and needed pliers. He went to work as a one-man factory, with demand far exceeding the supply. Internees needed them, too. I learned the story about the clothespins when I went into camp to have my medical pass checked. Ralph had deep calluses on his hands.

At last Trudl brought good news that Herbert had been

released by the Military Police, but Roy Bennett, editor of the *Manila Daily Bulletin* was still being held. A week later I met the Zippers secretly in a pre-arranged place near the Convent where Herbert told about his long interrogations by Japanese officers.

My medical pass had to be renewed at the Santo Tomas Office every month. It was much too far to walk. Stan, and sometimes Gale, rode with me in a pony *caratela*. I knew better than to ride alone. Although each trip was risky and hazardous, the joy of having a few moments with Ralph was anticipated for days before the trip. Sometimes, by getting to the gate just at lunch time when the Commandant's office closed for two hours, we could have two whole hours with Ralph and friends before getting our pass stamped to leave the camp. I always took whatever bits of news I had to share with internees.

Each trip I could see a change. Ralph was thinner; the faces around me wore tired expressions with deepened lines and wrinkles. On my third visit there were several friends I didn't recognize. Their hair was a different color! As more women and children became undernourished and ill, they were being released from Santo Tomas camp. Some were admitted to the convent where accommodations were set up in the corridors.

With more nervous and undernourished children in the convent, there were more quarrels and fist fights. As adults, our quarrels were more subtle and without any physical outlet. Tenseness and jealousies mounted as it became evident that some had come with large stores of food and much cash.

One of the newcomers, Irene Barnett, had come with a radio! Each night we gathered around in the darkness to listen to the "Voice of Freedom" from Bataan, then to news from San Francisco and Australia. Afterwards we argued over our different interpretations of what we had just heard. When the news came that Hongkong was lost, Mrs. Castleton was numb and silent. She said nothing about her husband in Hongkong with the British Forces.

Singapore *must* hold! It fell. We still wanted to believe and did believe that Bataan and Corregidor would last. The reports over "Voice of Freedom" were most encouraging. Headed by Carlos P. Romulo, this radio station propaganda kept the Japs on edge. They poured in more thousands of troops, then changed their chief of staff. General Homma promised the fall of Bataan by April 21st, and a high price was set on Romulo's head.

Rommie Romulo, the famous editor of *The Herald* newspapers, vice president of Rotary International, and one of the finest orators I have ever heard, was one of our favorite friends in Manila. Mrs. Romulo was an equally recognized civic leader and hostess. We worried over their inevitable fate if captured. They had four young sons.

Every hour of the day enemy planes roared over the tree-tops enroute to Bataan and Corregidor. But as long as we could hear anti-aircraft from American guns we had hopes. For the individual Jap soldier however, "orders to Bataan" were considered a death sentence. He would not be coming back. Often at night we could hear these soldiers weeping. In daytime, Filipino girls came into the convent showing off their newly acquired gifts of wrist watches or jewelry — a parting farewell from a Japanese soldier who was leaving for Bataan. It was strange how many of these watches had American names on them!

Trucks came into Manila almost daily, bearing bodies of Jap soldiers for cremation. In the tropical heat an unpleasant stench hung over the city, with no breeze or coolness to relieve the oppression.

On April 9th came news of the fall of Bataan. We listened in hushed silence to General Wainright's forced surrender speech. In one of his sentences his voice broke. At that same moment one could almost feel the pressure of a bayonet in his side as he continued to the end. I cried . . . Our only consolation came by underground news that Romulo had escaped. In the next moment we asked each other, "What about his family?"

EMERGENCY!
(April, 1942)

After his bout with Dengue fever, Gale had not regained his normal strength. His unwillingness to play showed his exhaustion. One night before bedtime he edged up to me. "Mommie, my tummy hurts." He felt feverish as I put him to bed. At nine o'clock he awoke with a rising fever and more severe pains. In our nightly blackouts care was difficult. I broke an aspirin. Some of it I got down his throat, the rest went on the floor.

From my past experience in the tropics I knew the meaning of such symptoms — bacillary dysentery. I knew, too, its seriousness. By ten o'clock diarrhea had started. I could get no doctor after curfew. Gale was too sick to be raised to his toidy. The best I could do was to sit by his side until dawn. Then one look at the bloody stool was enough. It was bacillary dysentery! His brow was burning with fever. I waited until he woke and then with Mrs. Castleton's help I gave him two tablespoons of castor oil, the first step in treatment.

An emergency hospital was just two blocks away. We sent for a *caratela.* Wrapping Gale in my arms, I hurried out to the pony cart. *"Sige na,* Ateneo," I told the driver. "Very sick baby." He swatted the pony.

Dr. Delena, head of the Red Cross hospital, examined Gale. "A few hours more and we couldn't have saved him. Get sulphanil-amide, one dozen tablets, twenty if possible," he told me. The nurse gave Gale an injection and started to fill a cup with castor oil.

"I gave him castor oil an hour ago," I said.

"How much?" She continued pouring.

"Two tablespoons."

"That's nothing. The doctor has ordered five tablespoons," she said.

Five more tablespoons! The thought nauseated me. I hurried out to the street, unable to bear Gale's struggle with the heavy dose of oil.

After looking up and down the street for the nearest pharmacy, I started walking along Isaac Peral, my head down in worry over Gale. He must have the sulpha tablets, yet how many places might still have such medicine? My pace quickened.

"Hi, Mrs. Nash." It was a familiar voice. I looked up to see Burt Fonger, president of the Junior Orchestra. He pulled up his bike, immediately sensing my worry. "What's the matter?" he asked.

"Oh, Burt, it's Gale, my three-year-old. He's terribly sick with acute bacillary. I've got to find sulpha tablets right away."

"I'll do it for you on my bike," he said. "I'll go to every *botica* if necessary." He took the ten pesos, all the cash I had, and rode off with prescription in hand.

I turned back to the hospital to comfort Gale and wait for Burt's return. This young man, sixteen years old, had come to the front so many times in the year and a half I had known him. And now his being outside of Santo Tomas camp was not by choice but by order. His parents, missionaries in Manila, had been interned with the rest of us in early January, but after a few days the Commandant had called a meeting of all missionaries in Santo Tomas. In a cordial talk, an official stated that the Japanese did not want to imprison missionaries. *They* were different and they would be allowed to return to their homes and live quite normally — as soon as they signed the little paper being handed to them. Burton's father, as head of the American Bible Society and an American citizen, refused to sign the paper, which in essence, was a pledge of cooperation with the Japanese Co-prosperity Order for East Asia. He was one of the few.

As a result, the Japs disliked Reverend Fonger heartily. They kept him in Santo Tomas and ordered his wife and son to go outside. Family separation with no means of support was another form of persecution. Burton was not one to remain idle. At the outbreak of the war, though too young for a driver's license, he had volunteered as an ambulance driver and was on hand to transport the wounded after each raid. Now he had started as an errand boy for the Philippine Red Cross, carrying messages and supplies to their different branches.

Within an hour Burt was back with the medicine for Gale. How grateful I was as I gave it to the nurse for administering. Poor Gale. He was too sick even to cry, his body wracked with cramps and a fever of 105°. I stayed with him until eleven-thirty, then hurried back to get lunch for Stan and to prepare class work for the children coming at three o'clock. I gave the lesson plans to one of the mothers who promised to take over my teaching and returned to the hospital at two-thirty. The doctor had seen Gale again and his report was favorable. The castor oil had worked and his fever had not risen since noon.

For days Gale was given only rice water, then gradually calamansi juice, the only fruit juice available. He was thin before, but now his skin looked transparent over his frail bones. He had been too near death this time to make a normal recovery. It would take time and special nourishment.

Right after his admission to this hospital, a tiny Filipino child was brought in with the same sickness, but it was too late to save him. He died during the night. Dr. Delena reminded me again that an hour's delay with Gale would have meant the same result. I shuddered and could not make the frightening thought leave. There were other children in the ward with Gale, but he seemed the quietest and frailest among them. He had been sick so often, yet never complained. The nurses loved him dearly. They said he often cried out, "Mommie," in his sleep.

As soon as my classes were finished each afternoon I hurried to the hospital. Gale had waited so long for me to come we both cried with joy at being together. When word reached Ralph of Gale's illness, he applied day after day for a pass to go to Ateneo Red Cross Hospital. Finally, with but a few minutes notice, a two-hour leave was granted. What a joyous surprise that Saturday morning for both Gale and myself as he walked in! We counted the minutes and I ran to the convent to get Stan. Although Stan was not allowed into the hospital, Ralph hugged him and talked with him just outside the entranceway. Ralph was noticeably thinner. Being separated like this was doubly hard for him, not knowing how we were and not having decent rations for himself.

Gale's progress was slow. It had been nearly three weeks now and he still had a fever in the afternoons. Could it be homesickness, being alone so much of the day? Dr. Delena agreed to let me take him back to the convent. The next Saturday noon, I went over to get him. The first trip I took his clothes and few toys. The second trip I carried him in my arms. Even though he weighed scarcely thirty pounds, the short distance of two blocks exhausted my strength.

We kept Gale in bed most of the day during the first week. His wanting to play outside was so encouraging but his diet would have to be watched with utmost care for several months. His appetite was so small and often the things he really wanted to eat he couldn't have or we couldn't get. His fever continued. We were baffled. My teaching and marketing took me away from him much of the daytime, yet if I stayed with him none of us would have food. I had no choice but to go on.

EARTHQUAKE!
(April, 1942)

I had finished my afternoon classes. It was five o'clock as I said goodbye to the children and, my arms loaded with books and supplies, I started for the convent. Mother Hope's great speed through the halls had unconsciously increased my own pace. My anxiety over Gale was also a factor. I hurried up the stairs. My load remained balanced until I started down the highly polished corridor to our room. Just as I reached the slight incline midway down the hall, my feet slipped. I stiffened to save myself. Books, pencils and papers flew in all directions as I fell with a thud on my tail bone. Stars went shooting before my eyes. I couldn't move because of the pain. Several girls rushed out from their quarters. Together they lifted me onto my bed. Surely my back was broken, I thought, as I lay stretched out next to Gale.

"Mommie, Mommie, what's the matter?" he sobbed, but I could not speak for minutes.

Mrs. Barnett appeared with a tall glass — a highball. "Drink it, Grace. It may help you," she said, lifting my head. My first taste of alcohol since New Year's Eve! With the first swallow, memories of that sad evening surged through my mind. Mrs. Castleton prepared supper for Stan and Gale. For thirty-six hours I could neither stand nor walk. Someone took my classes the next day. By that night I was able to walk a few steps.

It was about eleven o'clock when I was awakened by low, distant rumblings. The bed was shaking; windows rattled. An earthquake! Stan and Gale were sleeping soundly. The building was swaying now. We had to get out!

I climbed out of the net, and after trying to wake up Stan to no avail I loaded Gale into my arms, called to Mrs. Castleton, and started through the dark hall toward the stairs. My back twinged with pain. I had forgotten why. The rumblings were louder now and the building was shaking in large tremorous movements.

In utter blackness, I hunted for the stair railing. Others were awake and children were crying. If I could just get Gale outside I would go back for Stan before he could become frightened; he always slept so soundly. I had reached the first landing when suddenly I realized that the convent doors were locked. We were trapped!

I set Gale down on the bottom step, telling him I would be right back with Stan. Frantically I tore up the stairs, hitting the railings on either side as the building swayed. Stan was still asleep. "Stan, wake up, wake up," I said, pulling him across the bed. Sharp pains shot up my spine . . . agony . . . but I must get him out. Finally I placed him over my shoulders, piggy-back, and made my way out of the room in a half-stooped position. My spine had cramped.

Just as I reached the stair railing, Mother Hope called out, "Everyone remain quiet." Gale was crying at the foot of the stairs. Stan was awake now and, easing him off my back to the floor, I proceeded down to Gale. "I'm coming, I'm coming, Gale." The shaking subsided to small tremors, but the corridor was filled with women and children talking incoherently, sobbing and hugging one another. I brought Gale back upstairs and the three of us huddled in a corner. The presence of Mother Hope in any situation, and especially now, brought calm and a sense of protection to all of us.

The two boys finally went back to sleep after Stan's endless questions about this midnight upheaval. I lay awake the rest of the night, feeling the earthquake over and over. Worries after such a quake centered around the dangers of a tidal wave or a second series of shocks. By the second day we were hopeful. A series of small tremors that kept occurring throughout the day meant that the earth was slowly settling itself.

For days my every step was labored, yet only by continued exercise could I liberate those tightened muscles, so I had no choice. There was much to be done and not only Gale needed medical care — Stan was sick, too. Twice he had come down with severe tonsilitis and swollen glands. His tonsils must be abscessed, was the offered opinion.

Dr. Fletcher, our chief camp doctor in Santo Tomas, was allowed to call on hospitalized internees outside of camp one day each week. Ralph asked him to check on Stan. The next week he came to the convent. After one look at Stan's throat, he said, "His tonsils must be removed just as soon as it can be arranged."

The necessary details had to be covered and approved through the Japanese office in the camp. Early in May, Stan had a tonsilectomy at St. Luke's Hospital. Although we didn't have the necessary money to cover expenses, Dr. Fletcher went ahead. We paid ten percent and gave a note for the remainder. Stan was back in the convent in less than a week.

During this time I had to carry on with my teaching. Enrollment had increased both in music students and school classes and there were new worries facing us. There were rumors of our not being allowed to remain in the convent. They materialized the third week in May. "Everyone must be out by May 25th!" were the orders.

EVICTION
(May, 1942)

Like everyone else, the Catholic sisters were hard-pressed and simply could not house us any longer. Yet I couldn't take the boys back into camp, with Stan convalescing from his tonsilectomy and Gale with a continuing fever. Mrs. Castleton and I scoured the possibilities and found nothing.

Two days before the deadline of our eviction a solution came. The Ateneo Fathers in their college quarters offered refuge to the British women and children. Mrs. Castleton would go there. The Bousmans, a missionary family, generously took us in. I had been teaching their three children in music and now, on May 24th, we moved bag and baggage into their house.

Mrs. Bousman, truly a friend indeed, gave me a large room containing chairs and tables for my classes, and relieved me of cooking or planning meals. This was a tremendous help, for marketing and preparation of our scanty meals had been time-consuming in the convent. I paid the Bousmans an agreed amount toward food costs and continued giving the children their music lessons.

This family's hospitality and kindnesses brought our lives nearer to normalcy than any time during the war. And they were risking a great deal, having my underground school in their house, especially with the Japanese Military Telephone Headquarters just across the street!

I changed my class work to mornings and from 8:30 to 11:30

the room became a district school where children from kindergarten through fifth grade worked side by side while enemy planes droned overhead. There were other worries, too. The Union High School behind the Missionary Compound was occupied by a Military Recuperation Hospital, and in the open grounds between the buildings, soldiers bathed and sported themselves during the day. Just across from the front yard, officers were driving in and out of the Telephone Headquarters all day long. What would be the consequences if they should discover my activities?

My classes were becoming too large. I needed an assistant. Mrs. Hunter, who had been with us in the Assumption Convent, was living outside in the city now with her two small boys, and had little funds to go on. She accepted my offer. Her pleasant Australian disposition and manner with the younger children made our work go smoothly. We tried to give the best schooling possible under such conditions. My five fifth graders were industrious and eager. Each one was of a different nationality and each one spoke several languages. One morning in health class we were studying about the care of our teeth. One little girl offered a testimony. "My mother didn't clean her teeth when she was young and now she has diarrhea!"

Although Gale was still bedridden much of the day, he felt more secure because I was right in the next room. The children were solicitous over his welfare. "How is Gale today? Here is something for him," and they would hand me a cookie, a picture, or something special to give him. Stan's feelings were hurt. They never brought him gifts! Some days he would try to study in the school-room but the little attention I could give him wasn't satisfying and little storms of jealousy followed.

In the afternoons from one o'clock until six I gave music lessons; all sorts, to all sorts. After dinner there were lesson plans and papers to correct until midnight. I was too exhausted and too nervous to sleep.

Each evening at dinner with the Bousmans we discussed the day's toll — what abuses had been suffered that day by the Filipinos, receiving first hand reports from friends of the Bousmans. The stories grew steadily worse. Filipino prisoners from Bataan, released by the Japs, returned silent and disease-ridden, bearing scars and open wounds from physical abuse. We also heard about the extreme cruelty shown the American soldiers who were imprisoned in the Pasay Elementary School in Manila. Through the underground, a new list of the dead — American soldiers imprisoned in Cabanatuan and Camp O'Donnel — came through every few days, and we scanned it secretly for any familiar names.

The Bousmans lived only a short distance from Taft Avenue, a main thoroughfare. One afternoon Miss Flora Zarco, a Filipino friend, rushed in the back door, her eyes filled with terror from what she had witnessed on this main highway. A Filipino who had waved to American prisoners in a passing truck was severely beaten, she said, then spread on the sidewalk and left to die while two guards prevented anyone from touching him. Such incidents were plentiful. Manila became a city of ugliness and atrocities. There was no street cleaning or garbage collection, which was made worse by starving dogs and cats roving the streets in search of food.

One afternoon I took Stan with me to the Escolta shopping district. We were walking down the street when a pony *caratela* suddenly veered into the air. A speeding army truck had deliberately crashed into the two-wheeled cart that was carrying a Filipino woman and her baby. The impact threw the pony into the air, breaking the shafts from the harness and tipping the cart over backwards. I gasped, and grabbing Stan, pushed him into the nearest shop entrance, hoping that he hadn't seen what had happened. The army truck raced on, the soldiers roaring with laughter at the wreckage left in their path.

Stan *had* seen it and it took all of my control to answer his questions. There was no decent language left in my vocabulary.

Gale's fever persisted. The next week Brimos arranged an examination for Gale by their doctor, Dr. Moreta. He would fluoroscope Gale's chest for any signs of tuberculosis. That afternoon I cancelled my lessons to take both boys to his office. We rode in a *caratela* to and from the appointment. When the examination showed nothing, I was greatly relieved that it wasn't T.B. Yet what could be the cause of his lingering fever?

We had just stepped out of the pony cart at Taft and Herran Streets, preparing to cross the wide thoroughfare, Gale on one side and Stan on the other as I held their hands. Halfway across, the driver of an army truck had spotted us — enemy aliens! Pressing

64

the accelerator, he cut across the pavement towards us. Stan shrieked as the truck came head on at high speed. Somehow we jumped over the curb just in time, missing death by a fraction of a second and less than an inch! That night I could eat no dinner. I lay awake shuddering over our narrow escape.

The next order from the Japs ended our nightly radio news. "All radios must be registered. No short wave radios allowed. There will be a death penalty for disregard of orders." From then on, any news which filtered through was mixed with wild rumors and we never knew which was which. Their daily newspaper helped us some. By interpreting it backwards we could figure out many things. For example, each week they announced the sinking of the U.S. Navy, with the final blow coming when they published an editorial covering their greatest recent achievement: they had sunk our Navy Department! There has to be a place for laughter, and once again our captors had provided it.

If or when I had to go out alone, I chose transportation on the local charcoal buses — safety in numbers on these small over-crowded vehicles. Too often I would find myself next to an "unflavorable" soldier, his bayonet pressing against my side. One day a shop owner whispered a "good story" to me. It took place in the Arcade Cafe, he said, a downtown steak house. This Jap soldier had entered, ordered a table to be set with clean linen and shining silver. Without looking at the menu, he ordered a large steak dinner, a can of American beer, and a package of American cigarettes. Everything was served. The soldier carefully arranged it and rearranged it, stepping back to view it from all sides. He sat down again but didn't eat. The head waiter appeared. "Is something wrong, Sir?" he asked politely. "No, fine, all fine," replied the soldier, sucking in his breath.

"Why don't you eat? It will not taste so good cold," said the waiter.

"I wait for friend. He take picture. I send my home. They see what I have in Manila!" he explained, showing rows of gold teeth in his pleasure.

Manila was becoming filthy with ponies' excrement covering every street. Something had to be done. The local puppet government soon solved the problem: each *cochero* (driver) was ordered to carry a basket and be responsible for disposal of refuse from his pony. This order evoked great jokes and open laughter at the sight along every street as embarrassed passengers sat waiting while their driver "held the basket." Even the ponies seemed to smile! And as flies and mosquitoes increased, we agreed with the Filipinos that it was caused by the Emperor dispatching his *mosquito fleet* to Manila!

Despite all the suffering and hardships, the Filipinos managed to keep their wonderful sense of humor. Most of their jokes were made at the expense of their enemy, whom they outsmarted and heckled unceasingly. The stories of their successes went the rounds by bamboo telegraph. Too often, however, their daring feats resulted in torture and slow death when a quisling friend reported them to the Japanese for a price.

Gradually then, each *barrio* (town) became a closed family unit, following any newcomer with close scrutiny lest he be a collaborator! Some families were alienated from each other when certain members exhibited support for the Japanese. Such collaborators, while they enjoyed sudden wealth and position with the enemy, surely lived in dread of the time when our troops would return. And there were instances when these spies met sudden death. "They had served their usefulness," explained their Japanese employers.

Some of these roving spies had come from the Muntinglupa Prison — "lifers," set free by the Japs right after they had entered the city. This was one of their acts of beneficence, the freeing of vicious criminals with a promise of service to their liberators throughout the occupation. These criminals could be just as cruel as the Japs. They drew out information from their own people to help the Japs track down USAFFE guerillas and underground activities. Several Americans who were trapped by these traitors were tortured for days before their final death.

We were warned again and again by Filipinos to trust no one. Theirs was a loyalty upheld to the end as they continued their work against our common enemy. Army trucks were continually losing tires. When a Jap driver stopped by the roadside to nap, his tires were removed from his truck. Their warehouses were robbed regularly and the mountain roads became pitfalls when truckloads of troops were attacked by Filipino guerilla bands.

A request was made for Filipino truck drivers. One Filipino

who volunteered his services did so for a purpose. Assigned to the treacherous Baguio road, he took a truckload of troops over the mountain passes. At the steepest precipice he drove his truck over the cliff at high speed. His life for theirs . . . thirty to one, a good average. Such reports filtered back and forth, morale boosters for all of us.

Chapter Five

TONSILS
(August - September, 1942)

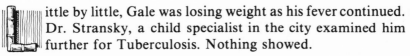ittle by little, Gale was losing weight as his fever continued. Dr. Stransky, a child specialist in the city examined him further for Tuberculosis. Nothing showed.

One afternoon as I read the thermometer, my eyes blinked. I looked again. His temperature registered 102. His throat glands were swollen. By evening his fever was 105.3. I was frantic. Mrs. Bousman filled the tub with tepid water and together we placed him in the deep bath to break his rising temperature. It helped and he slept peacefully. Early the next morning Dr. Daniels from the mission compound came. "Take Gale to St. Luke's Hospital immediately for special observation," he said.

Once again I bundled him into a pony cart and we started the long bumpy ride across the city to St. Luke's Hospital. Stan would stay with the Bousmans. When we reached the hospital, the Filipino nurses began their orders, wrapping him in wet sheets from head to toe. They watched over him every minute, sponged his brow and talked softly to him.

I kissed Gale goodbye and promised to return early the next morning. On my way out of the hospital, I met a Filipino doctor who often treated internees in Santo Tomas. He was on his way there now, he said, and would get word to Ralph about Gale.

The next morning, Dr. Fletcher greeted me at the hospital with word from Ralph that he couldn't get a pass but would keep trying. After examining Gale he gave the nurses further instructions. The fever had receded, but continued observation was necessary. He would keep Ralph informed, he said.

Gale's condition improved and after two more days I took him back to the Bousmans. This attack of fever and swollen glands had given the doctors a clue to the cause of his lingering fever. Covered abscessed tonsils, they believed. But before a tonsilectomy could be performed his general health must be improved.

Mr. Brimo had given me a bottle of calcium powder. I located several packages of Jello. A Swiss friend procured some iron tonic. For the next two weeks we loaded Gale with extra milk, Jello and the tonics. Still the laboratory tests for blood coagulation were not high enough. One more week, they thought.

Arrangements were made at St. Luke's for the operation the following Saturday morning early in September. Dr. Fletcher would be there. I arose at 5:30. In a drizzling rain, Gale and I started for the hospital once more. He was wheeled into the operating room at eight o'clock . . . I paced the floor. Gale had been so brave, so quiet. He had endured so much.

When Dr. Fletcher came out he was smiling. "Everything's fine, Grace. It's over. We found his tonsils filled with poison."

Gale's recovery was faster than Stan's had been, and the next day, a bright Sunday morning, I took him home, filled with hope over his chance for good health at last. It would be wonderful.

On Monday my classroom was filled. The children reflected my happiness over Gale's return from the hospital. They worked eagerly. It was noon already, time for dismissal. I was still on the porch when a pony *caratela* drew up to the gate. Someone was getting out. It was Ralph! I fairly shouted as he rushed up the steps and hugged me, then grabbed Stan. We three went into Gale. His little face beamed with joy. Ralph bent down to kiss him, whispering something to him. Gale's face lit up as never before.

"What is it, Daddy?" cried Stan.

"Guess, Stan," said Gale. Stan tried, but his excitement was too great, and Ralph finally told us.

"I have a pass to stay with you for one week," he said, his face one big smile.

Our eyes filled with tears of rejoicing. It was too good to be true. One whole week! I couldn't believe it. The Bousmans welcomed Ralph with open hearts. We were united as a family. I would not think ahead; not now anyway. The Japs had been good to us for once.

While I taught, Ralph stayed with Stan and Gale. He read to them; made toys out of empty spools by carving notches with his penknife. With two match sticks for the axles and rubber bands attached, he produced self-powered miniature tractors worth hours of play for them. Every minute was treasured.

On the fifth morning of his visit, Ralph awoke with a fever. He ached all over and his head was bursting. Dengue fever! This would mean he would be unable to return to camp on the seventh day. After recess that morning, Mrs. Hunter took over, and with a medical statement of Ralph's condition from Dr. Daniels and Ralph's pass, I started for Santo Tomas, hoping to get a one-week extension on his visitation pass.

When my turn came, I presented the doctor's signed affidavit with the pass. The Commandant glared at me after he read the paper. Quickly he stamped a date on Ralph's pass, then his chop-chop signature, and handed it to the interpretor with a gruff phrase in Japanese. The interpretor relayed the message: "Four days extension. No further extension. He *must* return on this date."

* * * * * * * * * *

Stan and Gale had been asking for a baby. "We want a brother or a sister," they repeated. They had knelt on their knees beside Mother Hope in the convent chapel. "Take care of Daddy and bring us a baby," were their two persistent requests. And more recently they had attended the Ellinwood Presbyterian Sunday School with the Bousman children. "Take care of Daddy and bring us a baby," they had prayed on Sundays. Each night their prayers had ended with, "Please send us a baby, God."

Soon after Ralph's return to Santo Tomas I knew their prayers had been answered. I was green with morning sickness. It lasted all day.

During his visit, Ralph made plans for the construction of a shanty in the camp so that when the boys and I returned to camp we would have a family shelter for daytime use. His office staff had met with him at the Bousmans. They would get the bamboo, sawali and nipa, and preassemble what they could before taking it to

Santo Tomas. October 2nd would be the date of delivery.

They were at the gate at 7:30 that morning waiting for admission. Meanwhile, a business racket had taken root in camp. Several internees had organized a construction committee, circulating information that "all materials for shanties must be ordered through them." It was a monopoly! They had procured the Japanese guards' assistance, based on a percentage plan. The guards were not admitting materials from any other source.

Ralph's men bowed low, asking for admission. Mr. Nash had left his signed request at the guard house the night before, they explained. They were refused admittance. Quietly they backed away, out of sight. They would try again later.

Bill Chittick, our close friend and chairman of the gate, knew of Ralph's plan. He knew also of trouble ahead. For two hours he finagled and planned, talking low to the guards. At last, when the road was clear, he quickly motioned the Filipinos in with their supplies on the hand cart — while the Japs turned their backs. They hadn't seen!

Waiting near the entrance, Ralph quickly led them to his assigned plot of ground. Together they worked several hours, pounding in bamboo posts, setting the foundation for the nipa roof. Late that afternoon they left in the same way — signaled by Bill Chittick while the guards had their backs turned. Ralph had procured the shanty for half of what it would have cost had the materials been purchased from fellow internees!

Each day Gale's health improved. We made plans to return to camp as soon as his temperature reached normal. I sent word of my plans to the parents of the students, saying that Mrs. Hunter would continue teaching some of the children at her quarters.

For my music students I outlined several months of work ahead. Burt Fonger wanted to learn other instruments besides drums and timpani, so I had started him on 'cello and orchestration lessons. An avid learner, he had managed to assemble remnants of our pre-war junior orchestra for Saturday rehearsals at the Bousmans while I was there to direct it. In spite of war and the dangers of retaliations, these young musicians who were not interned filed in with their instruments on Saturday afternoons. Their enthusiasm was contagious and the house fairly shook with the sonorous and some not-so-sonorous vibrations, while different ones took turns being the "lookout" for any uniforms that might appear. Even the parents came to listen from the Bousman's kitchen.

* * * * * * * * * *

I closed the school October 1st. Parents, friends and doctors had begged us not to return to camp, especially so when a few of them learned of my condition.

A note came from Ralph. He would get a pass to move us back to camp on October 6th. He had been assured of this in the camp office. This was in answer to my note to him on the third, saying, "Gale's temperature is normal today, the first time."

The morning of October 6th came, but I couldn't get up. It was an impossibility. Extreme dizziness and a terrible headache prevented my repeated attempts to stand on my feet. Tonia, our housegirl, had continued to come two days a week to help and together we had done a great deal of the packing in preparation for the move. She would return today, she said.

Mrs. Hunter came at nine o'clock to offer her assistance. I was too ill to talk. I had expected Ralph at nine, I mumbled. Ten o'clock passed; eleven, and he still hadn't come. It was raining and I was glad to stay in bed. We wouldn't try to finish packing, I told Tonia. By noon I had given up on his coming. I didn't want him to see me like this anyway.

At three o'clock my door opened. Ralph was bending over me, out of breath from running. His pass had not come through until 2:30 p.m. and he had to be back at 4:30! To get another pass would be out of the question. If we did not go today he could not help us. There was nothing to do but get going!

He tied bundles, labeled boxes and camouflaged our canned goods while I pointed out more things to pack. I struggled into some clothes while Tonia dressed the boys and assisted in the mad scramble. The entire household was in an uproar helping us. I had carefully counted my money after paying Tonia and Mrs. Hunter and leaving a last allowance for Mrs. Castleton the day before. The amount was much less than my previous estimate — 75 pesos less! I must have figured wrong, but there was no time to dwell on this now.

Two *caratelas* were being loaded with our strange assortment

73

of effects and after a round of goodbyes I started out the door. Tonia came running down the steps. "Mrs. Nash, Mrs. Nash," she called. I came back. She opened a powder box I had just thrown into the wastebasket, showing me 75 pesos rolled up in the lid. "You will need this," she said, pressing it into my hand. I gasped and hugged her. "Oh, Tonia," was all I could say.

The two ponies responded to their *cocheros'* commands, and we started off, Ralph and Stan in the first cart followed by Gale and me in the second cart. We were perched high on the board that had been tied on top of our luggage. Our main worry was to reach the gate of Santo Tomas by 4:15 and to get our belongings through the gate without having our canned goods ransacked by the guards. The ride was not an easy one. Both carts were heavily loaded, and the grade up to the Ayala Bridge was steep with a slippery down-grade afterwards. Ponies were no longer shod, and fell easily.

We were fortunate, reaching the gate safely and in time. It was heavily guarded with soldiers. One of the enforced regulations was to bow low to the guards before passing. The seriousness of it depended on the whims of the various soldiers. Ralph jumped down from the cart, but my cochero was having difficulty with his pony and I could see the guard was getting impatient, even angry, waiting for the Filipino to show his respect and humility. I tried to tell this poor old man what he should do but he stood there, hanging onto the bridle of his pony in dumb fright. The madder the guard got, the more frightened and stiff the driver became. I was sick with fear lest they make an example of this man, as they had with others recently. Faces were slapped daily, but severely beating a person, then stringing him up by his thumbs was something else. Finally the guard clumped over, shouting ugly syllables at the driver. He struck him with his bayonet. The bow came, low and long. Gale, sensing the fear, locked his arms around me.

We made it through the gate without much inspection, and drove to the office. It was 4:29 p.m. Ralph took our passes into the Commandant and then hurried to unload our baggage at the door of the Annex, our new quarters!

REUNITED IN SANTO TOMAS
INTERNMENT CAMP
(October, 1942)

"Little Moscow," — Room 64.

The Annex, Elementary Education Building of the University, housed the women with children. At one end of the building was the home economics kitchen with an adjoining dining area. It was now used for the children's meals and any adult "special" diet cases. Our committee saw that three meals a day, of one kind or another, were provided for the children. Adults received two meager meals a day.

Each of the classrooms in this one-story building had from twenty-five to sixty-five occupants. More than half of the occupants were small children. Room 64, the largest, had been the center lecture room. Now it was the living quarters for sixty-five women and children. It was known as "Little Moscow" because so many different languages were spoken by its inhabitants: Tagalog, Hungarian, Spanish, French, Dutch, Russian, Polish, French, and English now and then.

This was to be our room. Newcomers had no choice. We put up our cots and stuffed our bags underneath. Ralph used string to fasten our mosquito nets to the wires overhead, and after much effort we had quarters for the night. With tin plates, cups and spoons, we dragged ourselves into the chow line. Ralph hurried on to stand in the adult line for supper. Jeanette Fennel was on hand to help us get into the routine of things.

As the days went on, Gale still found it difficult to eat with so much shouting and crying around him. He was always afraid that I might leave him. Stan was excited, and always curious to find out what was what and who was who. He liked to dash away in search of new gadgets, playmates and sights.

The first night in "Little Moscow" was a nightmare — as were all the rest. A night's sleep was a rare possibility for anyone. Throughout the night the concrete floor resounded with the jangling of toidies being uncovered, covered, and sometimes dropped! Small children cried out with bad dreams or bites from bedbugs.

Mothers tended to spoil their children with over-attention, or beat them for the slightest misdemeanor. Parents were not normal; neither were the children. Overwrought with exhaustion, worries and hunger, they had little patience with each other. Day by day the situation grew worse. At meal time when children wouldn't eat, they were punished in the presence of others, and the more embarrassment a child suffered, the more belligerent he or she became. Depressed and angered, I sometimes felt I was going insane.

One family will always stand out in my mind, in their cruel, abusive treatment of their children. They had been brought into camp some months before, picked up by the Japanese from where they were hiding out in the hills. One of the five children had died of dysentery during these wanderings. The remaining four ranged in age from one to eight years. Their quarters were in Room 64. Mr. Layner* slept in another building. At 7:30 each morning fathers were allowed to come into the Annex to meet their families. But Layner was at the entranceway at seven o'clock to corral his family. Clattering the plates and cups, he stood gaping at the women who were trying to dress behind their mosquito nets. All doors to the classrooms had long since been removed by the Japs, and Layner had full view of the large room. As his children came forth he would demand a kiss between shouts of, "Shet yer mouth, will ya?"

The oldest boy, thin as a scarecrow, was the most abused. Once, in a rage, his father had thrown him across the concrete floor, then kicked him hard enough to cripple. Mrs. L. too, was sadistic in siding with her husband and often beating the children herself. Any interference from onlookers brought terse, threatening answers. One day a Hollander had seen all he could stand. "Mr. Layner," he said, "if I ever catch you mistreating your children again, I'm going to beat you up!"

"Shet yer mouth! God has given me the right to beat my children," said Mr. Layner.

"Ach!" replied the Dutchman, shaking his fist, "if God has given you the right to beat your children, so then has God given me the right to beat you!" But he slowly lowered his fist and turned away, knowing that any friction between internees would bring

---

*Real name not used here.

76

punishment to the entire camp.

A few days later, in the Annex dining area, Mr. L. was seated between his two youngest children. The smaller, frail child wouldn't eat her plate of slimy greens and rice despite her father's urging, in his usual burly manner. Angered by the child's indifference, he slapped her hard across the face. One of the mothers across the table spoke up. "Mr. Layner, don't ever let me see you do that again!" she said crisply.

"Shet yer mouth," he roared, "I am the son of God!" (He was a Baptist minister.)

"If you are the son of God, Mr. L., then give me an S.O.B. any time!" she said with finality.

Nipa Shanty

Ralph had finished the main construction of our shanty and by the second week we were able to have our meals together, away from the Annex. These small lean-to shacks being built all over the grounds afforded some semblance of family life, even though their upkeep required energy. To get away from the crowded rooms for a part of the day was gratifying. My spells of nausea were lessening and though I tired easily I felt relieved to have our family united

77

again. It was good, too, to be away from the city outside, not to fear being caught by the Military Police for my underground school, not to have to go out on the streets that were filled with soldiers. I felt much more secure in Santo Tomas among familiar faces, many of whom I knew and respected. For the most part, we were working together and making the best of our hardships. We found things to laugh about; we made our own entertainment in this sizable city behind the high *sawali* fence.

Our fifth wedding anniversary on October 24th was to be celebrated with a luncheon for several friends. We planned it carefully, choosing a can of lima beans to make a casserole dish and a can of fruit salad as a special dessert. Since there was no noonday meal for adults, any such occasion as this was anticipated for days beforehand.

The afternoon before our planned celebration, Ralph was noticeably not well. He was having chills, then fever. His body ached, he said. He started over to the hospital clinic for some aspirin. He did not return. A messenger brought word that he was put to bed there — Dengue fever, they thought.

I stood in the chow lines, got the boys fed, bathed and put to bed. Our anniversary was forgotten. The next day Ralph was too ill to have visitors. I was depressed and worried — he had worked so hard during the week before our return to camp, building the shanty, laying the bamboo floor strip by strip, and tying the nipa leaves in place for the roof. Yet in all the months while we were outside he had not eaten a single can of food I had sent in to him. Camp work and the near-starvation camp chow had drained any reserve strength.

I was washing clothes in the shanty when a bouquet of flowers was handed to me by a messenger from the Gate. Who could be sending flowers in a prison camp? I pressed the sweet smelling blossoms against my cheek and smiled, thinking, "Flowers keep on blooming in spite of the 'New Odor for East Asia,' and how sweet they smell!" Inside the bouquet there was a small piece of paper which said, "Best wishes, Bill." Anniversary flowers from Bill Chittick! He was one of the first persons I had met in Manila in 1936. He was best man at our wedding and now a fellow prisoner who already had saved many moments for us . . . and would save many more in the months to come.

I placed the flowers in a tin can on our homemade table; something of beauty to behold in our shanty in "Garden Court" — so named because this section of the camp had formerly been a garbage dump!

Ralph remained in the hospital and I was not allowed to visit him. What he had might not be Dengue fever. With this worry, the next few days were doubly hard, trying to keep track of the boys, standing in two lines for chow, and waiting in equally long lines to buy a few fresh vegetables brought in by Filipinos. This last task I dreaded the most. Guava fruit was plentiful and in season now. For some strange reason the aroma from this fruit which I had always liked, now sickened me. As I walked across the grounds and stood in line it permeated every breath I took. My nausea was overwhelming. The morning mush always lumped in my throat. Two or three spoons of it were all I could manage. There was still black coffee, but that gave little nourishment.

Although they missed their Daddy who was still in the camp hospital, Stan and Gale were noticeably more content in Santo Tomas than they had been outside. Finally a diagnosis of Ralph's illness had been reached. Dengue fever was not his trouble. It was yellow jaundice, hepatitis!

A week later I was carried to the hospital on a stretcher, too ill to speak. I had no idea what might have happened to my sons. The doctor was standing beside my cot, but I could say nothing. Acute enteritis, similar to dysentery and food poisoning, had attacked me. This was followed by several days of overpowering fever and sickness, then a slow process of regaining my strength.

The camp doctors watched my chart closely, marveling that I had not lost my baby. One eggnog each day was prescribed. Only a few patients merited such nourishment. What a delicacy, even though it was made with water instead of milk. Not a drop of canned milk could be spared.

Ralph, in the next ward from mine and able to walk now, was allowed to visit me a few minutes each day, and the boys were brought to the window below my bed. Jean Salet had volunteered to look after the boys, and with Jeanette's capable assistance I knew they were in good hands. Jean, an able college-aged girl and secretary at the American School where I had taught, was one of my most talented violin students.

On November 19th, my birthday, my breakfast tray included a note and a tiny package from Ralph. A bottle of perfume! At this moment more wonderful than a diamond bracelet! In the afternoon Jean somehow wangled permission to bring Stan and Gale up to the landing of the second floor where we could say "Hi" to each other. Two birthday cakes had been sent in through the Gate that morning. They were from two of the children I had taught in the underground classes. A third cake arrived the following day from the Bousmans. Made with rice flour and substitutes, those cakes represented more than the most expensive French pastries. They were enjoyed by many friends in the camp. Such thoughtfulness and sacrifices will always bring a lump to my throat.

Ralph's yellow skin and eyes were proof that the jaundice was taking its toll along with the intense hunger that comes with recuperation. But now another infection had begun — athlete's foot! Each day this fungus was spreading over more of his foot. He was not permitted to walk. The treatment prescribed was only aggravating the infection.

One of us *had* to get out of that hospital to relieve Jean and Jeanette of caring for our boys. Jean was already doing heavy camp work and there was a limit to what she could do. Yet each afternoon my temperature would go up; I felt weak and sick most of the time.

A week later on Thanksgiving morning, without a release, I walked out of the camp hospital and went to the Annex, Room 64, to resume my duties as a mother. The memory of that day will never leave me. I fought with all the willpower I had to keep from giving up. The unmerciful sun, my short temper and unkind words to my sons who were so glad to have mommie again, the long chow lines — I felt that I simply could not face life any longer. "Let me die and get it over with," were my prayers one moment; followed by, *"No, you've got to face it! They're your children! Keep going!"* came the answer. And to think that this was a day set aside for Thanksgiving!

Each visit to the camp hospital to see Ralph was more discouraging. He was quite helpless now. His foot was much worse — like raw beefsteak — and the treatment was agonizing. He refused any further treatment, saying that he would take care of it himself. I hurried to the Education Building to get some boric

80

powder from his room and he began applying wet packs throughout the day.

So many layers of flesh had been eaten away by the spreading fungus and the harsh acid in the medicine that it took several weeks for any improvement to show. With the help of "walking" patients he was carried to the garden for sunbaths each day. The healing powers of sunshine and the boric packs he applied the rest of the day gradually healed his foot. Early in December he hobbled on one foot over to our shanty. In a few more days he moved back to his room in the Education Building — six weeks from the time he had left to get some aspirin on October 23rd! In two more weeks he was able to take a few steps on both feet. Now we were a family again and he looked after the boys while I stood in chow lines.

Gale's birthday was December 15th and we decided a celebration was in order. Gale chose a few friends from the neighboring shanties and we found an ice cream freezer, bought some ice, and with coconut milk I made ice cream. Ralph turned the freezer while he dangled his foot over a chair for the sun treatment. With our fabricated pinwheels for favors, it was a gala afternoon. After the children had their ice cream there was enough left for the parents each to have a spoonful.

The next day Stan cried with an earache. His fever rose three degrees in a few hours. Ralph carried him piggy-back to the hospital three blocks away. He came back alone, saying that both of Stan's ears were badly swollen. Dr. Robinson would lance them at once. Then he hurried back to be with Stan. "Anesthesia is required. The doctor says it is urgent enough to use some of their small reserve stock there," Ralph called, halfway down the path.

I stayed in the shanty with Gale, waiting. When I couldn't stand it any longer, Jeanette Fennel took Gale for a walk and I started for the hospital. Just outside I met the orderlies wheeling a stretcher down the walk. Yes, it was Stan, still under the anesthetic, and they were taking him over to the children's ward next to the Annex. Each day I was allowed to see him for half an hour.

Stan recovered and we had Christmas together. Friends on the outside had sent in surprise packages with food, little toys for Stan and Gale; and a Christmas tree in camp, loaded with toys handmade by the fathers who had worked secretly for weeks.

There were scooters, hoops, dolls and kiddie cars. Even a Santa Claus with bells! What a day to remember!

MIDNIGHT EMERGENCY
(January 16, 1943)

We watched in the New Year without parties — women in the Annex and men in their respective quarters; each one in his or her own language making the same wish for the coming year: our early liberation!

On the afternoon of January 16th, Stan complained of stomach ache. He stayed on the bamboo cot in the shanty. His ear ached, too, he said. I got a hot water bottle from the clinic and put it against his ear. His stomach ache got worse and by seven o'clock he cried with pain on the right side of his abdomen. I hurried to the children's clinic which opened at seven in the evening and reported to the young Filipino doctor who was on night duty. "Take him to the main camp hospital for a blood count at once," he said.

Together, Ralph and I carried Stan, again turning to Jeanette to look after Gale. "The report will be sent to the Annex clinic," said the nurse as she finished the process.

We trekked back to the Annex with Stan to wait, hoping that the pain would let up. From the kitchen I begged for an ice bag after they had filled the hot water bottle again. Ralph could stay no longer. Curfew had sounded and he must go to quarters.

Stan cried out with pain, his ear and his stomach each vieing for first place. There seemed to be no relief. I was frantic with fear. Appendicitis! I knew the symptoms for I had been operated on too late. My appendix had ruptured when I was 13 years old. And mastoid was a dangerous infection! I carried him back to the clinic where I fanned him to keep mosquitoes away. He was too sick to be put into the crowded room under a mosquito net.

Stan's right leg was beginning to draw up now. The Filipino doctor became more worried. He would try to find Dr. Fletcher, head of the camp medical staff. Dr. Fletcher slept in Ralph's room and I hoped that he would waken Ralph, too.

In a few minutes Dr. Fletcher was there and examined Stan. He called me into the hall. "We must get him to a hospital fast. I don't know which will be first, the ear or the appendix, but we have no facilities to cope with either, here in camp. I'll get our interpretor, Mr. Stanley to call Philippine General Hospital for an ambulance and try to arrange for Ralph to go with Stan. We'll do everything we can to get speed," he said and hurried out.

I left Stan on the examining table with the other doctor while I went to our room to find pajamas, toothbrush and a towel for him. I wrapped them in a newspaper and hurried back. Fighting back my tears which he must not see, I tried to comfort him, while praying with all my strength. "Damn the Japs!" I said over and over under my breath between prayers. "Look what they have done to everyone!"

It was twenty minutes later when Ralph and Dr. Fletcher appeared holding a pass given by Mr. Stanley, the interpretor. The Commandant and other officials were not in camp that night. Another half hour passed before a white vehicle drove noisily and ominously up to the Annex. (Philippine hearses were always white.) *"I must be brave! I won't cry! I won't, I won't!"* I kissed Stan goodbye, then Ralph; and he lifted Stan on to the stretcher to be loaded into the ambulance. He quietly assured me that he would see that everything possible would be done for our first son.

I turned to the Filipino doctor who was embarrassed and so sympathetic. "What was the report on Stan's blood count?" I asked.

"12,000," he answered.

I shuddered, knowing that 12,000 meant, "Operate!"

"We don't know which was causing the high count," he added, "his ear or the appendix."

It was 1:30 in the morning and the crowded rooms were quieter than I had ever known them; only a small tot's cry and a few toidy lids bumping the concrete floor. I walked through the corridor and sat down on the steps outside. I could cry now, and I did — first silently, then a convulsive hysteria swept over me which I couldn't control. I had lost my nerve.

What if we should lose Stan! The thought and fear of it obsessed me. Mrs. Ferguson, one of the women from my room, had come out and was standing over me. She talked quietly to me until I got control of myself. Together we went into the room and I crawled under the mosquito net beside Gale. About dawn I fell asleep.

Sunday morning my eyes were dry and swollen. I clung to Gale's hand waiting for news, whatever it might be. Gale's first words that morning had been about Stan. Where was he? And why had I been crying?

I tried to explain what had happened and that everything would be all right because Daddy was staying with Stan.

About 9:30 that morning we left the Annex to go over to the shanty. Halfway down the path I saw Mr. Cullens, one of Ralph's thirty-some roommates, coming towards me. My nerves tightened and a cold fear swept over me. "News, what is it?" I called, running towards him. Calmly, in his slow Alabama drawl, he told me how Ralph had come into camp at nine o'clock which was the stated time limit on his temporary pass. In the office the Japs had given him an extension, but that meant he had to go outside immediately. A guard had escorted him to the Gate. He had asked to see me first but they had refused. Stan had not been operated on. The doctors had gotten sulpha for him and hoped it would lower the blood count. It hadn't gone any higher and they felt quite sure the next two days would bring it down. The ear infection was being treated. Any further developments would be reported. "Ralph says for you not to worry, Grace."

"Thank you, Jim," I said weakly and stumbled into the shanty with Gale. I collapsed on the bamboo cot, my body convulsed in tremors and my heart filled with gratitude.

Chapter Six

A CRUEL COMMANDANT
(January, 1943)

umors had spread through the camp that pregnant women were going to be taken out! I had laughed at the reports. It was just another silly rumor. Besides, Stan was on my mind every minute and I should be getting word soon.

It was Monday night. Gale was asleep and I was shivering under a cold shower when Jeanette Fennell came in. "How are you, Grace?" she called.

"All right. What's the matter?" I asked, recognizing a peculiar tone in her voice.

"Oh, nothing. I just came in to tell you that Mr. Holland and Reverend Foley would like to see you when you're finished."

A chill went through my cold body. It was news about Stan, I knew, for Mr. Holland was the internees' representative in the Commandant's office who arranged for outside passes and Mr. Foley was a minister. Still dripping, I got into my clothes and ran down the corridor to find the two men. They were waiting on a bench outside my room.

"What is it? How is Stan?" My words rushed out.

"He's doing fine, Grace, and they don't expect to operate," Mr. Holland replied.

"What is it then?" I asked, feeling great relief. If Stan's all right, then everything is, I thought.

"It's another matter we have come to talk about," said Reverend Foley.

Then in careful wording they revealed the new edict just made by the Commandant. It seemed there had been some unpleasant trouble over an affair between a promiscuous girl and married men in the camp. The Japs were angered. "The Commandant has ordered all pregnant women to be ready at 10:30 in the morning with their baggage, to be taken out of camp. The men involved are already being led to the camp jail for thirty to sixty days of solitary confinement," Rev. Foley said.

"Then I'll take Gale with me," I said quickly. As long as he could stay with me we could stand it. And they couldn't put Ralph in jail when he was with Stan in Philippine General Hospital! We had tricked them this time, I thought.

"We hope it can be arranged to have Gale with you, but the Japs have not disclosed where you will be taken," said Mr. Holland.

They left and as the news rolled over in my mind the whole idea seemed ridiculous. Perhaps it was the let-down after the heavy strain I'd been under that made me want to laugh now. Some women wondered why I was laughing. I couldn't explain, I said.

I walked to the front grounds, as Ralph and I often did after the boys were asleep, to hear a few recordings over the loud-speaker, followed by the camp news bulletin and Commandant orders for the next day. We usually sat with the Toynes, Jim Cullens and several others. I would go over and say goodbye to them.

I reached the Main Building just as the loudspeaker belched forth this new order from the Commandant. An ominous silence came over the crowd, then hushed whispers ensued as I walked on. "How many pregnant women are there?" "Some say 54, or 17, or maybe 81!" Speculations on the number were flying through the darkness.

Our group of friends became suddenly silent as I came into the huddle. They began with awkward phrases of sympathy. "What would happen to Gale?"

"He's going with me, of course," I said, never considering a different idea.

"Do you need any help packing?" they asked.

"Mr. Holland told me to take everything; canned goods,

anything I might want," I said, "but I can't get into our shanty until 7:30 in the morning, so I will be rushed," I finished.

"We'll be on hand," they said, as the gong sounded for "Quarters."

On my way back to the Annex I had an idea. What if I were too sick and could not be moved tomorrow morning? It would give me time to get word to Ralph to stay as long as possible in the hospital, time to plan a little strategy. Peanuts! That would do it! Dr. Fletcher had warned me against eating nuts, beans or any difficult-to-digest foods due to my internal condition after the Caesarian section I had had with Gale's birth. The doctor had sewn the uterus to the stomach lining — a real internal mess, he said. That had caused more than the usual discomfort during the first months of this pregnancy.

I hurried into the Main Building to the one "stand" to buy a large bag of peanuts, unshelled, then on to the Annex to tell Jeanette of my plan. Outside on the steps we talked and planned until after midnight while I ate *all* of the nuts, ready and willing to endure the suffering that was bound to come.

At six o'clock the next morning I awoke — feeling fine. The peanuts hadn't done a thing to me. I stalked out to the latrine, disgusted. Jeanette was up, too, worried over my probable indigestion, and in the semi-darkness we coaxed a cup of coffee from the kitchen staff.

I was first in line for breakfast but I said nothing to Gale about our going away until he had downed the gluey mush. I explained then that we were going out of camp to stay somewhere else. "What will Daddy and Stan do? Will they come, too?" Other questions followed, but he did not seem afraid as long as I would be with him.

At 7:30 Les Fennel opened the shanty for me, and together with Jim Cullens and Louis Croft we packed canned goods, several cooking utensils, and whatever else they thought I would need. I sorted out Stan's clothes which would stay in camp. Rosie and Jeanette put Gale's and my things into *tampipis* (native telescope cases). I packed my violin and the little music I had managed to keep, as dozens of friends pushed into the room to say goodbye and wish me well. Curiosity permeated the camp. No one knew how many were leaving or where we would be taken.

It was ten o'clock when Reverend Foley appeared wearing a long face. "Grace, the Japs say 'No take child.' Our committee has argued to no avail. They're going to put the children in Holy Ghost Convent."

I was enraged. "This will not be so!" I said. "Gale is still convalescing from his long illness and tonsilectomy. He's still frightened and shy and fragile. I'll go to the Commandant myself." I left my packing and ran toward the camp office, tears rolling down my face. I was too angry to know fear. Reverend Foley followed behind.

The Commandant, Mr. Kuroda, was sitting calmly at his desk. When my turn came I stood up before him, explaining Gale's illness, temperament and insecurity. His face showed no expression as I went on and on.

"I understand, Mrs. Nash, but I cannot change the ordah," he said, with his Harvard accent. "I am a family man, too. The ordah remains."

"Mr. Kuroda," I said, as tears streaked my face. "Punish me as you see fit, do anything — but do not make my child suffer. He has been close to death twice since our internment. Let him stay with me, I beg you."

The papers on his desk were blotched with my tears as I leaned over to plead my case.

"The ordah remains. You may go."

I turned and went out the door, bent in sobs. Beaten and defenseless, I walked back to the room where Rosie was telling Gale a story. He looked up . . . and grabbed me around the knees. "Mommie!" he cried.

Rosie and the others knew without my saying and they quickly unpacked and repacked, putting Gale's clothes in a separate case from mine. I sat on the cot holding Gale close to me until it was time to go outside. My luggage had been deposited at the Annex steps and friends were standing around waiting, saying farewells to another woman and myself. Her two children were older than Gale.

A dingy old bus drove up to the Annex. Our bags were loaded and we started off. As we passed the school room, several children jumped up to look out. "Mrs. Nash," they called, "we want you to come back so we can sing with your violin." I had started music classes, a song fest with them two weeks before.

Internees were flanking the long driveway through camp to watch the exodus of expectant women. "What, just two old married women?" I could imagine their words as the bus chugged along. "No young single girls in trouble? Why had the Japs been so excited?" They were definitely disappointed.

Gale sat glued to me. My eyes told him there was more to fear now. I kept my arm around him, my whole being wracked with grief and pain.

The driver would go to Holy Ghost Convent first to deposit the three children; then on to our prison, wherever that might be. Before we reached the convent I must tell Gale. How could I do it?

"Gale-boy," I began, "for a few days you are going to live with boys and girls like Benji and Ellen here. You can play with them and eat with them, and I want you to be a good brave boy and have lots of fun."

His lips began to pucker. "Won't you be there, too?"

"No, not yet, Gale. I will be with Mrs. N. and I'll think about you and know that you're all right."

"But I want to go with you. I don't want to be with the children, just with you," he sobbed, grabbing me with both arms.

The bus had stopped now and I got out with Gale while the driver unloaded the children's belongings. Mrs. N. hugged Benji and Ellen, asking them to take care of each other and Gale, too. Gale was clinging to me and I hugged him close, feeling utter despair and grief for him.

The surly guard clicked his heels. "Go now," he ordered. An American woman came out to assist the new arrivals. "Mrs. Nash," she said quietly, "I'll take Gale and look after him here. You need not worry." But he was hysterical and screaming as she took him from me. I climbed into the bus. Mrs. N. and I looked at each other and cried openly as the bus took us away.

ISLAND BANISHMENT
(January, 1943)

In the center of the Ayala Bridge over the Pasig River, there was a second bridge-road which turned at a right angle, leading to a small island. When the bus took this turn I knew where we were being taken — to a Spanish convent named "Hospicio de San Jose," the only structure on this tiny island. Before the war it had been known as a home for foundlings and the insane.

We were led inside by a Spanish nun in white robes. An American nurse waiting at the top of the stairs greeted us. "I'm Miki," she said with a warm smile. "Come this way." She took us down a long corridor lined with old men seated in their chairs. They were staring at us with searching eyes. The Spanish nun had hurried ahead. She turned and pushed open the short swinging doors, motioning us into a small room. This would be our "ward," Miki explained (the nun spoke no English) . . . "four small single beds, two on each side, end to end, with a narrow aisle down the center."

Our baggage was brought up and dumped on the beds. "Chow at one o'clock." After the Catholic sister and Miki had left, Mona and I sat on the woven *bohuca* cot frames and stared into space.

Before long Miki came back and putting her arms around us, she did her best to cheer us. She told us about the old men being housed there. "They're not able to take care of themselves," she said, "and too sick to be in Santo Tomas. They're the 'old timers' in Manila. Many have Filipino wives and children in the provinces. Some of them came out with the Thomasites right after the Spanish-American War, as teachers in the public schools here, training Filipinos in the ways of democracy. Their only hope now," she said, "is to live long enough to see the return of the American flag in the Philippines."

As the days went on we loved Miki and looked to her for comfort, laughter and help. The old men called her "Darling," and she furnished their small bits of joy and love so needed each day. Often her understanding and sense of humor prevented revolutions and petty quarrels among those eighty-five aged and sick male prisoners in late states of senility, TB, V.D., epilepsy and other diseases.

Her real name was Mildred Sherk. She was a registered nurse and wife of a mining engineer in one of the gold mines in Southern Luzon. At the outbreak of war, her husband was caught in Manila. Miki was left with the mine and Filipino employees. At the time of the invasion, she corraled the Filipino employees and after disposing of the gold in different forms down an old mine shaft they loaded a truck with supplies and dynamite and headed for Manila. To delay the Japanese forces coming from the south, they blew up bridges and trestles as they went.

Nursing the wounded in an army hospital in Manila until the Japs entered the city, she was interned in Santo Tomas then assigned to Hospicio de San Jose to care for the old men. Miki's husband reportedly had joined the American forces in Manila.

There were two other nurses with Miki. One, a British woman, widow of an American navy man, was fine and efficient in her brusque manner. The other I soon recognized as the "ugly" nurse from the children's hospital in Santo Tomas who had intimidated and frightened so many, including Stan. She had been transferred here to be head of staff. The old men feared her, too. Her terse and unkind answers and accusations to them made her a good example of what a nurse should never be, not to mention a missionary! Everyone turned to Miki for help.

In my utter despair over Gale, full realization of being here with these old men, separated in our quarters by only a pair of swinging half-doors, hadn't fully penetrated yet. All I could think about was Gale, hysterical and crying as he was torn from my arms. Mona's children had cried a little, but the older one, a girl of nine, had seemed to understand. She would look after her brother, she said. They would be better cared for in the Holy Ghost Convent than back in camp alone, reasoned Mona, especially when her husband was already in solitary!

Staring at each other, we started to speak at the same time. "Why had *we* become victims of the Japs' madness? Neither of us had broken any restrictions in the camp. But what about the girl who had? Were there others, too?"

Our questions were gradually answered. The next day a bus brought a third victim; Phyllis Lynch, an Australian girl of nineteen, taken from Sulpher Springs, a subsidiary internment camp for those who had money to pay for their food and lodging or for those who needed rest and special care. Phyllis was upset and bitter. A member of a famous roller skating trio from Australia, she and her friends had been caught in Manila when the war broke. In Santa Tomas she had fallen in love with an Australian boy. When the Commandant refused their request for a marriage ceremony, they were married secretly in the camp and then she got transferred to the small Sulphur Springs camp. Now her husband, Frank, was in the camp jail with Mona's husband.

We sympathized with each other and compared notes on our respective dates of delivery. Mona's baby, conceived in the Cebu camp where families were quartered together, could be expected the last day of April or first of May. Phyllis and I might have ours on the same day, May 7th. "Ralph's birthday," I added, "but what about the girl Mr. Holland and Reverend Foley had talked about? You aren't that girl, Phyllis, are you?" No, indeed, she certainly wasn't, she assured us.

The real reason for our being military prisoners and isolated on the island was finally revealed a week later when Mr. Holland arrived, leading a sullen-eyed girl into our room. He introduced her as Mary. Her eyes spoke defiance and bitterness.

We moved our belongings from the fourth cot and expressed our sympathy to Mary. She had nothing to say but a few crisp, bitter words, and for several days she stalked in and out without a word. Her gait was that of a streetwalker. Rumors were whispered among the old men, and gradually we pieced together her story.

Mona and I had exerted our efforts to get reports on our children. Mr. Holland had promised to keep trying with the Commandant to have Gale transferred to my quarters — it might be accomplished in a week or so, he thought. Meanwhile I had sent a letter to Ralph through the underground, explaining what had happened and asking him to keep Stan in the hospital as long as possible in hopes of avoiding a jail sentence. The Japs sometimes conveniently forgot.

One afternoon Miki came in with great news for us. The Filipino Doctora who was in charge of Holy Ghost Convent had secured permission to bring our three children to the island to see us. We would have one half-hour with them. Mona and I hugged each other in joy, then the sudden thought of their leaving after thirty minutes sickened us — we would *not* think about that today.

The next afternoon at three o'clock a pony *caratela* came over the bridge into the convent with our three loved ones. Gale was the first to climb out, his little face dry but tear-stained. We hugged each other closely, my eyes filling with tears. He bit his lip, but never a tear. We walked upstairs to my room in silence and he climbed on the cot beside me, with nothing to say. He just looked at me.

I asked him questions. Each one he answered with a yes or no, just staring longingly and pathetically, and every few seconds hugging me. "No," he hadn't eaten his lunch. "No," he hadn't played outside with the other children. "Yes," he had tried to be good. "Yes," he had cried, always.

The half-hour was gone! We started downstairs. He clasped my hand with all his strength and said with determination, "I'm not going to cry, Mommie, because the Doctora said if I cried I could never come to see you again."

A pain shot through me. So this was what he had been told. He kissed me, hugged me as strongly as his frail arms could do, then climbed up into the two-wheeled cart, his lips pressed into a thin white line as they drove away. I broke down completely.

Mona's children had been warned, too. They never shed a tear. But she and I cried long after the others had gone to sleep that night.

The next day I wrote to Ralph again, telling him of Gale's visit and how his forced silence and fear were killing us both. "Do something," I wrote. "Gale must be allowed to stay with me."

In the meantime, a note was delivered to me from Ralph containing a cheerful and bolstering report about Stan's convalescence, the extra food Filipinos had brought to Stan, the great kindness and care he had received from the hospital staff. I was relieved of worry over Stan, but my concern for Gale had deepened. Mr. Holland and the Committee had gotten nowhere, and evidently nothing would be done.

In spite of our worries we still had time to be hungry. Breakfast at seven o'clock consisted of a small piece of *puto* (blown-up, aerated rice bread) which left no feeling of having swallowed anything, and a cup of hot water with a slight coffee-colored appearance, sickeningly sweet. Six hours later we had lunch which was a small portion of badly cooked rice (mixed with lime and stones), some mongo beans (loaded with gas) and a stunted, thumb-sized banana. By four o'clock we were so hungry we could talk of nothing else. In desperation I began opening my canned goods — one can of something each afternoon divided into four equal portions. The others had no food with them. And this was never enough.

The food in Santo Tomas had never been satisfying in taste, quality or quantity, but here in San Jose it was even less and *worse* in taste. Although our pregnant conditions made our hunger more intense, we wondered how these old men could last on such meager fare, as well as the nurses who worked so hard.

Miki appeared at our swinging door. "Girls," she announced, "Dr. Moreta is coming this morning. He will see you in the clinic, so be ready at ten." Dr. Moreta! The elderly Spanish doctor who had been so helpful to us during Gale's illness months before. He was a family doctor to many of my friends and a highly respected surgeon. He was assigned or had volunteered to be in charge of medical needs for the old men and ourselves.

A few minutes before ten o'clock, to our surprise, he appeared in our quarters accompanied by Miki. Mary sat sulking on her bed, showing no sign of courtesy as he greeted us.

"So this is what the Japs have ordered — pregnant women with diseased old men," he began. "Excuse me, ladies, if I get profane. We'll get even with them and you'll have the finest babies in the world! Let us begin with a complete checkup, blood count and all."

One by one we went into the clinic for our examinations. When my turn came he asked about Stan and Gale and was deeply concerned about our family separation and the boys' health. He listened to my case history, one normal birth then a caesarian section and the internal mixup. After examination he assured me I could have a normal delivery. He would tell my friends of my whereabouts. I mustn't worry.

His assistant, a young Spanish graduate, would do the followups in routine examinations, he explained. Miki later filled in with details that Dr. Moreta's weak heart prevented him from climbing stairs. Visits to the convent would be difficult for him.

Results from the tests showed that we were all sub-normal. My blood count was very close to pernicious anemia. My blood pressure was a low 80. Mona was in poor condition, too. Within a week came Vitamin B and iron cocktails! Soon we were also given a series of liver shots.

One day I asked Miki how Dr. Moreta could procure these tonics for us when such medicines were not available at any price. "We don't ask him, Grace. He is a wonder and a godfather to all of us. Say nothing about it." Many months later I learned that he was sending thousands of pesos worth of medicine to our military prisoners in Japanese camps. I prayed that somehow he might escape the enemy's claws. He hated the Japs with a vengeance and was directing all his energy, skill and means to combat the suffering and sorrow they were inflicting everywhere. "Anay," he called them, the parasite ants that work from the inside, leaving only a surface shell behind.

UNDERGROUND HELP
(February, 1943)

Phyllis and I made a resolution to walk at least two miles a day. Mona found walking too painful — a half mile was all she could do. With the hot, dry season coming on, along with the dust, we realized that any walking would have to be done in the early morning and/or late afternoon. The grounds were small so we measured the approximate length of the drive, one end to the other. It would take eight to ten round trips to equal one mile!

Each morning after our small lump of breakfast *puto,* we started out. The old men who came down for their walks snickered at our bulk and our speed. Now and then they would pace along with us, chatting and reminiscing, but most of the time Phyllis and I marathoned the dirty slag alone. We became staunch friends, sharing our childhood experiences, comparing customs of our two nations, and in general, philosophizing.

Phyllis had had a colorful show career. Her training in ballet and circus acrobatics, then into roller skating, had been thorough and tough. She was most interesting and talented. Her speed in knitting appalled me — and she could read and knit simultaneously! My needles tangled, crossed and dropped stitches. Now, with her inspiration I struggled to increase my proficiency, succeeding to the extent that I managed to knit a pair of string socks in one day by racing with myself on each row, then each ten rows.

Ordinary string, which had been so cheap in pre-war days, was now inflated in price like everything else. Ralph and the boys needed socks. Luckily I had purchased a large cone of string in camp. (Wool was too hot and unavailable at any price.)

A week after Gale's visit, several Spanish girls were permitted in the convent to see the old men. One of these girls mentioned that she had gone to Holy Ghost Convent the day before to see the children there. Yes, she had seen Gale, the little boy who was sick in bed with a fever. They didn't know the cause, she said. But I knew — it was grief and homesickness! He would never be well as long as he was separated from us. I was desperate. What could I do? A heavy depression settled over me. This was Friday.

On Sunday afternoon when families of the old men were allowed to visit, I was summoned downstairs secretly. Our prison papers stated that we were now military prisoners. Contact with any outsider was forbidden. Because the Japanese were too busy and short-handed to keep a guard at the entrance gate, the responsibility for carrying out their restrictions fell to the elected monitor for the old men. He was sympathetic to us, and a visitor had been smuggled in. Who was it?

I tiptoed downstairs, unnoticed. An American woman, Mrs. Kephart, greeted me. She was outside of camp because of her small baby born just before the war. Women with children under one year were not being interned.

"Grace," she whispered, "it's so good to see you. We want to help you. Mrs. Boni, Mrs. Rifkin, Mrs. Larcher, and myself." They were all parents of children I had taught in the American School and were outside of camp for similar reasons as Mrs. Kephart. "We want to bring you food," she said.

I could hardly hold back the tears. Their concern and generosity had come at a time when I was in the depths of despair over Gale, and hunger, too.

"How would it be if we sent you a hot meal each day?" she continued.

"Mrs. Kephart, there are four of us here and we are all hungry. I appreciate your great kindness but I couldn't possibly eat when the others are just as hungry as I am. They do not have contacts in Manila. I know it is out of the question to send food for four."

She thought for a moment and then said, "Suppose we each send one meal for four, once a week. I'm sure the others would be happy to do this. We each have a Filipino house boy who can deliver the food, say around five o'clock on Mondays, Wednesdays, Fridays and Sundays." She kissed me and said she would send someone to Holy Ghost to check on Gale. Donning her dark glasses and large brimmed hat, she hurried out.

Stunned and speechless, I flew upstairs to tell the others of our good fortune. My words spilled out incoherently. "Food! We're going to have food," I cried, trying to explain how and from whom. Mona and Phyllis expressed their appreciation and excitement. Mary said nothing.

At an opportune time I told Mr. Reyes, our monitor friend, of the plan. He promised to watch for the Filipino and to see that we got the food; no names would be mentioned.

On Monday afternoon we couldn't stay away from our one window which looked out on the entrance gate. The late afternoon sun blazed in on us. Five o'clock came and passed. No sign of our expected meal. Phyllis checked and rechecked her watch . . . 5:15. Had the plan fallen through? We tried not to show our anxiety, but I felt doubly responsible, having given them such hope for food. At 5:20 a bicycle was coming toward the gate. We twisted our fingers, bit our nails, and fervently prayed. Yes, there was a food pail swinging from the handlebars!

In a few minutes there was a knock on our swinging door and Mr. Reyes slipped the bucket through with a knowing smile. That meal and the meals which kept coming on those red-letter days were heaven-sent. Several more women joined the group of four to lessen the drain on each of them. Later Mrs. Rifkin asked to take every Sunday, sending us fried chicken or some delicious fare each week. We lived for those days, counting the hours until five o'clock.

The next secret visitor who came to the island was Trudl Dubsky Zipper. She was like a fairy godmother, sneaking in when few dared, and risking the spying of the Japs who watched her and her husband's activities closely. Bearing fruits and sweets, she proceeded to tell me of her visits to Philippine General Hospital to see Stan and Ralph, and to Holy Ghost Convent to see Gale. She had taken him candy and cookies and told him stories while he lay in bed. Both Stan and Gale knew and loved Trudl and Herbert, so Trudl's visit must have cheered them and brought hope to Gale. The Zippers were teaching privately in their apartment, and Herbert, despite the Jap's weekly visits to check on his progress in reorganizing the Symphony, was still managing diplomatically not to do it! I knew they had little to eat themselves, yet Trudl continued to bring fruits and supplies to us, plus bits of encouraging news.

From the first arrival of food from our benefactors, Mary, without discretion, had seen to it that her portion was the largest. The three of us, especially Mona who was a true missionary, wanted to help Mary who was only seventeen and showed the need of correction and understanding in every way. Her Spanish mother in Manila had refused to get in touch with her. No one had a good word for her. So we shared everything we had and purposely gave her little extras. Her language as well as her table manners were revolting and most of our efforts seemed futile.

Our greatest blow came when we discovered that she was taking things! Mona and Phyllis had obtained several tins of canned milk. I had nearly a case of milk, procured when I was teaching. Mary had bought several tins from one of the old men. We had rationed ourselves to one can per week, drinking a small amount each night at bedtime, but Mary downed a can a day.

One night as I took my can from the shelf, it felt surprisingly light. I had opened it only two days before. As I tipped it to pour, only a few drops came out. Mary was out of the room. I turned to Mona and Phyllis. They were astonished. It couldn't be. We decided to mention it in front of Mary, without any accusation. She was not in the least responsive. Soon we noticed other things missing, not only food. Finally we took our problem to Miki, who bore the brunt for everyone's feelings and upsets. She talked to Mary as only Miki could, but still no change.

Mary became our added cross to bear. We tried to turn aside the thought of venereal disease which she most likely had, and we scrubbed our tiny lavatory each day with a weak disinfectant solution available. Mary never did her portion of room cleaning, never shared in her responsibility for anything.

One day the Spanish nun came in while Mary was out. She, too, had found that Mary was taking things from the dining room, and with a translator, she told us we must keep all of our canned goods under lock and key. She would furnish us a small cabinet placed in the corridor outside.

Because Mary was Catholic, she was watched more persistently by the Sister. Father Kelly*, a young Irish priest, red-headed and personable, came to see Mary one morning. Perhaps he would be able to help her, we thought. When she returned to our room her eyes were red and swollen. From then on, he came to see her nearly every week to take account of her sins and to know if she had attended Sunday Mass in the convent chapel. Our hopes would soar, only to be crushed the following day.

It had been three weeks since our forced exodus from Santo Tomas. On this morning Miki called to me after breakfast. "I want to see you, Grace." I hurried into the clinic before the regular line of old men had formed.

"Mr. Holland just called me from the Commandant's Office in Santo Tomas," she began. "He said the Philippine General Hospital ambulance will stop here to pick up something enroute to Santo Tomas. 'Tell Grace,' he said." At first I was puzzled, then I suddenly knew what the message meant — Ralph and Stan would be on that ambulance going back to Santo Tomas, and if I were downstairs waiting outside at the proper time I might get to see them. Miki hugged me and said, "I'll keep that ambulance here as long as I dare, Grace."

I lost no time in getting outside, setting up a folding chair in the grass as close to the entrance gate as possible. It was only eight o'clock but I would stay right there until they came. I planned

---

*Father Pat Kelly was a member of Irish Mission to China, located in the 300-year old church and convent in the Ermita section of Manila. Long suspected by the Japs for their sympathies and help to the Americans, Father Kelly and the other priests were locked in the upper floor of an apartment building that was filled with Filipinos. Petroleum was thrown on the foundation, and the building was set on fire. All of the mission priests died there except Father Fallon, who was later found dead of shrapnel wounds in his schoolyard.

hundreds of things to say, but always my thoughts came back to my one worry, Gale, and the necessity of getting him back to one of us, either in Santo Tomas with Ralph or here with me. I kept hoping that if Ralph weren't put in solitary, Stan and Gale could stay in the Education Building with him.

The tropical sun was beating down on my head, but I couldn't go inside. I might miss them. I squinted at the bridge road until my eyes were blinded with dark spots. Suddenly the gate opened and in drove the ambulance. I raced behind it up to the entrance steps. Stan shouted, "Mommie, Mommie, I'm all well now!" In trying to reach the other side of the bus where Ralph was seated, I did not hear the rest of his words. He put his hands out to me. "We can't get off, Grace. How are you?"

I interrupted, breathlessly crying, "Ralph, we must get Gale moved from Holy Ghost. He's sick with fever again. I can't stand it any longer. Do something! Do something!" My voice choked with sobs.

The guard was hurrying the bed frame into the bus. "No wait — no time!" he yelled. The driver jumped in, complying with the order.

"I'll see that Gale is taken care of, either sent to you or to me," Ralph called. "Take care of yourself, dear — don't worry. Stan is fine. I'll see to everything." The bus sped away.

This had been our thirty seconds of communication. The nervous tension in waiting in the hot sun, the running I had done, now spent itself in a convulsion of hysteria. I staggered blindly, hunting for my chair. Everything went black in front of me and with a dizzying nausea I fell against a pillar supporting the small overhead roof and steps.

Miki found me and helped me inside. The rest of the day I spent in bed, unable to speak or eat. That night I dreamed once again of the terror and fear of the Japanese, separating and hurting us.

The next afternoon a call came from Mr. Grinnell, head of our camp committee at Santo Tomas, saying that Gale would be brought to me from Holy Ghost Convent the next afternoon by Mr. Duggleby. Stan was being sent out of camp to the Bousmans (the missionary family who had sheltered us months before) and

Ralph was already in the camp jail beginning his 30-day sentence in solitary confinement.

In contrast to my despair on the day before, I now felt a surge of joy. Even though Ralph had to be in solitary, Gale-boy would be with me and I could give him the protection and love for both of us. Stan would be in good hands with the Bousmans whom he liked so much. The world looked hopeful.

Mona, Phyllis, and even Mary, expressed their happiness in my new joy. With Miki's help, we shifted and pushed until there was room for one more very narrow cot beside mine. The male assistant brought it in, accompanied by the Spanish nun.

I could hardly wait for Gale's arrival. The girls knew that our outside meals would henceforth be shared by five, but they weren't unhappy about it. Mona tried not to show her longing to see *her* children who had been taken back to Santo Tomas to be with their father. Reverend Newland was out of solitary; paroled after one week with an apology from the Commandant: "Very sorry," he had said, "big mistake." But they had refused to change Mona's sentence. She must remain with us. Her two children were sleeping in the Annex in Santo Tomas with one of the mothers responsible for them.

From the beginning of internment, the Japs openly resented the consideration and respect shown to women by our American men. They hated to see the men doing all the heavy work — garbage detail, kitchen cleanup, carrying water, and helping with the children.

As yet Mona had received no word from her husband. Many times she had sent notes to him asking that he send her several cans of milk from their stock of tinned foods. She had opened her last tin of milk. Completely unselfish with her few belongings, she was reluctant to accept from others. In our conversations she had told us of their former mission work in Tibet, the hardships of their life there with unclean food and long hours of work with the natives. She was genuinely in love with her husband and children, yet as time went on we knew that Mona had carried the brunt of responsibility and work in both family and missionary assignments. Her heart was in the missionary field with a zest beyond her physical strength. Her face already wore deep lines of toil and suffering, doing without dire necessities. In camp, Reverend

101

Newland customarily studied and read scriptures while Mona did the family wash.

When Gale arrived the next afternoon, I didn't cry, but he did — so great was his joy of seeing me and knowing that he wouldn't be taken away in half an hour. Mr. Duggleby slipped a note into my hand as he handed over Gale's *tampipi* of clothes and few toys. It was from Ralph.

Underground communications were fantastic and harrowing; dangerous to those who risked carrying messages, yet breathtaking and exciting to us. Tom Poole, Mr. Duggleby, and one of the old men who went to Santo Tomas camp for treatment twice a week helped to keep our spirits up.

Although Gale was noticeably thinner and slightly feverish in the afternoons, he gradually showed improvement and had a better appetite. There were problems, of course, trying to keep his hands clean, especially when the old men would give him candy. They would call him to their bedsides, offering him a trinket or a piece of *puto*.

A more serious problem was the mutual dislike that was developing between Mary and Gale. I had been careful not to show any negative reaction toward Mary. Her language was no different in front of him and she had spoken quite crossly to him many times. Especially noticeable were her groans of resentment if he cried out in the night.

One day he edged over to my side and whispered, "I don't like Mary, Mommie." This personal feud between them continued the rest of the time that Gale was with me. I never dared leave him in the room with Mary. Her temper was no average one, and his remarks could easily ignite it.

Another reason for concern was the sudden affection shown toward Gale by a man in the next room beyond ours. He was the only patient in a room by himself, recently released from an isolation cell in an asylum. A wealthy businessman before the war, he had gone insane soon after internment. He was recovering and was pronounced "no longer dangerous." His wife was in Santo Tomas camp. In his recovery he longed for his grandchildren back in the States, and Gale became the answer to this longing. He imagined Gale to be his grandchild. It was a continuous struggle to prevent him from taking Gale into his room where he would describe his hallucinations, holding up a picture of his wife and dramatizing her, talking about his grandchildren and calling them by name. He also developed a fixation for me, hunting me out to confess his past ways in business, and in the evenings insisting that I play the violin for him.

I had often played for the old men at night in the unlit corridor, answering their requests for "Rock of Ages," "Tenting Tonight," the "Blue Danube," "God Bless America," and even hillbilly music. Now, soon after supper each evening — long before dark — he would be pounding on our swinging doors. "I want the 'Old Refrain,' Grace! Play it for me. Right now!" There would be no let-up until he could hear me tuning the strings.

There were other annoyances, too, such as the horrible profanity, spitting and hacking of the old men sitting their days away just outside our doors. We could never shut out the sounds because our halfway doors were open above and below. There was one old man whom I'll always remember. I can still hear his loud-spoken accounts of the wonderful hangings he had performed in Shanghai and Hongkong, as executioner par excellence! If we heard it once, we heard each story twenty times, interspersed with mention of "my wife at that time." He had never said exactly how many wives he had had, but we did know that he had twenty-two children — some of whom came to see him on Sundays. His profanity was rich and profuse and he finished each episode with a loud hack and long spit toward the spitoon across the corridor, often narrowly missing one of us walking through the hall.

I thought I had become immune to profanity in my college days when I was a violinist-stroller in a Chicago restaurant and bar, and an erstwhile drunk would give vent to his abusive vocabulary. But this was mere child's rabble compared to what we were hearing, both from Mary and from the old men in the convent! The blasphemy that was vilest and loudest occurred on certain nights of the month — during full moon — when one of the men, an epileptic, had his worst spells. Unfortunately at this time each month some native liquor was smuggled into him and in no time he would be dead drunk in one of his terrifying spells, shouting unearthly blasphemy as I had never imagined possible. Miki was the only one who had any control over him. She and Mrs. Breson, the English nurse, would take turns staying up all night with him, changing his bed and trying to quiet him. The head nurse would not go near him. "He is a sinner!" Some months later we learned that his liquor supply came from a Jap soldier-friend.

On such nights I, too, would be awake, fearful that Gale would be aroused and frightened. And at least once every night some man would have a nightmare, walk in his sleep and raise up the dead with his ghostly cries. We got used to that and could almost sleep right through such minor disturbances, but one night I was awakened suddenly by our doors swinging back. I raised up to see a shadowy figure of a man inside our room. I was terrified. He was standing in the narrow aisle between Mary's and Gale's beds. "What is it?" I asked weakly. "What do you want?"

He backed out of the door just as the other girls awakened. We got up and looked into the hall. Ronnie, the male orderly, was hurrying down the hall to rescue one of the men who had gotten lost. "It's all right, girls," he whispered. "I'll take care of him."

Up to this time we had not thought of being molested and now we laughed over this sudden and foolish fear. It was a joke for many days after that, especially when we learned just which old man it was!

Several times after that, different ones burst through our doors in the daytime by mistake and much to their embarrassment. Our doors were just like theirs, they said, so the monitor, Mr. Reyes decided to tie a large white tag on the door with "LADIES" written on it.

One of the old men, a Scotsman, was interested in gardening and drew Gale's attention to his planting. Gale was excited . . . he would have a garden of his own. Each morning he would finish his rice bread and hurry outside. One morning his dreams came true — two cornstalks were peeping through the ground.

The first Sunday after Gale arrived, Stan was allowed to visit us on the island. A missionary minister who came to conduct a service for the old men brought Stan with him. I still smile when I think of his arrival. Any news that Stan had could never wait, and this day he had much to tell.

First there were shouts of "Mommie" piercing the stillness of a Catholic Mass in the convent. I rushed outside to reach him before he shouted more. As Gale and I raced down the hall, he shouted so loudly that even the old men who complained of deafness could relate the story. "Mommie, I'm here! Daddy's been put in jail and I'm staying with the Bousmans 'til he gets out! I want to see Gale, too!" followed by a complete repetition for emphasis.

Our few hours together made me realize how much stronger Stan was. His apparent good health accented Gale's frailness. As he kissed me goodbye and ran pell-mell down the steps to the outside world, my concern over Gale increased.

I had sent a small box of canned goods into camp for Ralph, asking that they would be taken to him in solitary. The two portions a day of cold line chow would leave much to be desired and these cans might help to keep up his strength and his morale. I learned later that he received none of the cans until after his release from the prison-within-a-prison.

Chapter Seven

FALSE ALARMS
(March - May, 1943)

The day after Ralph's release from solitary his request to have Stan and Gale come back into Santo Tomas to be with him was granted. Because of crowded conditions in camp (others were being brought in from southern islands and other camps), the Japs were allowing some of the men to sleep in their daytime shanties. Accordingly, Ralph was permitted to have the boys with him in the shanty.

Gale, homesick for his Daddy, was anxious to return to Santo Tomas when I explained that he and Stan could be with Ralph in our shanty both day and night time without the crowds of others. Arrangements were made and Gale said goodbye quite happily. I had packed some of the canned goods with his clothes. Half of our original supply was already depleted.

For Mrs. Breson's birthday, we planned a surprise and invited all three nurses to come to our room at eight o'clock that night. We had fixed a fruit salad, adding one can of fruit cocktail to the native fruits, and from one of the *muchachas* we had bought some inferior cookies to complete the feast. A week before we had talked about entertainment for the occasion. I penned some lyrics which we set about practicing in a whisper to the tune of "Solomon Levi." Our dramatic rendition made the floor show a success and we all laughed harder than we had in months.

To the tune of "Sōlomon Levi" we sang:

Verse I

We are four pregnant women,

107

And we come from Santo Tomas;
The Japanese are mad at us
Because we have done thus;
Our husbands have been put in jail,
Our children taken, too,
All because the Japs now say,
"To propagate — no can do!"

Chorus

We're with the old men,
Living in San Jose;
We all eat together
But three meager meals a day;
But here we have our liver shots,
And iron cocktails, too;
And in between some Vitamin B,
With all that it can do!

Verse II

But now we must confess to you,
Our duties here are nil —
Just sit and think and knit and sit,
Of which we've had our fill;
But also we must add to this
That we have not lost face,
Because we're doing all we can,
To propagate the race!

It was a rollicking evening.

It was true, we had no camp duties, no chow lines to stand in, no KP work. Our days seemed to get longer. Idleness does not help endurance. So we sewed frantically, knitted furiously and wrote amorously. There was little reading matter to be had, and little of that was worth reading.

Mary did little except to mope on her bed, reading whatever she could pick up in true story romances. She was larger than we were, although her baby was not due until July. We talked about the importance of daily exercise and not overeating, especially with starches, which was all that the convent diet consisted of. Her high blood pressure was giving the doctor concern. She ignored the doctor's advice, ate more and exercised little. Sometimes her disdainful attitude, even her presence, stretched our nerves to the breaking point. Even the old men showed their disapproval.

The days I had visitors went much faster. Nearly every week Mrs. Graemiger, a Swiss lady whose children I had taught, rode bravely into the Hospicio, her bicycle loaded with fruits or surprise articles. Her visits always pulled me together. Emotionally and spiritually, I felt more whole. Then Tonia, my Filipino housegirl, began to come once a week on her way to Santo Tomas. She insisted on washing my sheets and any dress I might want. Sometimes I added Mona's sheets with mine, knowing how hard it was for Mona to do them in a tiny tub where she had to bend over in painful position.

I had been so confident that the war would be over before my baby would come that I had given away dresses that were getting snug. So many in Santo Tomas needed them. Once again, friends on the outside came to our rescue with maternity dresses for the four of us. Some of these were third-hand and before imprisonment would be over, they'd be sixth and seventh-hand. Nothing wearable remained unworn.

For several days now I had felt intermittent pressure pains that would almost lift me into space — then no more until the next day.

On April 25th during siesta time, we heard Dr. Moreta's voice in the hall. I had just "surfaced" after the strongest labor pressure yet. Perhaps I should report this condition to him. Pulling my robe around my extended waist, I stepped out into the corridor. Miki, Ronnie, and Mrs. Breson were leaning over and working on one of the old men while Dr. Moreta was listening to his heart. He motioned to them to stop. "This poor fellow is a prisoner no more," he said quietly, and they covered him with a sheet.

He turned, and seeing me, said brightly, "Well, how is Mrs. Nash today?" Maybe he didn't know I had seen the death that moment before. As we walked toward the clinic room, I described my symptoms. After examining me, he turned to Miki. "A new life for one just finished." Then he said to me, "Pack your things, Grace, and come along to the hospital!"

Life and death, I thought, all in the same call. We're only transients . . . life on lease. I hurried to the room to pack. The others were excited and rushed around trying to help. In our haste and hulks, we kept bumping into each other.

The old men, in spite of the death among them, rallied to this newer excitement, my delivery. Those who were able to go down the steps ushered me to Dr. Moreta's car, wishing me their best — in other words that it would be a boy. As Dr. Moreta drove out the gate, I realized it was the first time I had been in a real car since the fateful ride to Santo Tomas in January '42.

At St. Joseph's Hospital, Dr. Moreta told the nurse to prepare me for examination. Although my labor pains had quieted, I was terribly excited. Anxiously, I prayed for more pains, quick!

"I don't think it will be tonight," he said after the examination. "Perhaps tomorrow, we'll see." Then, his eyes twinkling, he added, "Wouldn't you enjoy a private room for the night? You don't need to go back right away. Just take a little vacation here."

My disappointment was sharp over the delay in delivery, but it would be a real treat to stay here overnight. I thanked him and said it would be wonderful.

With all the sudden privacy and change in environment, I slept very little that night. Too nice, I thought, imagining what the others would say when I returned the next day. The thought of the old men's probable laughter would be humiliating — but I must face it.

This was the first of a series of embarrassments, and by the third false alarm I had developed a complex. Leaving and returning in the daytime wasn't quite so humiliating, but having to return after curfew at eleven o'clock meant wakening the sisters, the monitor and any light sleepers. It was absolutely disintegrating! Each time I said goodbye, they laughed and said, "Oh, yeah?" or, "See you tomorrow." The head nurse, horrified over the possibility of my giving birth in the convent, insisted on timing my pains — but they couldn't be timed. And she would become irascible, accusing me of deliberate stubborness. Before the Hospicio Convent would accept us, the nuns had been assured by the Japs that our babies would be born in a hospital, *not* in the convent. This was to our benefit.

These overwhelming pressures continued, with the discomfort and agony lasting from one to many hours, then suddenly stopping. Nights I would pace the hall for what seemed like hours — then a few hours of sleep to gather strength to face the next day. Dr. Moreta, so kind and patient, had tried to console me with messages of "a few more days, maybe a week, but be brave, Grace." The difficulties I was having stemmed from the previous Caesarian section, when the uterus was sewn to the stomach lining. Now, in these final months, the pressures I was feeling were due to a pulling away, or a tearing of the sutures.

The four of us had often talked about names for our babes. I had written to Ralph for his suggestions and had mentioned one or two names I liked. The name "Kerry" for a boy had interested me. His note came back suggesting his father's name, Harry. But there was already one grandson, Edward Harry, his sister's boy, and I had never held a particular fondness for that name. Suddenly I remembered that April 29th was the Japanese Emperor's birthday. What if this baby were born on April 29th! On second thought, I burst into laughter.

"What's so funny," asked Phyllis, looking up from her knitting.

"Well, if I should have a son born on the Emperor's birthday, April 29th, don't you think Hari-Kari would be a good name?"

They howled with glee — anything for a good laugh. After that third false trip to the hospital, Phyllis had a better idea. "Grace, if you do have a son, I think you ought to name him Douglas."

"Why Douglas?" I asked innocently.

"Because he's so late in coming — like MacArthur!" she answered. Her remark brought gales of laughter, but my baby still didn't arrive and I became more anxious and weaker each day with the continuing hours of labor pressures.

Long before dawn on May fifth, I awoke when Mona got up. It was past time for her baby to come. Each night we had repeated our wish, "May this be your last night with us, Mona." She was weary from the discomfort and extra weight.

"Mona, are you all right?" I whispered.

"Yes, but I think the time has come at last," she answered. "It's only 1:30, so I won't call Miki yet," she added calmly.

I stayed awake with her, anxious because of her past history. Her babies had come fast, she said. At four o'clock we awakened Miki who thought it best not to call Dr. Moreta until a bit later. I was more worried than Mona, but at 6 a.m. Dr. Moreta's car pulled in and we escorted Mona down the stairs. At the last minute, Miki decided to go with them and the three drove away.

We waited for news like anxious relatives. Finally at noon the telephone in the clinic room rang. Miss Earl said she would answer. We waited in the doorway. Ah, Mona had had a son, normal and fine. All was well. We returned to our room with sighs of relief and joy. Miki would give us the details when she returned.

Which one of us would be next to have our baby? Phyllis or I?

May 7th dawned, the day set by both of us. It was Ralph's birthday. I had made another pair of socks for him the week before and sent them to camp; not much of a gift, but the thought was much deeper than the material expression. I longed to be with him; my heart ached to give expression to my love and appreciation. I thought of the care he was giving our sons, being both Father and Mother to them despite his long hours of camp work. When Stan and Gale had visited me two weeks before, they were neat and clean, full of praise for their Daddy. They told me how he could make delicious pancakes out of their mush and flip them in the air; how he had carved toy acrobats out of scraps of wood. He washed their clothes, scrubbed the shanty, and bathed them each night before they went to bed. "And guess what Dad's making for us," said Stan. "It's a bus, a beautiful bus!" broke in Gale. "This long." He measured an arm's length. "It's going to run, too — with a real motor," continued Stan. "He started to build it in solitary — while I was at the Bousmans, remember?" I would be hearing more about the bus later.

Mona's children had also come to visit, loaded with their laundry, and she had spent the day scrubbing her children and their clothes.

My pains began early on the morning of May 7th, and I paced the driveway in the hot sun, forcing back tears, yet hoping that labor would continue. It lasted until eleven o'clock, then no more. I lay back in bed for a siesta.

About five o'clock, Phyllis cried out, "Maybe, Grace, maybe." She rushed around the room doing nothing. By six o'clock she was sure and hurried down the hall to take a shower.

Her baby girl was born just before midnight on Ralph's birthday. How ironic, I thought, that Phyllis would have Ralph's promised present!

Mona and Phyllis had their babies. Mary and I were left, still on the island with the old men. Somehow I must grin and bear it. The next night Mary told me much of her life history, about her planned marriage to the man in camp whose wife and children were outside. For the first time she took on an almost mellow feminine nature. I was sympathetic and hopeful for her.

The following Sunday was my worst day and I broke into uncontrolled weeping. I hated the staring eyes of the old men each time I had to go through the corridor to our communal lavatory, and I felt as if I were going insane. In my mind I cursed the bungling mess the missionary doctor had made in the needless Caesarian section he had performed when Gale was born. I abhorred the tropical heat.

Maybe a shower would calm me, at least I could turn the water on full force to cover the sound of my crying. It did help and I gave vent to my emotions, crying bitterly for half an hour, the shower drowning out my heavy sobs.

Back in my room, I began to think about all the women who had sent food to us so faithfully. In a few minutes I composed verses of thanks to send them, making copies for each one, as follows:

> *Once again pen and paper I take,*
> *To write thanks to you ladies*
> *For those delicious meat, steaks,*
> *Salads and pastries with vitamins five,*
> *That during these months have kept us alive!*
>
> *(With courage undaunted,*
> *Regardless of rumor*
> *Over what next may happen*
> *To darken our future . . .)*
>
> *And now that the end of confinement is sighted,*
> *I'm due to take leave of the "Old Men's Home,"*
>   *delighted*
> *As never before, to enter hospital gates and*

delivery room door,
Bent double with labor and backpains galore.

They soon will be over, and out of the mist,
Another "new Nash" for Manila we'll list;
(In spite of the wartime, "Production now ceased,"
Nash models keep coming, here in the East!)

May this babe be the stronger for Dad's
*   sentence in jail;*
(Double internment itself, still proved no avail)
Old men and neurotics, and civil war talk,
Should make for strong will, good character and walk;
Topped off with a rich sense of humor
To balk any prejudice, spite, or small talk.

And as I think back o'er this long preparation,
Your kindness and gifts helped build our
*   great nation.*
My hope is — that since so many have helped to
*   bring "Nash '43,"*
That of all models yet, the finest (s)he'll be!
And have what it takes for success and strong faith,
In a life that is better than that we have faced.

> *Yours sincerely,*
>
> *Grace Nash*

I had just finished the copies when Miki appeared in the doorway. "Grace, how would you like to go to the hospital and stay there until your baby arrives?"

What relief it would be to get away from all of this, and the old men's curiosity and kidding. "But how can I do that, Miki?"

"It has all been arranged, Grace. Dr. Moreta will call for you in half an hour," she said.

"Who got the room for me? I can't afford to pay for living at the hospital!"

"Dr. Moreta will tell you all about it. Don't worry. And, Santo Tomas office has agreed."

Mary offered to help me pack, and promised to give my notes of thanks to the houseboy who was bringing food the next day. I took the other notes for Mrs. Graemiger and those not in the meals' pool with me to send through underground channels.

For a final and fourth time, I bade farewell to my senile friends. I kissed Miki and wished Mary good luck, then settled into the seat beside Dr. Moreta. On the drive to the hospital he disclosed how Mr. Brimo had engaged a private room for me in the hospital and that I should not worry about bills or costs. They were taking care of everything. "Just don't mention it, Grace," he finished.

Words are not adequate to express the gratitude I felt that day — and still feel to this day — to such great people as the Brimos, the Zippers, Dr. Moreta, and countless others. I haven't mentioned the surprise which Dr. Moreta brought to the Hospicio on the day before Mona went to the hospital. To each of us he presented a large *tampipi* of baby clothes, decorated on the top with a hand-painted nursery scene and pretty ribbon bows. Inside was a complete layette, including a large rubber pad, two nursing bottles and nipples — items no longer procurable in stores. He explained that some months before he had told his many patients of our predicament and with their help he had fitted the cases — another way of getting even with the Japs, he said, smiling. We were speechless.

I felt much easier at the hospital even though my labor troubles continued. The nurses tried to check the regularity of pains — as long as they lasted — and then marked "false alarm" on the chart.

There were a number of ambulatory patients at St. Joseph's Hospital who had managed to stay out of internment camp. One of these, a well-known perennial bachelor, Mr. Hoskins, introduced himself. He knew Ralph, he said, and on his behalf he invited me to have lunch with him the next day.

Mr. Hoskins was a connoisseur of fine foods and had spared no cash in building up his reserve supplies. He prepared his own meals, not eating the hospital fare. His special dishes were "out of this world," I exclaimed as I feasted to the bursting point.

We had lunch together often after that, I being too weak-willed to refuse the good food he prepared. He was ever solicitous over my negative progress and we enjoyed many hours in pleasant conversation.

Mona left the hospital for Santo Tomas a week after I arrived. I had tried to help her with care of her baby and herself. She was still weak and frightfully hungry. On that Saturday morning I, too, was exhausted. My labor had started at one a.m. and had not let up since. I gave Mona a note for Ralph. It was frantic sounding, I am sure, as I wrote that I was in such pain, hour after hour, and I couldn't stand it any longer. Mona said she would see Ralph and explain my condition to him. "Don't give up, Grace," she said, bidding me goodbye. By four o'clock that afternoon I was desperate. I called the Filipino doctor and begged him for an opiate, something to relieve me long enough to muster strength. Finally, seeing my hysteria and the chart, he consented.

Sunday morning I awoke with a dull numbness and indifference. My face was swollen and my will power gone. When Dr. Moreta arrived, he was told of the previous difficult day I had had. He wanted to make an examination. I had been on that uncomfortable table so many times that I hated it with a vengeance. "By the end of this week you'll have your baby, I'm sure," he said hopefully.

I was a joke in the hospital now. The nurses giggled when they saw me walking the floor each day and night. "False alarm," they would say, "not tonight!"

The phrase, "next week," had been said all too often. How long could this go on? Certainly not much longer and me still be alive, I thought. Yesterday it was sixteen hours, I thought bitterly. Sunday all I felt was a deep depression. Only a few times had the pressure carried me into space.

About 7:30 that night a nurse looked in. "Telephone for you, Mrs. Nash."

I didn't understand. The rule of "No internee may talk on the phone" had been rigidly enforced.

"Telephone for you," she repeated. "Come."

I rushed into the office. It was Ralph's voice. I nearly fainted! He had gotten permission to call me, he said. "I was so worried. I had to hear your voice. What does the doctor say, Grace?" I answered him, discouraged.

To my question about his health, he told me a carbuncle had developed on his shoulder. He was suffering great pain and could not sleep. But it was heaven just to hear his voice, and I slept more peacefully than in many nights.

The next day was quiet. I took my morning walk around the hospital grounds and settled down to read at siesta time. I had been there ten days now.

About 2:30 my eyes lost focus with the heavy pressure of pain again. I dreaded the hours ahead, but after each pain I tried to read again — until the next one would carry me away. The pains were coming more often now, and harder each time.

With a suddenness, I rose from the bed. This was it, my time had come — at last — I knew. I hurried to take a shower, calling Elsie Cotterman, a new patient, to assist me. I made the high step getting into the tub all right, but getting out I couldn't make the necessary clearance with a heavy pain beginning again. Elsie maneuvered and tugged, and finally got me out without mishap. I raced back to the room, only to be seized again. They were coming in earnest now. I paced the room while Elsie ran to tell the Doctora to call Dr. Moreta.

"Not this time," the Doctora replied, "it's just another false alarm."

Snooks McClure, another patient and good friend, came into the room.

My whole body was in a series of tremors now, but I kept on walking, reaching for the bed post each time around. It was after five o'clock and they still had not called the doctor. I was frightened that he might not get here in time. Panic swept over me as I realized that neither the staff doctor nor the Doctora knew anything about my internal entanglements.

"Snooks," I said, perspiration dripping from my face, "command them to call Dr. Moreta at once. The baby will be born in this room if he doesn't come right away."

At six o'clock the Doctora reluctantly made the call. Good fortune that Dr. Moreta was still in his office. He understood her immediately when she said, "Dr. Moreta, Mrs. Nash would like to see you."

My walking was finished. I lay in a trembling heap on my bed, my body shaking in a heavy and continuous palsy. If only I could lose consciousness.

A NEW NASH!
(May 24, 1943)

In the distance I heard the sound of the elevator door closing. Dr. Moreta had come at last. He was the only one who used the elevator. A sense of relief came over me. He was at my side, speaking so reassuringly now.

Turning to the Doctora, he said quietly, "Please remember this: when a woman begins to shake, there is no time to lose. She must get to the delivery room." It was too late now for any preparation. Dr. Moreta, his young assistant, Dr. Ricardo, and the Doctora hurried into their hospital gowns and gloves. Snooks was by my side as they hoisted me once more onto the table, my legs aching in the uncomfortable position.

I begged for ether, the first time I had ever longed for its effect. Snooks held my hand as I inhaled it fast and hard. I saw Dr. Moreta reach for the forceps as I went under. A strange but so real a vision came to me . . . *I was feeling all the pain, submerged in its totality, and I knew that the Japs were trying to prevent me from living through it. I knew that if I failed, they would win the war . . . I was on the other side now . . . and how could it be explained to Ralph? . . . If only I could get back and tell him, and then we would win the war . . . terrific pain . . . I must pull through, yet I knew . . . one more such pain would be the end. "This is the last one," I sighed aloud.*

At that moment my baby cried. In joyous relief I rose up on the table and opened my eyes to behold a wonderful bit of pink and white humanity! I was pushed down again while the cord was cut and the baby placed in the glass incubator. An eight-pound boy! We would win the war!

I was very much awake as the stitching got under way, conscious of what seemed to be endless feather-stitching. "I've counted eleven stitches," I said, "How many more?"

"We are just finished; three stitches in all," replied Dr. Moreta, laughing.

He had scarcely finished the sentence when, instinctively or from habit, I raised up and stepped onto the floor. The attendants gasped and swung me back on the table. What a patient, they must have thought.

Dr. Moreta came to my side, congratulating me on the superb specimen he had just delivered. I hugged him, planting a kiss on each cheek. "Thanks," I said, too overwhelmed to say more.

I was back in my room now, receiving congratulations and joy from Elsie, Snooks and the nurses on that floor. Roy Leslie had been born at 8:01 p.m., and weighed in at eight pounds, one ounce, on May 24, 1943.

Uppermost in my thoughts now was to get word to Ralph. The camp office would be closed, so no possibility of a message tonight. Dr. Moreta had promised to call the Brimos, Zippers and others as soon as it happened, regardless of the hour. In all of my excitement and happiness, I slept but ten minutes that night. Over and over I was picturing our wonderful new baby, Roy, and reunion with Ralph, Stan and Gale.

It was just 7:30 the next morning when Trudl Zipper appeared in the door, smiling from her eyes to her toes. "Grace," she said, "I have just seen your new son, and I'm on my way to Santo Tomas to sneak word in to Ralph." She bent down and kissed me. Trudl always had a way of knowing my desires without my voicing them. Assuring her that I was fine, she left on her mission, bicycling the several miles to camp.

During the preceding weeks many false reports had gone to Ralph about our son's birth. Each time the let-down and worries that followed became more difficult for him — especially when such information was passed along and internees had stopped to congratulate him on the new girl, or boy, or whatever. One Saturday night during a movie being shown to the internees (usually a Japanese propaganda movie), the loudspeaker interrupted: "Mr. Nash is wanted at the office, immediately." Whispers started through the crowd that Mrs. Nash must have had her baby.

Ralph rushed to the office. Each shanty area had an internee night guard whose duty it was to see that there were no "illegal meetings between men and women, as well as no burglarizing." The guard from Ralph's area was standing in front of the office. "Your older son is crying, Ralph. He needs you."

Disappointed, Ralph hurried to the shanty to find Stan quite hysterical. Gale, playing 'possum,' appeared to be deep in sleep. "Daddy, Gale wakes me up all the time. He teases me and I can't stand it any longer."

Things were settled immediately and Ralph remained at the shanty while rumors of all sorts circulated the camp — rumors that had to be corrected the next day, and the next.

On a Sunday morning a week later, Gale had awakened saying that he had a baby sister. Even though it was only a dream, he convinced Stan, and before Ralph had returned with their breakfast mush, they had set out to tell their friends. Later that morning they told it to their Sunday School class, which took more days and patience for Ralph to undo.

Trudl arrived at Santo Tomas Gate. Bowing low to the guard, she asked for Mr. Chittick. He was not there yet, but she managed to speak to another American on duty who promised to relate her message to Bill Chittick, who in turn would get it to Ralph.

Before Bill had gotten to the Gate, her message had gone its way, at random. In her written note to Bill she had mentioned about the delivery by forceps and that there were streaks and marks down the baby's cheeks, not realizing that the streaks were caused by the Argerol put into his eyes.

Ralph, suffering agonies with the huge carbuncle, was in no mood to put up with more false rumors and when several internees started to congratulate him on his new son, he'd had too much of it, and said so. It was nearly noon before Bill could leave the Gate to deliver the message personally. He had looked for Ralph in all the places he might be, when Mrs. Fennel told him that Ralph had gone to the camp hospital in great pain.

When Bill found Ralph, he was being operated on. The doctors were cutting out the carbuncle. It was no minor surgery, they said, being the largest carbuncle they had ever seen — and the results could be dangerous if the drainage of poison should spread through his system.

I have often wondered how Ralph endured the suffering, mental and physical, through those days. On this day, Bill carefully told Ralph the news Trudl had brought, omitting any mention of the marks on the baby's face.

While Ralph was in the camp hospital, forbidden to move for

several days lest the flow of drainage go the wrong way, the Fennels and Crofts in our shanty area took care of Stan and Gale. He appreciated their help and expressed his gratitude to them. It was not pleasant, however, to find later that unkind remarks and criticism were being passed by a few hyper-critical neighbors. The Fennels were always first to offer assistance in a crisis. Jeanette and I had helped each other often, and now her sincerity helped to balance the scales against so much evidence of two-faced friends. Gradually I would learn of the sharp accusations against Ralph, blaming him for all our troubles, family separation and all. It enraged me at first, especially when I had been the one to persuade him that surely the war would be over before a baby would be born, and that it would be a good time to start our third child. I would never disclose these malicious bits of gossip. He had suffered enough.

Long after prison camp was over, I would find this faded copy of a pencilled letter I had sent him by underground from St. Joseph's Hospital, as follows:

From the hospital

My Dearest,

If only you could see our third son! He is so precious, not like a new babe — he has so much expression and understanding, and beauty. Ah San, our old Chinese amah who took care of Stan, saw him today. "All same, like Stanee," she exclaimed. (The highest compliment she could give.)

Am writing this in a wheel chair, my second day out of bed. Last night I had a sleeping pill, with eight hours of most wonderful sleep! And, for both of the night feedings, I had more milk than Roy could take. Yesterday, however, I started Roy on twice-a-day supplementary feedings with Elsie Cotterman who has enough milk for a nursery! Her baby, born three days ago, is beautiful, too.

Dr. Moreta said he is going to get some kind of injections for me which will help my nursing. Enough sleep will be a great boon, too. I'm drinking gallons of liquid and eating well.

Tell Stanley and Gale I'm very proud of them for being so grown up and well behaved, especially when you're feeling so bad. They'll be so thrilled when they see their little brother that it will make up for their long waiting.

I need more booties and diapers for Roy. The booties I have here are too small — his feet and his appetite are like mine, I'm afraid.

My return pass extends to June 20th, and I shall see how strong I am after I get on my feet and am taking full care of the baby. A nurse is helping me now. My nursing of Roy is the main concern that will govern my return to camp, as much as I want to get back to you all.

Please thank Mrs. Hill for the lovely baby bib clips, and when anybody asks, tell them I am doing fine and feel like a new person — which I am!

We have two baby books for Roy, in which I hope to keep accurate records, including his prenatal history. So many people have had a part in his arrival, from food and clothes, to hospital and delivery, encouragement and morale . . . that he is bound to be a "special model" — which you can easily recognize already!

Give Phyllis and Mona my love, and tell Rosie, the Fennels, and the Crofts of how much I do appreciate their help and kindness to you and the boys . . . You can probably expect us around June 15th, if all goes well.

Love,

Grace

P.S. Are you about finished with the carbuncle pain? What fun we shall have, all together, soon.

In a message from Ralph two weeks before, he had described the toy passenger bus he had cut from a cigar box. "Not a single nail in it," he wrote. "It's blue and silver, exactly to scale, with seats, a steering wheel and doors that open when touched, and with a clock-works motor to run it. The boys love it. We took it out on a test run last night after chow — on the concrete walk behind the mess kitchen. A hundred or more internees watched, and cheered. "It's a good model for busses that I plan to build after this is over."

At the outset of our double prison sentences (solitary and island isolation), the Japs had promised that each expectant father could visit the hospital after his child was born. Mona's husband had visited her in the hospital; Frank, Phyllis' husband, had come, and now Ralph had applied for his pass to come to the hospital on Friday, the earliest date the doctors would consider letting him sit up in a jolting van. The pass had been granted, and he had sent a note to me saying that he would bring the baby clothes I needed. Unwittingly, I had sent most of the layette from Dr. Moreta, back into camp, freshly laundered and ready for our return. The hospital had no supplies at all.

All of my thoughts were focused on Ralph's coming visit. On Friday morning the nurse helped me dress Roy in the little green *camisa* I had made from scraps of voile left over from the bed jacket I was wearing. What a beautiful child! At nine o'clock the hospital van was leaving for Santo Tomas, taking some supplies to camp and bringing back my favorite husband!

Having no watch, I counted the minutes. I borrowed some lipstick, sparing no effort to look my best. Roy's bed was next to mine and he was dressed up like the prince he was.

I waited anxiously for the sound of footsteps on the stairs just outside of my room. Snooks was watching, too. At 11:30 she came into the room, her face showing anger.

"Grace, the hospital car is back and here are some of the baby things you asked for. Ralph's pass was canceled just as he was ready to leave!"

I was too angry to cry and the rest of the day I was depressed and morbid. This was one more way our promise-breaking captors had found to break our morale. There was no predicting what they would do.

In the Orient it was thought that white women could not nurse their babies. From the beginning of this pregnancy I had made up my mind to one thing — *that I would nurse this baby*. I had not succeeded with the other two boys beyond a few days with no more

123

than a "first course." Each day in this pregnancy I had concentrated on being able to nurse this baby. The idea was planted in my subconscious and now I was more eager than ever. Tea was a good milk stimulant and I had saved the two small packets of tea from the British-South African food kit distributed the year before. With a glass of carabao milk, a portion of rice, and ten cups of tea each day, I should be able to feed him every three hours. Although he was crying some between feedings, I knew somehow I could supply his needs. The Brimos smuggled in two bottles of French wine and I drank a small amount each day. I gulped quantities of water and tea during the night. Finally I conceded to two ounces of formula once a day, opening the one can of Klim powdered milk which had been given to me some months before.

Various friends in Manila managed to sneak into the hospital against Japanese orders and bring me gifts of food and clothes. The Bergs, a German couple, sent in a large box containing three new dresses and four ten-peso bills! A tin of Ovaltine from Alice Clements was delivered to my room. Surprises! Surprises!

On the last afternoon of my stay at St. Joseph's I had a secret visitor. She introduced herself as Mrs. Brady, American wife of an Irish lawyer, therefore they were not interned. In a low whisper she explained that Mr. Brady had obtained 3,000 pesos, requested by Mr. Duggleby in Santo Tomas for camp loans. (In normal times, 3,000 pesos were equivalent to 1,500 U.S. dollars.) Would I take this money back into camp?

I thought of the many times Mr. Duggleby had smuggled notes to me from camp, how he had negotiated to get Gale to the Hospicio with me, and brought Gale himself. And Mrs. Brady, too, had sent food into St. Joseph's for me without my knowing her. It was a risk, I knew, but I gladly consented.

Thinking about the problem of hiding money, I found a solution — I could put it in the hems of my new dresses! That night I stayed up late, sewing the bills smoothly and carefully into the hem of each dress and skillfully packing the dresses in different places of the *tampipi*. My hands were shaking with nervousness.

After a short sleep (repeated attacks by bedbugs, hospital noise, and my excitement), I got up and finished packing. I must figure some way to get more sleep, I thought. It would surely help my nursing.

Dr. Moreta came to make his final examination. Once more he begged me not to return to camp, to accept one of several invitations from friends and remain outside. I said no to him. "I must return to my family, Doctor."

I was still very weak, but there was one problem that made me more nervous than anything else. My bladder was unpredictable and uncontrollable! Without warning when I stood up, the floor would be drenched. In embarrassment I told him. "What can I do, Dr. Moreta?"

"Don't be worried. You're drinking so much liquid, you know, and your strength has not yet returned." He gave me a shot of strychnine to alleviate the condition. Then he pulled a small box from his pocket. "This," he said, "is what I've finally located to help the nursing mother." He gave me one shot of the medicine and told me to take the other vials to the camp dispensary to have it administered every other day. It was an Italian fluid of some sort to stimulate the milk glands. Expensive, I knew, but he refused to disclose the source or the cost. "Just a present," he said.

On June 9th, seventeen days after Roy's birth, we were loaded into the hospital van with Elsie Cotterman and her infant. She seemed much stronger than I, despite her baby being five days younger than Roy. Dr. Moreta asked me to repeat the promise I had made: that I would *not* stand in any lines. "That is the one condition on which I discharge you. Remember!" he said, waving us away.

Chapter Eight

WE ARE FIVE!
(June, 1943)

he rainy season had started. As we drove through the gates of Santo Tomas, I noticed how emaciated and ill-clothed the internees looked — more worn and gaunt than when I had left six months before. Yet I was glad to be returning to this so-called hell-hole. Our family would be reunited once more and this time there would be five!

In the steady, slow rain, the ambulance van stopped in front of the Commandant's office for inspection of luggage and checking in. I strained my eyes looking for Ralph, but as we stepped out there were only three people I knew — Elsie's mother-in-law and two passersby.

Where was Ralph? No one offered any clues. Suddenly Les Fennel appeared. "I'll attend to your luggage, Grace. Just take the baby and go to the shanty out of the drizzle," he said. "Ralph will be along soon." He offered no explanation. I whispered to him to try to avoid any thorough check on my luggage, and then, with Roy in my arms, I started down the path.

Our shanty was at the far end of the grounds, but scarcely halfway there I heard screams of "Mommie, Mommie," as Stan and Gale came running to meet me. They hugged my legs, begging to see their brother. "How much does he weigh? How tall is he?" Questions flew out, two at a time, without waiting for answers.

Mrs. Fennel had heard their shouts and came to welcome us, too.

"Where is Daddy?" I managed amid their exclamations.

"Daddy's at the hospital with his carbuncle," they both answered at once.

I laid Roy on the bed so they could see their new brother.

"Isn't he the sweetest baby you ever saw?" Stan said.

"Aren't you glad you borned him?" Gale said, beaming.

I looked around the shanty — everything neat and clean — I marveled at its home-like atmosphere. Jeanette was admiring our baby and the boys dashed out shouting the news to their friends. I could hear their voices. "We have our baby brother . . . he's seventeen days old . . . twenty-two inches long . . . weighs eight and one half pounds," they were repeating over and over.

I turned around. Ralph was in the doorway. Jeanette quickly left us. We silently embraced, tears in our eyes. His shoulder was enormous, packed with ten thicknesses of dressings. I could read in his eyes the days of suffering and pain. He was much thinner, too.

From the moment of our return, our lives took on a new meaning. Stan and Gale lived for their baby brother, admiring him untold times each day, rushing to get dressed each morning in the shanty in order to come to the Annex where Roy and I slept. They would quickly peek through the mosquito net to see him. "Mommie, I've forgotten what he looks like!" And after gazing at him, "Our sweety-pie! Isn't he the cutest baby you ever saw? Aren't you glad you borned him, Mommie?"

The next day in the shanty Stan became very serious. "Mommie," he began, "remember when we were at the convent and we asked you for a baby? You said to pray for one. Gale and I both did . . . and then at the Bousmans, too. Well, which place did God answer our prayers? At the Catholic Mass with Mother Hope, or at the Sunday School where the Bousmans lived? I wanna know."

Fortunately my luggage was not searched at the Gate and the peso bills were not discovered. I unhemmed my dresses and turned the money over to Mr. Duggleby the next night.

There were no toilet facilities in the shanty area, and the long trek to the Annex latrine was difficult for me. Always laden with at least one toidy, I balanced it like a tight rope artist as I walked over the cobblestones in the daily downpour of rain. My own condition gave me no warning and many times I was saved from embarrassment only by these same rains. Between the worry over my bladder problem and hemorrhoids, I was never comfortable, sitting or standing, but I would not give up the fight to nurse my baby.

I drank tea, water and one glass of ovaltine each day; I was always starving. Often Stan and Gale would take part of their food and put it on my plate. "That's all right, Mommie — more milk for our sweetie-pie."

As soon as Roy was two months old, I opened one of our three tins of vacuum-packed rolled oats, a special gift from Dodo Jansen, wife of the Swedish Consul in Manila. Each morning I cooked a tiny portion for him. The problem of ants in the tropics made it necessary to use food immediately. It could not be left out even ten minutes or the ants would be carrying it away. Also, we were continuously fighting flies. I had cooked the oatmeal now, and had turned away to pick up Roy and put on his bib for feeding. When he had finished most of the oatmeal, I tipped the dish to spoon out the last bite. Just as I was about to put the spoon in his mouth I saw that there was a dead fly in it! "Oh, Roy," I said, hesitating, "here's hoping that fly hopped in during the cooking and was sterilized." I removed it and Roy finished the oatmeal with a satisfied smile.

My room in the Annex was no longer Room 64 (Little Moscow where I had been before), but a smaller room where English was the principal language. It was far better, although we were still crowded and, as I soon discovered, not too congenial. But we *had* agreed to the rule of taking our children out of the room if they cried during the night. The rainy season was in full swing now. The roof over the corridor did not extend to the entrance of our room. Streams of water poured down just at the doorway. If Roy cried, my only solution was to nurse him back to sleep. With every two hours or less of awakenings, my supply of milk was depleted by morning.

Worried over his intermittent rousings, I examined his bed, loaned to us from another internee and loaned to her from Mrs. Kephart. I could find no bedbugs. "They might be inside the mattress," suggested a friend. We opened the mattress — yes, plenty.

By special permission we sent the mattress out of camp to be redone. But Roy's restless nights continued. Finally we bought a bottle of creolin — almost prohibitive in price, it was so needed in camp for bedbugs. I boiled water, and day after day Ralph and I put creolin solution into the wood seams of the bed with a medicine dropper. Yet nothing would flaunt the beasts. I despaired, as our life with the bedbugs went on.

Ralph's camp duty began soon after six o'clock each morning, before Stan and Gale were awake, so they had the freedom of the shanty until he returned after eight o'clock with their tray of breakfast mush. Now their chief thought was to get to the Annex to see Roy each morning. Before I came back with the baby they had spent the time in other ways. They wrestled in their pajamas and jumped on the cots, and one day tried a new game: standing as tall as possible on their cots, they had a contest to see which one could urinate farther out of the window in the early morning. It was much more fun than using the toidy in the corner. One morning a shanty occupant passed by at that very moment. He narrowly missed being hit in the eyes! This incident must have sobered them, for nothing was ever said to Ralph. I only learned about it many months afterwards.

Each day brought us new pleasure in Roy's smiles and cute ways. Stan and Gale ran errands to the Annex, they stood in lines holding a place for Ralph. They were upset if Roy so much as whimpered. "He's hungry, Mommie . . . maybe he wants water again. . . maybe a pin is pricking him!" Ralph, too, was solicitous and delighted in carrying Roy outside whenever weather permitted. On the paths people stopped to greet him. Old men stopped to look at Roy, and *we* never ceased admiring him. For the first time Stan and Gale put forth a united front. Instead of jealousy and envy that Stan had felt towards Gale during his long illness when people had been so attentive to him, each one forgot his individual wants and troubles in his affection and love for their baby brother. They became a closely allied protective team.

VIOLIN CONCERTS
(July, 1943)

Music casts its spell, weaving intricate patterns of the past again and again. Realities of the present become submerged by memories which rise to the surface with all the senses refreshed! Certain pieces will forever belong to certain people in my memory of their courage, their sacrifice, their friendship, during our struggle for survival in the Japanese prison camp.

A few weeks after my return to Santo Tomas with Roy, Cort Linder, former pianist with Horace Heidt's orchestra (what fond memories I had of his music in the Drake Hotel in Chicago! magic nights of dancing) came to our shanty. Cort was director of the recordings played each evening over the loudspeaker in camp. Now he had a new idea. He discussed his plan of presenting a half-hour "live" program each week, finishing with, "Would you play violin selections for the first program, Mrs. Nash?"

After so long a time without practice, I knew this would require hard concentration during the two weeks ahead, but my answer was, "I'll do my best, Cort." In flashback, I recalled the last program I had done, a Vesper Musical Service at the Bousmans' church last September, and the memory of a Japanese officer in the audience flashed before me. It was in the Ellinwood Church where Ralph and I had been married in 1936. My thoughts were interrupted by Cort.

"Who will accompany you, Grace?" He had long since given up his professional career, having come to the islands in a business capacity.

"I'd like to have Melvin Toyne," I said, "if he can fit it into his camp schedule." Melvin and Helen, his wife, taught in Santo Tomas school for the children. Melvin also worked in the children's kitchen and played harmonium for religious services in camp. But he consented, and we prepared a program of well known violin classics. Ralph looked after Roy while I rehearsed, often bringing him to the tiny radio room to listen. He sat very still on Ralph's lap, content. Cort was on hand, too, and his meticulous criticism and suggestions were invaluable.

On that scheduled Friday night, I hurried to get Roy nursed and asleep in time to get to the studio, hoping that my nervousness would not reduce my already scant supply of milk. Thirty seconds. We were on the air. The room was so small that drawing my bow one inch too far meant clashing with the wall on one side of the room or the piano on the other side, but I played with all my heart.

As we reached the final chord, Cort turned on the "talk back"

131

microphone and we could hear the heavy applause outside. Ralph rushed into the studio, kissed me, and said, "It was wonderful, darling, wonderful!" Rosemary Parquette spoke next. "Your tone is different, Grace, so much bigger and richer!" In her burst of enthusiasm, her usual British reserve was gone.

Others made similar remarks and I, too, sensed a difference in my tone. Despite no practice for months, my tone had deepened and warmed. Rosemary's remarks suddenly brought back what my teacher, Max Fischel, had told me years before. "To play the violin, Grace, one must know suffering. You have not suffered enough." His words had angered me then. Now I understood. As I hurried to the Annex to feed Roy, our ex-seaman friend, Skipper Williams, stopped me. "Mrs. Nash," he said, "you played 'Danny Boy,' my favorite. Thank you."

The next morning an elderly man came by our shanty. He introduced himself and then said, "You played Max Fischel's piece last night!" Tears came to his eyes as he continued, "Max was one of my dearest friends in Chicago. The joy of hearing his composition, 'Bohemian Dance,' again is something I shall never forget, Mrs. Nash. You took me out of prison!"

"Max Fischel was my violin teacher at Chicago Musical College," I said. For the next half hour we talked about our late mutual friend, his great personality, humor and kindness, and we forgot for the time being that we were in a prison camp. Each time I played after that, internees expressed their enjoyment and the pleasant memories certain pieces had brought back to them. Melvin and I tried to play old favorites on each program to lift the hearts of our tired and hungry fellow-prisoners. Our Christmas night program seemed the saddest to me when we played Schubert's "Ave Maria." With the events that were to follow, it would bring even greater sadness to my heart.

Roots and rumors! Roots were our bulk, and since December 7th, 1941 rumors had been our vitamins. We masticated some, toyed with others that we could not swallow, and welcomed any new ones we could set our teeth into, any hour of the day.

One of our best and most persistent rumor-vitamins throughout internment was "repatriation." It always came from "reliable sources." We had hashed and rehashed the subject, even swallowing it, only to have it return again and again like the semicooked beans we had each week. Finally it materialized in October, 1943 when the Commandant announced that a certain number would be repatriated; the list to be made up in Tokyo, of course.

We knew there was little chance that our names would be on that list, but even a ray of hope is better than none at all. Most everyone agreed on one thing — the sick and aged should be given first consideration. Tokyo had other ideas. Slowly the names leaked out. Other than members of the Diplomatic Corps and State Department and a few missionary doctors and nurses, there were names that left little to our imagination as to why and how they had gotten on the list! The Repatriation Ship was soon renamed "Reputation Ship" and jokes and verses were repeated about these certain individuals who had "paid" their way by diverse means.

Some of the doctors and others asked to give up their spaces for certain sick internees. The answer was, "You do not have to go, but *we* will select the one who will take your place."

In the meantime, permission to send letters on the S.S. Gripsholm "Reputation" was granted — one letter to each family, to be censored first.

After a long study of what to write — information that would pass their rigid censorship and still contain news of our existence — Ralph and I drew up a letter. The most important item, of course, was the birth of our third son. And we dreamed of the excitement back home when our letter would arrive.

Santo Tomas Internment Camp
Manila, Philippines

Date: September 12, 1943

To All Our Families,

Please be advised that we are all here together and keeping reasonably good health — no serious illness during internment but our share of usual ailments. ***Keep all Insurance paid up.***

Kindly inform all close relatives because this is the only letter to be transmitted in many months.

The big joy of our life here is a son, the third,
Roy Leslie, now three and a half months, a perfect
Nash Model, most handsome and strong. A natural
birth, May 24th, eight pounds; now fourteen
pounds. He is a combination of all good qualities
from Stanley and Gale, even to appearance. Grace
manages to nurse him successfully — Thank God.

Our living is in a 9 x 12 hut of grass, except
Grace and baby sleeping in dormitory.

Ralph Nash

Sunday, October 24th, we were celebrating our second
wedding anniversary in prison camp with a few friends in our
shanty, when we saw Bill Waldo in his shanty across the path from
ours, staggering as he tried to get a drink. He was ill with flu or
Dengue fever probably. We called over to him to offer our
sympathy.

Bill and Josie were a handsome couple and outstanding in
their camp service and character. Josie always had a pleasant smile
in spite of internment, and Bill was mayor of our "Garden Court"
shanty area, recently elected to the Board of Directors for all
shanty areas in camp. He was a star athlete. Our boys admired him
in hero fashion and often sought out his advice. Bill slept in the
shanty and Josie joined him during the day. (Husbands and wives
were still separated in their living quarters.)

The next afternoon, in a heavy downpour, I returned to the
shanty after rehearsal with Melvin. Ralph and the three boys were
marooned inside. An ambulance from San Lazaro Hospital
splashed by me and turned down our narrow foot path. The
significance of this particular ambulance did not penetrate for
several seconds. I hurried into our quarters just as it backed up
against Waldo's shanty.

Ralph stood up to see who had driven in. "What happened to
Bill?" I asked. He motioned to me not to speak so that the boys
would not know. I realized then that San Lazaro Hospital in
Manila handled serious contagious diseases. Stan and Gale were
peering out the small opening, frightened by the sight of a hospital
van.

Ralph whispered to me, "They think Bill has polio."

I gasped. Bill with polio? It just couldn't happen to him, I thought. He was one of the strongest and finest men in camp. I watched, terrified, as the several attendants maneuvered him on to a stretcher and out through the window opening into the ambulance. Dr. Fletcher was there beside Josie, who quickly packed a few of Bill's things and gave them to the attendant.

What would Josie do? How terrible for her! Then I thought of our three boys. What if they might contract polio? Our shanties were scarcely an arm's length from each other! "I won't think about it, I won't!" I said to myself, trying to shut it out of my mind.

The next few days were nightmares of waiting for news of Bill. He was in an iron lung . . . had nearly died the night before, but rallied again. There were still hopes for his recovery.

The following Friday, Melvin and I played again for the camp. I could think of nothing else but Bill's suffering. After the program a group from Garden Court shanty area gathered in front of the Commandant's office. Permission had been granted to call the hospital. We waited outside, fervently and silently praying. Al Cutting, one of Bill's closest friends, came out of the office. His face told us before he spoke — Bill was worse again. Paralysis was reaching his throat.

The next night Bill passed away. Josie had been with him, allowed to go there several days before. After the funeral she went to Remedios Hospital. We were thankful that she did not return to camp, to the constant reminders of Bill, surrounded by the grief of their friends.

For months afterward everything that happened in Garden Court brought Bill to our minds. The boys looked for him in the mornings. We still expected to hear his cheerful voice and to see Josie and Bill eating their food across the way. We missed them sorely and our grief did not lessen for many months.

This was the second case of polio since the beginning of camp. Luckily no more cases followed. Even the little boy, Bruce Cutting, whom Bill had held on his lap the day before his illness struck, did not get the disease.

With November came the typhoon season. One morning the rains were coming down too furiously to make it out to the shanty. I stayed in the Annex with Roy. It was a madhouse of marooned children. Wet laundry filled the lines that stretched through the corridor, sending up a stench of sour mildew and unclean diapers. The place reeked of putrid dampness. By late that afternoon, the wind had increased and typhoon signals were hoisted. Shanty dwellers were told to reinforce their shacks, strengthen the foundations, however possible. By nightfall the floors in the Annex corridor were under water.

I lay under the mosquito net with Roy, listening to the terrifying noise of wind and rain slashing at the windows, pounding the roof. A typhoon was raging in all its fury. What would Ralph and the boys do out in the shanty? How would they manage? There was no way of finding out. The water continued to rise outside the open doorway. It must be waist deep in the shanty area, I thought. Maybe at this very moment, ten o'clock, our shanty and others, too, were floating in the lake outside. To sleep was impossible. At 1:30 a.m. I heard sounds of children's voices. In my *bakyas* (wooden sandals) I clopped over to the corridor. There were Stan and Gale wading toward me in great excitement. "Mommie," called Stan, "we came over on a barrel. Daddy and Mr. Fennel tied us on top and pushed the barrel through the water."

"We sat on top," added Gale. "The water is so deep, it's over our heads."

"Daddy said to stay with you. He's gone back to hold on to our shanty," explained Stan.

The sides of my net bulged out with three squeezed into a single bed, but finally we dozed off for the few hours left.

I didn't see Ralph until nearly noon the next day when he told me of the harrowing night's experiences. He had tightened up the shanty and tied the window flaps, then gone to sleep, exhausted. Sometime later he awoke, and putting his feet out from the net to step into his *bakyas*, he hit water, knee deep. No *bakyas*. They had floated away. He floundered through the water and darkness, finally hoisting the two wooden chests of our clothes out of the water, onto the table. Les Fennel was outside warning occupants of the "high tide." Together they had located the barrel to bring the boys over to the Annex.

The days following were both harrowing and funny, as shanty occupants began the search for their belongings. Ladies' undies had floated into bachelors' shanties. An empty whiskey bottle went ashore into a missionary's habitat! Canned goods had lost their labels and exchanged owners. Even precious toidies were lost, and found. Perishable foods were ruined and all tinned goods had to be aired and dried to prevent rust and swelling. Most of the labels were missing. Our greatest loss was the beautiful toy bus. It was blown off the shelf during the night and swept away in bits and pieces in the rising waters. Many times Stan and Gale recounted that trial run and the cheering crowd. "It was perfect, Mommie, and the prettiest bus we'll ever see."

I opened the chests containing the boys' clothes and gasped at the sight. Everything was a sickly pink in color. As I removed each piece, some were cherry red! Two bright red Santa Claus stockings we had saved from before the war had bled their colors throughout the chest into every piece of clothing! Despite the damage to gas and water mains, no one got typhoid fever. There was much to be thankful for, and before long camp routine was back to normal.

A week later, Roy was stricken with tonsilitis. Six months old! We were filled with fear and panic. Once more Rosie Rosenbaum came to my aid. "Some aspirin, Grace," she said, handing me two tablets wrapped in a tissue. By the second day Roy's fever had subsided and we rejoiced to see his sweet smile again.

FOOD FOR CHRISTMAS
(December, 1943)

On Gale's fifth birthday, December fifteenth, his second birthday in prison camp, we celebrated in great style — our first American Red Cross Comfort Kits were distributed. Stan and Gale were holding a place in line until I could come. Their excitement over the food that might be in the kits was beyond the imagination of well-fed boys and girls.

At last two of our names were called over the speaker, Roy's and mine. With the two good-sized boxes loaded onto a little cart, we took them back to the shanty where Ralph and Roy were waiting. Ralph carefully lifted out one section of the first kit. Fingers were all thumbs in the excitement and we wanted to shout to the rooftops when we beheld the delicacies inside: one pound of powdered Klim milk, a package of processed cheese, vitaminized chocolate, canned meat, packet of bouillon, prunes, tiny vitamin C-pills so needed to offset the all-starch camp food! And there were four of these units in each kit! It was simply unbelievable! This wonderful food! We cried with joy and gratitude.

When arrival of food packages had first been announced, we were told that the cigarettes contained in them had to be removed, due to a victory slogan on one brand. In anger, the Jap guards had slashed open the boxes with their bayonets and, under close scrutiny, a group of internees were instructed to hunt out all the cigarettes.

To our astonishment as Ralph unpacked the other units in our kits, we found packages of cigarettes that had been overlooked. We had a special treat now for our friends, and secretly in the days to follow we shared this unexpected luxury. No one must find out — it might get back to the Japs.

The following day, Ralph, Stan and Gale received their kits, and what enjoyment we all had, adding a carefully measured amount of delicious-tasting American food to our line chow each day. Our health and our dispositions improved. In addition to the food kits there were medical supplies, vitamin tablets and clothes to be distributed. After long and careful planning by our committee, each internee was given one bottle of multiple vitamins and instructed to take one each day. Later the clothes were distributed. The medical supplies were stored in the camp hospital.

Many internees began selling the contents of their kits to other internees — vendors who were buying up supplies of canned goods, etc., to sell later at exhorbitant prices and huge profits. We followed our instructions and made our own rules about using our canned goods sparingly. Secretly we traded some of the cigarettes for a small amount of Pablum for Roy.

Ten days later, we had our second Christmas in camp. Internees were better fortified in their physical condition and we all had renewed hopes for an early release. Some argued that there was no need to use their canned goods sparingly. "Eat now and be in good health for the day of liberation," they said. Our rumor-relays never slackened, taking us sky-high with hopes on one day, then dropping us into the depths of despair the next.

My own hunger never seemed to let up, and from one nursing to the next I despaired over my small supply of milk for Roy. "If only I had some beer, that would do it," I said lightly.

Late that afternoon, Bill Chittick came by for a chat. "How are you getting along, feeding Roy?" he asked.

"I'm struggling, Bill. If I had some beer, he'd be happier, though," I said laughingly.

"If that's what you need, Grace, you should have it."

I soon forgot our conversation. But hardly a week later, Bill came down our path with a paper market bag. It was topped with newspapers. Probably his laundry, I thought. "Hello, Bill." We talked of the usual things, including a few rumors, of course. He had access to choice bits of news in his work at Santo Tomas Gate. Stan and Gale went outside to play.

"Grace," he whispered, looking in each direction for anyone within earshot. "I've brought you some Japanese beer!"

I gasped, still not believing him. Such a risk was unthinkable.

"It's under these newspapers. Guard it and don't let a single solitary soul ever know. Hide the empty bottles which I must return later. I'll be back next week for them, and I might have some more for you then."

I wanted to hug him, but instead we quickly changed the conversation to routine matters as the sound of footsteps neared our shanty. He left to get in line for his chow.

With no doors on our shanty — just open spaces, as required by the Japs — each morning and afternoon I draped baby blankets over the clothesline inside. Surrounded by our camp stools and table, I bent low to open one bottle of the magic "tonic-intoxicant." Pouring it into a battered cup, I drank it as if it were water, relishing every drop in anticipation of what it would do for Roy.

It did help, noticeably, but for two hours after each drinking I had to avoid any proximity to my best or my worst friends, lest someone find out. Roy profited in secret and I looked forward each day to that cup of warm beer for its startling results!

Bill appeared the next week as promised, exchanging the empties for fulls; a second bag of beer for a nursing mother in a prison camp! No one ever found out until long after imprisonment was over. Nor did I find out that Bill had nearly lost his head, literally, in his third and final coup d'etat for me. He never told us

139

until his visit to the States several years after our release.

Bill was a friend in deed, many deeds before and during prison days. A few months later, he smuggled in several packages of "mickey mouse" cash for us, arranging the IOUs at a good rate of exchange. This money enabled us to buy fresh vegetables and fruits, such as pechay, syncomas, bananas and papayas which were brought into camp at different times by Filipino vendors. Although thirty "mickey mouse" pesos (Japanese-printed paper money) would buy very little, that little staved off beri-beri for the time being.

EPIDEMICS BEGIN
(January, 1944)

Soon after Christmas, an epidemic of dysentery started among the youngest children in camp. Roy, now eight months old, was one of the victims. He was isolated in the children's hospital, and I was not allowed to nurse him or to see him. Within forty-eight hours my milk supply was gone, and although he was not as ill as many of the children, I wore a long face. Two days later, Gale became ill. In less than half an hour I knew it was bacillary dysentery. We rushed him to the hospital where Roy was. I sat up most of the night, fearful and anxious. I could hear faint cries coming from the hospital across the field from the Annex and I imagined them to be from Gale and Roy.

Thanks to the hospital supplies received in the December Red Cross shipment, their recovery was more speedy and sure. Within a week we were five again. For a long period following dysentery a soft diet must be rigidly enforced and now that Roy was on a Lactogen formula, slightly stronger than water, this necessary starvation diet left him crying from hunger much of the day. The cause of this bacillary epidemic was finally discovered. One of the kitchen staff in the Annex who pureed the squash, spinach, and *camotes* (native sweet potatoes) for the babies was a carrier of the disease. Although she did not suffer from the disease herself, her contact with the food had transferred it to others.

Before dysentery had been quelled, another epidemic hit the camp: whooping cough! The nightly retching coughs were terrifying. I found myself lying awake, counting the seconds after each long whoop until there was relaxed breathing again. Then another series of coughs began. Fortunately, Stan and Gale slept in the shanty, away from the crowded Annex, and I hoped that Roy's natural immunity from my nursing would protect him from getting it. We were also trying to keep Gale and Stan away from the gangs of children in their playing in hopes of missing this epidemic.

Gale started coughing first, then Stan, and finally Roy. Heavy doses of vitamin C were administered, but they whooped in spite of the C injections. Gale suffered the most and for weeks not a meal stayed down longer than half an hour. I made extra-bland food and puddings, using canned milk, sugar and native cornstarch, but every attempt was futile. He gagged for minutes over the laundry bucket with Ralph or me holding his head, his frail body shaking from the strain. We couldn't let him out of our sight because each attack was worse than the previous one. His stomach muscles ached from the stretching, and each day he looked sadder and thinner to me. Nights I lay awake wondering if Ralph would waken in time to help him.

Stan had a few severe spells, but most of the time he kept his food down. Roy had coughed in little whoops, but had not choked. One evening I was gathering up our belongings to go to the Annex for the night when Roy began to cough. I picked him up but the coughing continued. He couldn't stop. Each time I waited in agony for his breath to return. Ralph had gone to the camp faucet to wash our supper dishes, a block away. I was seized with fright when I saw Roy's face turning blue. In a flash I grabbed him by the feet, turned him upside down and began shaking him. When I turned him right side up, he was breathing. I sat down, hugging him to me and thanking God once more. When Ralph returned he found me as pale as a ghost, holding Roy in my shaking arms. This proved to be the only serious attack that Roy had. Slowly he, Stan and Gale came out of their weeks and weeks of whooping.

Before the whooping cough epidemic had finished its rounds, measles began to spread. So many children were taken with either, or both, it was necessary to use one section of the main dormitory for mothers and older children. A few children had measles, whooping cough and dysentery simultaneously. When they returned from the camp hospital weeks later, they were but shadows of themselves, and now they had lice! Ralph and I worked tirelessly to keep our three boys by themselves, close to the shanty.

Sometimes it was like trying to isolate one's bed from bedbugs! Impossible. But the boys did not contract the measles.

Gale, still weak from coughing, continually fell down on the slag paths. I could tell his cry instantly and would rush out to find him running toward me, his knees dripping blood. We had no equipment for disinfecting and doctoring his wounds, so we had to go to the Annex Clinic and into the waiting room filled with other children and their equally distraught mothers. There we would wait, Gale whimpering with pain and in dread of the disinfectant and cleaning out of the dirt. Somehow the bandages would slip off, and as I look back, I never remember Gale's knees being completely healed before he would fall and scrape them again. His chief joy these days seemed to be his baby brother and this made up for the hardships and suffering he endured.

Among the various gangs of children in Santo Tomas, there were a number of over-sized bullies. One day Gale, who was usually one to mind his own business, was the victim. This older boy in a neighboring shanty area decided to experiment on Gale. In front of two other boys, his onlookers, he clasped his hands around Gale's throat and slowly tightened them. If an adult had not chanced by at that moment, his experiment would have continued to the end! The man brought Gale home trembling with fear, and for some days Gale found it difficult to swallow or talk.

"Something should be done about such children," was the repeated cry. But this boy always did things so quietly and effectively — without any parental discipline — that there was no coping with the problem. We had to watch to keep him away from our boys, and keep our children close by our shanty steps — the only solution. This same youngster had previously cut off most of Gale's hair, chopping it beyond repair — but that was a minor misfortune and in a month or so Gale looked like himself again.

Early in Roy's life, his brothers had longed to take him for a walk, to show him off. But he wouldn't be walking for some time yet. Ralph found the frame of a discarded doll carriage. Using Roy's outgrown bassinette for the carriage, he bolted it onto the frame of the doll buggy and painted it in blue and ivory — a deluxe model!

With Roy outfitted in a blue *camisa* to match his carriage, Stan, Gale, Daddy and Mommie strolled down the path — Easter parade on Thursday! The bumpy slag path was not conducive to a smooth ride, but Roy took it without a whimper. Every pleasant day after that the carriage had to be tried with Gale and Stan taking turns driving. Because the carriage was slightly top heavy and the paths bumpy, either Ralph or I always went with them.

One afternoon when I was busy and Ralph was on camp duty, I gave them permission to take Roy out alone. They had promised to stay on the path between the shanties and I could hear them gathering their friends and admirers for Roy as they went along. Suddenly there was a baby's cry in the distance. I hurried out. Two paths over, I saw a crowd gathered. Stan and Gale were putting things back into the carriage while an adult held Roy, who was crying at the top of his voice.

Back in the shanty, Stan tried to explain how it had happened. He and Gale were more frightened than Roy. They carefully examined him from head to toe and back again to make sure he hadn't been bruised when the buggy had dumped him on the slight incline.

From the time Roy could sit up, he would take no ride lying down. Life was too exciting and he responded to each and every passerby. Balancing the carriage to correspond with his movements was far from easy, and an older person had to be at the helm to insure his safety.

Gale and Stan still never seemed to tire of their baby brother, even though their work increased with his growth. They hauled buckets of water, ran to the Annex for his clothes, to the Annex kitchen for his bottle; they carried the surplus bedding and diapers morning and night from Annex to shanty and back again. And Gale, even more dependable, would sit in the shanty staying close to Roy while I reported to latrine duty every other day. So often my assignment coincided with Ralph's camp work. Stan, too, would plan on looking after Roy, but after five or ten minutes his curiosity and active body took him out of the shanty. Some friend had come by and coaxed him out to see something, he explained. But Gale would be right there, steadfastly watching over his brother.

"Mommie, you should see what he can do now. He can bite his toes!" And a complete account of Roy's every move would follow.

Chapter Nine

ANOTHER MOVE
(LOS BANOS)
(April, 1944)

ore camp restrictions began. Every hour, half hour and sometimes every three minutes, the loudspeaker blasted out new orders from the Commandant's Office. Surely with the pressure of orders and changes of orders, our prison term would not be much longer. We remembered so clearly the ominous statement made by the Commandant earlier: "As long as we are victorious, we can afford to be magnanimous." Now we were receiving the implied turn-around in treatment. Rations were cut and the all-important package line was being closed in two days. Santo Tomas would be placed in complete isolation from contact with the outside as far as internees were concerned.

On the final day of the package line, we received a wonderful surprise from Trudl and Herbert Zipper — one hundred pesos (mickey mouse currency)! We knew they could little afford such sacrifice but we tucked it away most gratefully with our small reserve for future needs.

More people were being interned in the already congested quarters. In order to make space available, on February 1st came the order permitting families to live together in their shanties. We welcomed the news despite our small one-room shack. Without delay, we heaved and lugged our belongings from the Annex out to the shanty. It meant having our things in one place only. Ralph and I could spend the evenings together sitting outside after the boys were in bed, not going separate ways to different quarters. Our family would be under one roof.

Ralph built an extension on one side of the shanty which gave us more foot room, although with the addition of Roy's screened bed and my single cot, there was little floor space left.

The number of guards had been increased around the camp, and sentries were stationed inside the camp walls at every turn. Rumors became more whispered and more abundant. There were air raid practices and less food. Yet our morale rose higher. "Our time is coming." "The Japs are jittery." "Just a few weeks more!" "Oh, make it soon!"

All electrical equipment had been confiscated days before. One afternoon Tom Poole, head of the camp electrical work department, of which Ralph was a member, hurried over to us and whispered, "Come over to Room X after nine o'clock roll call tonight." He said no more but went on his way. Ralph knew about this particular room in the Main Building. It had once housed the camp barbershop but now it contained special equipment. He also knew what Tom had in that room, but he said nothing to me other than, "Don't tell anyone about our plans for tonight, Grace."

I knew better than to divulge such top secrets, even though I always listened to, and usually repeated to others, all favorable rumors. With the three boys asleep, we asked one of our neighbors to check on them. "Going to the Main Building for a few minutes," we explained. In the Main Building we walked along the corridor and Ralph indicated, without pointing, the door for our entrance. We continued on and then retraced our steps. "You go in first, I'll follow," he said. He had explained the knock code to me before we had left the shanty.

We hesitated until the corridor was clear of people, then affecting nonchalance we made our entrance. No lights in the room. We were quickly guided to one side where another door was immediately opened for us. I was in a state of creeps by this time. In one corner was a group of shadows — people crouched close to a radio. Someone handed me a pair of earphones. Trembling, I stuck them on and listened. I was hearing a real news broadcast from Australia! This was followed by the news commentator, "Winters," whom I recognized from earlier transcripts heard in the convent, outside. Then came the most thrilling part — KGEI, news from San Francisco! Shivers went up and down my spine . . . hearing, actually *hearing* a voice from the United States. It was more thrilling and wonderful and lasting than the news itself, which I soon forgot. Twenty minutes of contact with the outside world and America! May I never forget its significance to me that night, as a hungry prisoner of the Japanese. (Tom Poole had assembled this radio from spare parts procured outside. Commandeered to repair radios for the Japs, he always asked for "two" replacement parts until he had enough to make this radio.)

We stole back to our shanty in silence, knowing that we dared not tell one person, yet how I longed to share my excitement with everyone, I was so buoyed up in spirit, positively exuberant. It lasted for many days, and that night I dreamed again of being home in Ohio.

Everyone in camp had pet dreams of their past comfortable life, but mine seemed to be of one particular sort. I would be shopping in Cleveland or Chicago and just as I'd reach the door of that department store it would be closing time. If by chance I had gotten inside, either I had no cash or no check book. In several dreams, accompanied by a friend, we had decided to stop for refreshments — always chocolate cake and ice cream — in which case, either the store was fresh out of it or, again, as we pressed the latch the doors were being locked. One time, however, I woke up happy, unbelievably happy, with the taste of chocolate cake a la mode still in my mouth!

Somehow good news balanced bad news. On February 21st most of us received letters from home. They had come in November, six months before. The Japanese were deliberate as well as sadistic. When the announcement came, we practically stampeded to get to the office counter. And within the next hour the same people were weeping with homesickness, shocking news from home, or no news at all.

Ralph and I had four letters from different members of our families. Each day of the next week we sat down to read them over again, and each time we finished them in tears. I often wondered whether the anguish was greater from receiving the letters, so thoroughly censored, or receiving no communication. Which was harder to bear? After each reading we tried to read between the lines and imagine what had been censored out, then we brooded over our longing for families, freedom and the United States.

Now and then extra food was brought into camp by the

Japanese to be sold. Often the lines would start at 4 a.m. and extend miles in length before the selling started. We depended on Stan and Gale to bring us rumors of anything special that would be sold, such as peanut butter or cornstarch. While Gale held a place in line, Stan would rush back to get one of us. They were also developing the art of scavenging and worked hard at the trade.

Our only protein in camp chow consisted of fish heads and tails, already high with stench when they were delivered. Fermenting radishes added to the flavor and savor. I often wanted to stop breathing altogether! The flies multiplied; and a few cases of measles, dysentery and chicken pox continued. Our boys managed thus far to stay free of any further developments of contagious diseases.

Santo Tomas had become too congested. On March 23rd, the Commandant ordered a selection of five hundred internees for transfer to Los Banos, a new camp forty-five miles south of Manila. A certain number of families could be included in the five hundred, they said. The whole camp was alive with the news when applications were requested.

That night a group from our shanty area gathered together to discuss the pros and cons of such a transfer. The Los Banos Camp was in the heart of coconut and banana plantations. It had been started the year before when eight hundred men from Santo Tomas had been sent to organize it. Their wives and girl friends had joined them in December, 1943. Several of our friends had been among this group and through the underground we had heard encouraging reports of better living conditions, less congestion and better food. Burt Fonger and his mother had joined Mr. Fonger there. He had been one of the first eight hundred. After family separation for nearly two years, they had been united in Los Banos Camp.

After the group discussion, Ralph and I sat up most of the night weighing our chances for survival — better in Los Banos or Santo Tomas? Transportation facilities for foodstuffs were becoming more difficult, and would certainly get worse as time went on. In Los Banos one could survive on coconuts and bananas — whole food — and the Japs could not use transportation as an excuse for not feeding us. After thinking about measles, chicken pox and diptheria, which the boys had not succumbed to yet, and the fact that there would be fewer children and less chance for

148

contagion in Los Banos, we decided to put our names in for transfer to this new camp.

The next morning I hurried to the office to sign up before the family quota had been reached.

The next two weeks were filled with excitement, work and worry. There were air raid alerts, changes announced in departure date, emergency roll calls with surprise searches of both shanties and building quarters; crating and packing of our luggage.

Finally on April 7th we were loaded into shaky Japanese army trucks, on top of our mattresses and other luggage. Ralph and I had stayed up all night to make sure everything was in readiness by 4 a.m., as ordered. We then waited in the blackout until 6:30 for their trucks to arrive. Now, as we rode through Manila to the outskirts and *barrios* beyond, our hearts were saddened by the sights. It was a city misused, its people mistreated, its heart broken! A few Filipinos stood along the roadside, straining to see our faces, yet not daring to wave. They looked thin, hungry and frightened.

Roy slept through the whole trip, bundled in my arms. Stan and Gale took turns napping against Ralph's shoulder. There was comfort in having our family together in this transfer. Our hopes for better food and quarters in this new locale bolstered us, and we were eager to reach our destination. As the trucks jolted into Los Banos Camp, we craned our necks to find familiar faces among the crowd. Faces were gaping at us, some with friendly welcoming smiles, others with negative, disgruntled expressions.

No one came forward as we jumped down from the truck. We soon realized they had been forbidden to speak or fraternize with new arrivals until all inspections and assignments to quarters were completed. From experience we knew there would be plenty of deliberation by the Japs. We stood for three hours in the blazing sun, waiting to go into the crowded barracks to receive our orders. We had given Roy a cup of milk at eleven o'clock to help stave off his hunger, but Stan and Gale, with nothing since 4 a.m., were weak from hunger and midday sun.

At last assignments and orders were completed. Bill and Rosemary Parquette raced over to us, grabbed us and took us to their small cubicle where we celebrated with a hot lunch of fried rice and mongo beans! A delicious and wonderful reunion. Revived and happy, we started out to find our quarters and haul

149

our luggage across the open fields from where it had been dumped.

The first weeks in Los Banos Camp were all but killing ones with the hard work to make our quarters livable. But we all persisted and in two months time we had better and slightly larger accommodations than in Santo Tomas. The camp food with the added noon meal was worth all the hard work of moving. The grounds were beautiful and green, temperatures were less torrid than in Manila, and in total, we were glad to be here rather than in Santo Tomas. The boys' shoes had worn through. They went barefoot now without danger of imbedded glass and crockery that had existed in our shanty area in Santo Tomas, once a garbage dump. Roy began walking just before his first birthday.

Jim Cullens, the Parquettes, Frank Ale, Harold Bayley, and Mrs. Breson, a British nurse friend from the Hospicio Island days, were in Los Banos and spent much time with us. Roy-Boy, as they called him, was the main attraction, with his happy face and mannerisms. Jim Cullens became our "Uncle Jim" who took Roy for long walks to see the ducks, pigs and chickens belonging to the Japs, and a pet monkey that belonged to one of the internees.

Soon after our arrival it was announced that each family could send a 25-word message to *one* address. We worked and re-worked the following message home:

> *"We are doing better here in partitioned barracks and garden space, family groups living in units. Roy is most perfect baby, now eleven months. Gale, Stanley fine. Love to all, Ralph Nash."*

One day at the water tap, waiting to fill my jug, Skipper Williams, our pirate and sea captain friend in Santo Tomas, appeared. "And how are my buccaneers today? It's been many a month, hasn't it?" He patted Roy's cheek and tweeked his toes. "Wait just a minute, I won't be long." He hurried off to his barracks just beyond the water spigot. I had filled my jug and with Roy in one arm was turning to leave, when Skipper, out of breath, handed me a newspaper-wrapped package. "For the wee one," he whispered, "I've saved it for him."

It was a whole can of powdered milk, saved from the one Red Cross Kit a year earlier — enough to make a gallon of full strength or two gallons the way we diluted it. "No, Skipper," I stammered. "You'll need it yourself."

"Never touch the stuff," he said gruffly. He looked at Roy a long moment and then turned away. In tears I called out to him, "How can I repay you?"

Half-jokingly he called back, "Just play me 'Danny Boy' at your next concert." Later, with Rosemary accompanying, I played "Danny Boy" with a silent tribute in my heart for Skipper who was sitting in the front row.

Skipper's lot had been one of the hardest during imprisonment. A salty British ship's captain in salvage work in the China Sea, his ship had been bombed from under him in Manila Harbor. During the first months in Santo Tomas, he and his Norwegian seamen had all but starved to death. They had no contacts or acquaintances in Manila to get food to them when the Japs had not bothered to feed internees, and everyone depended on Filipinos and friends not in the camp to throw food over the fence. The British community was known to have the largest store of canned goods, yet they did not concern themselves over the plight of their fellow countryman. Smugly and indifferently they had turned their backs, subsisting quite well themselves.

In the camp, Skipper* became one of the favorites, admired for his exciting lectures about his adventures on the China Sea. With his unique sense of humor and unbeatably salty stories, the grounds would be filled with listeners long before the scheduled hour of his talks. It was always a refreshing evening, one which would make them forget prison walls.

LT. KONISHI
(May, 1944)

One of the many reasons for our wanting to leave Santo Tomas was to get away from the continuous threats and mental heckling carried on by a special Japanese officer, Lt. Konishi. Although titled "Lieutenant," he outranked all officials in the camp, including the Commandant. Insofar as we could find out, he

---

*See "The Gallant Buccaneer of Los Banos," First Person Award Story in *Readers Digest,* February, 1959.

had been sent to Santo Tomas as a personal emissary of General Homma, well known for his hatred of the white race. Lt. Konishi's special and diverse ways of carrying out this hatred were unlimited!

In Los Banos Camp we found a tolerant and fair Commandant, one who was concerned with the welfare of the internees insofar as his superiors' orders and restrictions would allow. We breathed a deep sigh of relief and satisfaction almost daily. Burt Fonger's father was the head of our Camp Committee, an efficient diplomat and humanitarian, yet one who never sacrificed his integrity or self respect as an American citizen.

Mrs. Fonger taught subjects in the camp high school, and Burt was taking courses offered for first year of college, besides his double work assignments in the camp. Their morale was high and their gratitude for family life after their long separation showed in their faces. When the teenagers presented their original camp show, Burt was one of the leaders responsible. As an eagle scout he led the younger boys' cub scout troop. Stan was a member. Everyone admired this tall, gaunt youth with the heavy black beard.

Our better food, more agreeable Commandant and happier life was short-lived. Two weeks later Lt. Konishi arrived to instruct us in the inferiority and degradation of the white race and the superiority of the Imperial Japanese as exemplified by General Homma. As described by Earl Carroll*, he was "the most hated man ever to enter Santo Tomas; a squat, sloppy, filthy-bodied little Jap." Now he was the bane of our existence in Los Banos Camp. Our rations were cut severely; petty persecution, continuous orders and change of orders began. And there would be more, and more, and more.

About this time news came into Los Banos that shocked us. At first we wouldn't believe it, then a few days later it was confirmed when a truck arrived from Santo Tomas with Tom Poole aboard. He told us about Helen Toyne, Melvin's wife and fellow teacher

_____

*Earl Carroll: Colossus of Philippine Insurance, by Ed. C. de Jesus and Carlos Quirino. The Underwriters Publications Co., Inc., 1980. (Earl Carroll was a leader in our Santo Tomas Camp Committee and the only member of that committee to survive the war.)

with me in the American School before the war. She had died suddenly on May 24th, 1944 from an infected mosquito bite which had spread to her brain within a few short hours! Helen was a dear friend, the one who had befriended us that first horrible night of internment, sharing space for Stan and Gale under the mosquito net with her daughter, Mary Helen. She and Melvin had contributed so much to the camp. Their high morale and tireless efforts were an inspiration to others. Helen's run-down physical condition must have contributed to the cause of her death, I thought. We bore our grief silently, as we had many times before. So many of our cherished friends were gone, it seemed, yet each loss made us more determined to carry on, to live for them.

Chapter Ten

ENEMY SOLDIER /
VIOLIN CONCERT
(June, 1944)

or some time I had wanted to give a serious musical
program in Los Banos. The only classical music heard in
camp were recordings played on Sunday evenings. Now
with encouragement from a number of internees, I persuaded
Rosemary Parquette, a splendid pianist to accompany me. There
was a reasonable sounding piano in the empty barracks down by
the guard house where we could practice. It was daring, in the face
of fear and starvation, to present a live concert like this with only a
few weeks of scheduled rehearsals. But we went ahead.

Outside the fierce heat beat down on the nipa-thatched roofs
of our barracks that stretched in rows along the foothills of the
Makiling Mountains. Together we made our way to the empty
barracks at the far end of the camp, Rosemary carrying my violin
and music, I carrying Roy. Ralph was doing camp work.

Inside, we carefully closed the heavy barn-like door. While
Rosemary dusted off the rickety piano, I cleared a section of the
slag floor where Roy could play, then took out my violin and tuned
to a questionable "A" from the piano. We began the concerto.
During Rosemary's piano interlude I glanced down at Roy. He was
listlessly putting pieces of slag into his tin cup. His sweet face . . . his
spindly legs . . . The despair I felt found expression in the slow
throbbing tones of the Adagio Movement of the Bruch Concerto
I was playing. But my thoughts were on the coconut trees and
banana palms beyond the high fence — heavy with fruit. I thought
of Stan and Gale out searching for weeds and scraps of Japanese
garbage, of Ralph working an additional two hours in burning sun

for an extra cup of rice. Lt. Konishi knew how to break one's spirit and morale, how to procure civilian labor with enforced starvation!

All at once a shadow crossed my vision at the entranceway. My bow scratched and bounced off the string. A Japanese soldier was staring at me from inside the barracks door! Still playing, I drew back toward Roy. Rosemary's hands faltered over the keys . . . but we must not stop.

The soldier's boots crunched against the slag as he came slowly toward us. A sickening wave of fear swept over me as I struggled on with meaningless notes. It was too late to get Roy and run. We were trapped, and no one would hear our screams. His heavy breathing was close, he was standing over me, sucking in his pleasure. I jumped with fright as he shouted, "Play Mozart!"

Our music broke off. "Minuet from Don Juan," I whispered, "Key of C."

The guard backed away, grinning and sucking noisily. As we reached the last note, he cried, "Beethoven!"

We began the "Minuet in G." Rocking slowly with the music, his eyes never shifted. I could feel them staring at me. We played on, praying that he ask no more.

The piece was finished. I would put my violin away, gather up Roy and get out. But he rushed toward us, uttering sharp, incoherent phrases. A few feet from me, he stopped and clapping his hands, the Japanese words spilled out, *"Dom arigato, dom arigato!"* Bowing low, he backed his way out of the barracks, his bayonet scraping against the slag as he disappeared.

We stared after him. He had said, "Thank you."

In the hungry darkness that night I lay restless under the mosquito net. I felt he would come again. This was not the end.

Several days passed without sight or sign of him. Then one afternoon as the heat settled like a steaming blanket over the camp and Roy's fretful cry was quieted, I pulled back the door curtain for air, and gasped. There stood the soldier. He grinned and thrust a piece of paper into my hand. His eyes scanned the cubicle. *"Boisan?"* He pointed to Roy, then waved his arms as if to play a violin. "Music!" he pointed to the paper he had handed me.

156

I looked at the paper. On it, in legible English, was written: "Bring piano friend, play music in empty barracks. Today. Bring baby."

I looked up from the paper, wanting to refuse him, but he had disappeared. I knew better than to ignore the order. I wakened Stan and Gale and told them, not of the soldier, but of a practice appointment with Rosemary.

Carrying Roy and my violin, I summoned Rosemary, and together we went to the designated barracks. As she creaked open the door, one of the guards in the sentry box beyond turned from his forward stance. It was the one who had come to my cubicle. He had managed to get guard duty at this outpost.

We started to work on a Handel Sonata. We had come to make music, to practice seriously, and section by section we rehearsed, going back over the difficult spots. In our concentration we had somehow forgotten the soldier, until reaching over the piano for the next piece of music, I saw him standing in the darkened shadow of the huge door, motionless. How long had he been there?

We continued our practice. Meanwhile, Roy had edged his way over the slag toward the khaki puppet. Quickly I put down my violin and went to get him. The guard motioned me back to my playing. *"Boisan,"* he said, "Likee, likee." He lifted Roy off the slag and, dusting off a section with his dirty handkerchief, put him down again.

An hour went by without further interruption. As we prepared to leave, he bowed and said, "Music to-to-morrow."

"Tomorrow," we repeated. At least this enforced daily practice should make for a good program, we agreed.

For three more afternoons we went to the barracks, practicing before the watchful eyes of this strange enemy. And each day came the words, *"Dom arigato,"* followed by one new phrase in English. "Five year soldier. Cello, Formosa before." The second day, "Tired of war, want peace. Play cello." The third day it was different: "To-to-morrow no music. Night watch."

We didn't see him again until the night of our concert, and then only his face peering in over the open window ledge at the side of the barracks in the darkness.

That Sunday evening, June 16th, Ralph and Bill Parquette, with help from various internees, had transformed the central barracks, usually reserved for lectures and religious services, into a beautiful concert hall. They had built a real stage surrounded with festoons of tropical foliage — palms and highly colored leaves. There was even a footlight and one overhead light, giving the worn upright piano a regal setting! We, too, had done our best to look beautiful, each wearing a white cotton formal smuggled into camp two years before, and the best available borrowed makeup — with native flowers in our hair!

The audience, clad in shorts and *bakyas,* was attentive and responsive. Never could we have played to a more appreciative audience, we thought. Ralph had placed Skipper's chair in a front row position.

As our program progressed, so did the bugs. How lucky not to be a singer, I thought, until a giant mosquito lit on the elbow of my bow arm during that wonderful Adagio, slow movement of the Concerto. It took its fill of my thin blood, with rest periods for digestion!

A second moment of horror came during a fast piece, Praeludium-Allegro by Fritz Kreisler, when a huge something fluttered down my neck! It wriggled and turned. I accelerated my tempo, Rosemary rushing to keep up with me. At intermission I dug it out and we went back for more. Our concert ended with several encores, including "Londonderry Air" for Skipper.

* * * * * * * * *

I had all but forgotten our episodes with the guard when one afternoon in the cubicle, listening to Stan practice on his tiny violin, I stepped over to pull back the curtain for needed air. There stood this same guard, listening! Grinning and bowing, he backed away out of sight.

The next afternoon after chow the soldier sent for Stan to bring his violin to the main gate. "Yes, Stan, you must go," I said. "There is no choice." I walked part way with him, and waited on the path.

He was back in half an hour, carrying his violin, bow and a paper sack of native fruit. Yes, he had played for them — more pieces, he said, and then they had given him the fruit.

The following week our rations were cut again and the Commandant's orders forbade *any* contact or speaking between guards and prisoners. I felt sure the incident between this guard and ourselves was closed.

One afternoon Stan came running into the cubicle. He pulled the door flap closed and, out of breath, began telling me, "Here, Mom," he said, pulling a small package from inside his ragged T-shirt, "a Jap soldier gave this to me down by the vegetable cleaning stand. He said, 'No tell. Give to Mama-san. Tell nobody.'"

Together we tore away the newspaper wrapping and stared at the contents. Brown grains of raw sugar, maybe half a cup, and a few tablespoons of ground coffee which gave off a pungent aroma. Delicacies we had not had for months! I pushed back the tears.

Making a syrup from the sugar, I put a spoon of it on the boys' mush each night before bedtime. The Parquettes and Uncle Jim shared our coffee until the dried grounds, re-used so many times, could give no color to our brew.

Fearful lest someone might have reported Stan's meeting with the guard, I questioned him further as to how the contact had been made. "I was going along the path, Mom, and this soldier cut across the compound toward me. I bowed from the waist, like our orders. He bent over, too, and shoved the package into my hands saying those things I told you. That's all." It had been a daring daylight contact, I thought, and worried over what might happen in the days ahead.

HUNGER CONTINUES
(July, 1944)

With Lt. Konishi's cutting of food rations, an epidemic of some sort was bound to come among the children. Now it was measles. Gale was the first one in our family. So many were already quarantined in the camp hospital that Dr. Nance agreed to let us take care of him in our cubicle. Our quarters were at the front of the barracks so we could isolate him. By hanging blankets over the window openings, we could protect his eyes from the bright sunlight. As with the other illnesses, Gale was very sick. On the last day of his quarantine period, Stan came down with measles. A few days later, Roy followed. Six weeks of isolation with measles . . . but we were thankful to have had them with us. They came out of the siege thinner and weaker, but the fever and spots were gone.

Our Los Banos barracks were of quite different construction from the university buildings in Santo Tomas. The wooden plank floors and thin *sawali* walls of woven narrow leaf fibers often separated, leaving space enough for "outsiders" to enter from beneath the floor and depart, or travel from one cubicle to the next. Accordingly, one afternoon a stranger appeared in our barracks — not a war prisoner, yet evidently interested in fraternizing. Our first announcement of this newcomer was the sound of frantic screams from two cubicles down the corridor. Everyone rushed to the scene and a mad scramble ensued. The occupants, two elderly widows, were waving their arms, directing the search as beds and boxes were shoved back and forth. Nothing in sight . . . so we all followed to the next cubicle. "What is it?" Everyone was too busy to answer. Finally someone volunteered.

"A large iguana, member of the lizard family — about half the size of a young alligator. It's been seen several times in other cubicles but always evaded capture."

About a week later I was practicing for a camp show when a motion crossed my vision. It came from the corner of our cubicle, close to the floor. As I looked again, Iguana was peering up at me through the space between the floor and *sawali* wall, his beady eyes sparkling, his red tongue flicking! Not daring to move, I kept on playing for what seemed like hours before he slipped back down out of sight. I kept thinking about the story of Heifetz in Manila, years before, when he was in the middle of a concert in the old Manila Opera House and a huge python had slithered onto the stage, charmed by the beautiful music.

We saw Iguana again a few days later when he came sliding across the beams overhead and crawled into an empty carton above us. Then we lost track of him, and for awhile everyone seemed to have forgotten about him. Curiosity over his whereabouts renewed in a few weeks when hunger became more acute. "If only we could find Iguana," they said, "for some nice, juicy steaks!" But someone else must have made the conquest.

There were fewer cats and dogs in evidence in the camp. As days went on, several times we heard an unearthly screech in the night, then silence. The next day there would be a faint odor of meat cooking in someone's cubicle, and passersby would linger. Even the odor was a treat!

For months and months there had not been meat in the camp chow, and the little bit we had had consisted of five kilos of carabao bones rejected by the army. When Ralph would bring the chow buckets, Stan and Gale were sure to be at the cubicle waiting to peer into each of the two small cans, one with rice *lugao* (rice cooked in quantities of water, like liquid library paste), and the other with a weak broth of greens and just possibly a few half-inch squares of gristle, a great good fortune! They would spoon out the gristle and put it aside for dessert to fondle this tidbit in their mouths long after chow was finished.

Uncle Jim, an experienced gardener, had helped us spade our three or four feet of hard adobe clay outside our cubicle and he had planted several okra seeds and butter beans. I scorned the idea of planting such things. "We won't be here to use that, Jim. You're wasting valuable energy." But his foresight was right, and we harvested each little plant and started more. The papaya trees which we had planted right after our arrival in Los Banos were tall now and ready to bear fruit, but alas, not one papaya came. Out of the five trees, three were males and two were morphodites that only blossomed, endlessly and endlessly.

Jim's earlier experience as a pharmacist also helped us to stave off beri-beri with the bitter tonic of iron he brought us each day. During his camp work at the piggery, he and several others had planted a small patch of *camotes* — native sweet potatoes. This crop took six months to mature but the green tops would grow quickly and profusely and could be eaten as greens. While his friends selected the young, tender leaves for their portions, Jim picked only the large tough leaves that he knew contained lots of iron. With added pigweed leaves, I cooked some every noon, chopping them fine for Roy's portion. He was eating line chow with the rest of us now, but he hated the bitter taste of the *camote* tops, just as we did. But by noonday his hunger drove him to eat what was offered — and there was nothing else in sight until he swallowed the greens.

Fuel had become a serious problem, too. The boys searched the camp grounds for scraps of wood, often dragging back a tree branch to be hacked into small pieces that would fit into our small clay stove. Dry wood was not to be had.

While Stan was in school for two hours each morning, Gale was busy with Roy, taking him for a walk to distract him from his hunger, or scavenging for food, rusty nails or fuel. One day he brought back a treasure. "Look what I have for you, Daddy." It was a rust-eaten shovel head without any handle. "I found it in a ditch," he said proudly.

Shovels were scarce in the camp and hard to come by. To procure one from the camp supply was difficult and then for one hour only — after gardening hours. Ralph somehow found wood for a handle and fitted it into the shovel. It proved invaluable. Jim used it to spade our little plot deeper, and Ralph little by little began digging a foxhole in front of our cubicle. The Japs had previously announced that our forces knew nothing of the where-abouts of Los Banos Camp, and if we wanted protection from our own planes we should dig our own trenches.

By now the children were all scavengers, as well as grouping in gangs for mud fights and play-warfare. One of the trees in the camp had branches low enough for a child, hoisted up by others, to swing and get a hold. Having witnessed a youngster in Santo Tomas fall from the top of a tree, I had warned Stan against climbing any tree. One night at bedtime, Stan had not shown up, so I started across the field to locate him. A high school girl called to me. "Mrs. Nash, have you seen Stan?"

"No, Eileen, I'm looking for him. Have you seen him?"

"Oh," she said, excited, "two boys just carried him into the Clinic."

I raced across the grounds to the hospital, my heart beating against my throat. There he was, on the examination table, alive and weeping. "I fell from a tree," he sobbed, pointing to his leg which was swollen from the ankle upwards.

An assistant to the doctor looked at his leg, getting cries from Stan as he touched the tender places. "I think it's only a sprain," he said, "but hot packs should be applied. We had better keep him here tonight," he added.

I had had little experience with broken bones, but I was skeptical about its being only a sprain. The swelling was increasing

162

and the area was turning blue. "Please have Dr. Nance look at Stan when he comes," I asked the clerk at the entrance.

It was getting dark and I hurried back to tell Ralph. With Gale and Roy in bed, I returned to the hospital to be with Stan. Dr. Nance had come and was examining our six-year old. "A broken bone," he said, but the leg is too swollen to set now. Perhaps tomorrow."

Stan was moved into a ward and hot applications were started. I kissed him good night with a promise to see him first thing in the morning. I returned to Ralph with the verdict. We dreaded the weeks ahead for Stan, with his leg in a cast, but did they have anything to make a cast?

Stan emerged from the hospital on the third day, hobbling along disconsolately on a rubber-tired brace which Dr. Nance had skillfully made into a cast from a previous casualty. Suddenly a familiar voice came from behind. "Well, blow me down, if it ain't Long John Silver Nash, peg-leg and all! What have you done to yourself, lad?" Skipper was back with us, and under the spell of his enchanting nonsense, "Long John" was swinging briskly about, looking alive again; and the younger children, organized by Skipper as junior picaroons, vied with each other in their imitations of "Long John" Nash.

After six weeks the day finally came to have Stan's cast removed. We went with him to share in the big moment. He was impatient to get it off. "Ah, there!" he beamed as he stood up from the chair. Pains shot through his toes and up to his knees. He quickly sat down again. It was pathetic to see his struggle in learning to walk all over again, a few steps at a time, to his school class. He was still walking like Long John Silver, never touching his heel to the ground and carrying a hitch that resembled a peg-leg. Each day Ralph took him by the hand, making him slowly put his foot flat on the ground, but the next minute, in a hurry to get somewhere, Stan was back in his accustomed stride. He walked with a slight hitch for two months. He needed milk and eggs, and calcium to replenish his system, but *lugao* (rice paste) and a few greens were still our fare — in lesser amounts each week.

Chapter Eleven

BURT FONGER, EAGLE SCOUT
(August, 1944)

he continued cuts in our rations were lowering everyone's resistance. Burt Fonger was noticeably thinner now, yet his grin and buoyant spirit remained steadfast and he was still doing a double shift of camp work. One night they carried him to the camp hospital on a stretcher. It was Dengue fever, they thought.

On the fifth day, just at noon, I was pouring the weak broth of greens into the boys' plates when someone came running into our cubicle. "It's Burt! He's gone — malignant malaria." Starvation disguised itself in strange ways!

Stan and Gale stopped eating. Big tears came into their eyes. A hush went over the camp as the news spread like a rolling todal wave. I was stunned. I hurried to his parents' cubicle, searching for some bit of comfort to offer them. My lips were dry, my body numb. It was Mrs. Fonger who comforted me.

As I started back to our barracks, fellow prisoners were plodding along the road, heads bowed. There wasn't even a whisper. I sat down on the steps, thinking back . . .

It was September in 1940. Burt Fonger was fifteen when I first met him on a lazy Sunday afternoon in Manila. He was summoning me to the Union Church nearby.

I put down the phone and with some misgivings hunted out an old baton from the desk. Slipping it in beside my violin bow, I closed the case and started out.

As I turned into the driveway of the church, a loud blaring sound vibrated in my ears. I wanted to turn back, but the eager voice I had heard over the telephone led me on. I pushed open the door to the recreation room. The noise stopped suddenly as five teenagers put down their instruments. The dark-eyed boy behind the drums was grinning. His face flushed as he stood up.

"I'm Burt," he said. "This is Milt at the piano, Jay with the trumpet, Dave and his harmonica, Joe and his fiddle. We wondered if — well, we want to have an orchestra. But we need some help." His feet shifted. "You can tell that we need help." They all laughed. He rubbed his flushed cheek and wrinkled his nose. "We don't know much. But if you'll help us we'll work hard — won't we?" There were loud cheers of approval.

And so that next hour and a half marked the first rehearsal of what became the Junior Symphony of Manila. Within a year it grew from five to forty-five members.

I got to know Burt first in a musical way — his enthusiasm, his eagerness for criticism, how he took hold of every suggestion and carried it through, his capacity for hard work, and his contagious grin — qualities which made every rehearsal rewarding.

We were preparing the program for our first anniversary concert when the song, "God Bless America," swept Manila. Burt was whistling the melody as he came into rehearsal one afternoon. It didn't worry him that we lacked scores, for he knew I would arrange them.

What a big moment for all of us — that concert night. There were new white suits, red and blue ties. Burt had measured the ribbons for those ties, set up the music stands, arranged the microphone for the broadcast to all the islands.

Dated September 5, 1941
MANILA DAILY BULLETIN

JUNIOR SYMPHONY GIVING
CONCERT TONIGHT

Eagerly anticipated for several weeks, by numerous Manila parents, friends of the young musicians, and other interested music lovers is the first anniversary concert of the Junior Symphony of Manila, which will be given tonight at Heilbronn Hall, American School, beginning at 8:15. The second half of the program from 9 to 9:30, will be broadcast over radio station KZRH.

Mrs. Ralph Nash is the director of the orchestra, which is composed of 45 young people ranging in age from 10 to 19 years. They are . . . and Burton Fonger, percussion.

The concert was about to start . . . young players eager and nervous. Some had had their instruments for only two months. But Burt was grinning. And after each number the players looked back at the drums, at Burt's grin to regain their confidence.

When they came to "God Bless America" they played it with all their hearts. The audience stood and sang the chorus. "God Bless America" and "America, the Beautiful," two melodies that I had blended in harmony . . . too bad that score was burned . . . the minor note in the trumpet call of the introduction, like an ominous warning of the war ahead.

We had great plans for that young orchestra comprised of many nationalities. Twelve concerts were scheduled for that Christmas season of 1941. We had bought more instruments with the proceeds from the anniversary concert in September, and best of all, a set of timpani.

Burt helped to unload them from the truck. "They're swell kettle drums," he said, as he took out the sticks to try them. "H'mm, I forgot they have to be tuned. But I'll get the hang of it, and a smooth roll too." Before each rehearsal he was there practicing, often staying after the others went home.

His face was one big broad smile the night of the Scout Rally in late November when he played the timpani for the first time. And after the orchestra numbers he stepped out from behind those drums to become an Eagle Scout. We were proud of Burt that night. Putting away the music afterwards, he said, "Gee, I'm looking forward to those Christmas concerts. Ya know what? — we're getting better all the time."

We never played those Christmas concerts, for the war took

away our plans. Instead of Christmas music there were bombs and air raid sirens. Burt was an air raid warden and drove an ambulance to and from Cavite Navy Base with the wounded. He was sixteen years old then.

The city fell . . . imprisonment . . . family separation because Reverend Fonger refused to sign the paper presented to missionaries by the Japs. Burt was a messenger for the Red Cross outside, when Gale was taken with acute bacillary dysentery . . . he was riding his bike. "I'll get the sulpha, I'll find it — if I have to go to every botica in town. "I could hear his voice loud and clear, and he was back with it within the hour. It saved Gale's life.

Burt continued his messenger work even after he had to wear the red arm band signifying that he was an enemy alien. It was a risk to be seen on the streets in Manila. He went on with his high school studies without teachers to guide him. At the Bousmans, he came to me for cello lessons and orchestration, and mustered together the remnants of our orchestra for those underground rehearsals on Saturday afternoons.

When his father had been taken to another camp, Los Banos, Burt and his mother were admitted to Santo Tomas. I had returned from the hospital with our new baby, Roy. One morning Burt appeared in front of our shanty. He was grinning hard. "Hi, Mrs. Nash," he said.

"It's about the orchestra. Some of the gang have their instruments here." He shifted from one foot to the other, rubbed his cheek nervously, while the other hand dug deeper into the pocket of his ragged shorts. "I thought if you'd help us . . ." He looked away.

"But we're not equipped, Burt," I said.

"We could try."

"Where could we rehearse?" I asked.

"I'll find a place and get the kids together." His eyes sparkled. He snapped his fingers.

"But the music, Burt!"

"I brought a few books with me and I'll copy the parts."

"Yes, Burt," I said.

"Thanks a lot." His feet shifted again. He slapped the bamboo post that held up our nipa roof. "Have to run now. My camp work. I'm on the garbage crew." A huge grin wrinkled his features. "But I'll get the gang together. So long."

The next afternoon right after chow he rounded them up and we met under the "lean-to" on the small camp playground. Players tired and hungry, violins with strings missing, trumpets with sticky valves . . . I could see their hearts weren't in it as Burt put the music on makeshift stands of broken chairs. But his enthusiasm and the spirited rhythm that he beat out on his snare drum rallied them. They blew on their cracked reeds, bowed their two strings and pulled out sticking valves until the red sun dropped out of sight.

The next week there were fewer players for there was too much work in camp, even after sunset. But he didn't give up until we were refused the "lean-to" for rehearsals.

"We tried anyway," he said smiling "It won't be long, this war. Then we'll start all over and be twice as good."

"That's right, Burt," I said.

A few days later he bounded into our shanty. "What d'ya know? Mother and I are going to Dad's camp in a few days." His grin had spread over the whole of his face.

"You'll be together at last! It's wonderful," I said.

"Change of commandant, I guess. Mother's excited as all get out." He laughed and stroked the dark shadow of a beard on his chin, then dug his thumbs into his belt. There were folds in the waistband of his shorts, a new notch in his frayed belt.

"Dad'll be surprised. I wonder how he's making out. It'll be great to see him. Oh, he's all right, of course. He's got what it takes. Gotta go now. Be seeing you — at a steak dinner!"

I met Burt months later, but not at a steak dinner. It was in Los Banos camp. I hardly recognized him until he grinned. "Funny how those steaks didn't get done in time," he said.

He was taller and thinner and his beard no longer a dark shadow. Its heavy growth added years to his appearance. He and his gang put on a camp show and we laughed until our sides ached. People forgot imprisonment that night.

* * * * * * * * *

169

My thoughts were interrupted as someone brushed against me, putting a note in my hand. It was from Burt's mother, asking me to play the violin for the services in the little chapel on the hillside at three o'clock. "Andante Cantabile," Schubert's "Ave Maria," she mentioned.

I stared up at my violin case on the shelf inside. I rubbed away the dust that covered it and unsnapped the lock. Folding back the silk cloth, I saw the four strings, loose across the bridge. But I had no feeling. My body was like an empty shell, the soul torn from it. Slowly I lifted out the instrument and turned the pegs to tune it. My hands were shaking as I tried the bow.

"No, I can't," I cried, putting it back into the case. How could she ask me to play at a time like this? Then my hand brushed against the open letter.

"I think Burt would want you to play, Grace," it finished. The note fell to the floor. My fists clenched. "You will play! You must!" I cried.

Just before three o'clock I went to the little chapel. Looking back I could see the staggering lines of prisoners coming up the hill. The Scouts, followed by the Cubs, led the way. Stan was walking with the Cubs.

And then Burt's parents came. The Japanese commandant took his position beside them. A silence settled over the nearly two thousand people who stood on that hillside against the tropical sun.

I lifted my bow to begin the "Ave Maria." A verse from the Bible was being read aloud. My heart cried out bitterly, my hands trembled. How could I play? Hunger takes away strength. And now . . . What is the use of trying to go on? Hunger . . . imprisonment . . . a slow death!

I had no courage, no strength to face it. Everything seemed to blur. Again, the present faded. *I was back in October, 1940 — the gala concert celebrating the Commonwealth of the Philippines . . . five thousand people filling the Rizal Stadium. Burt and his gang were in the audience. "We'll be there," he had said. "Wouldn't miss it."*

The program was starting. Offstage, I stood waiting, nervously clutching my violin while the Constabulary Band played the national anthem, then a spirited overture. Gold braid and polished silver instruments glittering under the lights.

It was time for my solo. As I was escorted on to the stage, a great sea of faces engulfed me. Fear blanked my mind. How could I play? Then there was a movement in the audience. Someone was standing, cheering. It was — yes! It was Burt, smiling, standing up, leading the applause. His gang beside him . . . Burt . . . I would never forget . . .

My eyes scanned the hillside. But he wouldn't be there today to give me that courage and confidence. Yet, I could feel his presence. I blinked away the tears. I felt a surge of strength, my bow stopped quavering.

"Oh, God, let me play as I've never played before!" The melody soared in smooth even tones. Yes, I was playing for him . . . Burt's smile . . . "Ave Maria."

The fortitude and strength of Burt's parents in facing their deepest sorrow were beyond our capacity for such bravery, yet it made us realize that we MUST carry on. We did, with more determination than before. Burt was not gone. His spirit lived in our hearts and would live there forever.

Burt Fonger

Chapter Twelve

INCREASING HUNGER
(September - December, 1944)

For some time Rosemary and I had been urged to play a second concert for the camp. At the end of August, despite our hunger, we started practicing in earnest. Unwisely, perhaps, I tackled a new concerto. Although it was not too difficult, my technique and memory weren't responding as I had expected.

Our rehearsals were usually at 8:30 in the morning. With no food until ten o'clock, after a night of little sleep, much tossing and gnawing hunger, we had neither strength nor will for concentrated practice. As the day for the concert grew near, my nervousness increased. It was scheduled for September 24th, a Saturday evening, only a week away.

On Thursday morning, September 22nd, I went to the empty barracks for our rehearsal as planned. Rosemary and I had grown accustomed to distant bombing practice by Jap planes, with or without any announcements. This morning we were hearing distant detonations as we started to play.

After a few minutes, I stopped playing. "Rosemary, do you hear the noise?"

"Oh, yes, Grace, it's just more target practice. Don't get excited."

We began the next movement of the concerto. The rumblings became heavier. "It's not practice," I said, still playing. Looking out through the open doorway, I noticed Jap guards grouped together. They were stretched on tiptoes, craning their necks and waving their arms toward the sky.

My bow trembled on the strings. I stopped. "Rosemary, come. Let's get out!"

Quickly closing my violin case, I grabbed the music and pushed my way through the barricade of guards who were peering into the clouds. Rosemary followed close behind. As we hurried toward our barracks, internees were standing in the road, pointing into the sky north of us.

I began to run when the monitors shouted, "Everyone inside quarters. Air raid alert!"

I could see tiny specks by the hundreds high in the clouds. I heard continuous heavy thuds. My heart was beating faster than my feet as I raced on. I was the last person outside, and my whole being shook with happiness as I reached our quarters. American planes, at last!

Ralph was inside with the three boys who were jumping up and down on wobbly floor boards. Gale grabbed little Roy, hugging him as he danced around the cubicle. "Sweetie-pie," he said, "just think, we can have an apple in just a few days now! An apple, Sweetie-pie!"

Gale didn't even know what an apple tasted like, nor what it looked like, yet it symbolized freedom to him — an American apple! The bombing continued past noon. We had no morning mush, but our hearts were high — and we opened a long-saved can of meat to celebrate.

We welcomed the complete blackouts every night. Rumors flew over the camp faster and heavier than the bombs we heard. Several of our bachelor friends brought us some tins of milk from their long cherished stock. They were all so sure that a few more weeks at the most would bring our deliverance.

The Japs were noticeably jittery and non-committal, but we welcomed their air raid alerts like manna from heaven. Needless to say, our concert was cancelled. I was more than thankful for the reason causing its cancellation.

The number of guards was soon doubled and the order was repeated with stronger threats about "no communication of any kind allowed between any guard and internee". . . Again and again our rations were cut, but we could stand it, we said. It would soon be over.

Day after day we looked into the sky, expecting and waiting. The hours passed at a snail's pace. By eleven o'clock each day the children were weak from hunger. They stumbled to their cots to lie down, their knees buckling under them.

Our papaya trees were still not bearing fruit, so one by one we dug them up. Slicing off the pulpy roots, I boiled them for hours. They were tasteless and indigestible but the heavy lump they made in our stomachs gave us the feeling of having swallowed something.

Roy always finished his portion of mush first. Stan and Gale would make theirs last as long as possible, but Roy's sad cries for more always brought tears to their eyes and they would spoon out some of their mush for him.

Roy loved the two or three tiny butter beans in the noon broth. Butter beans were his brothers' favorite, too, but they often took theirs out of the broth and put them in Roy's plate. They were starving yet they couldn't endure the thought of his hunger. We still had a small amount of powdered milk set aside for Roy — the can Skipper had given us. Longingly they would watch him drink it, saying nothing.

In certain cubicles, however, there was case upon case of canned goods, protein foods which had been collected at reasonable prices by several internees at the time of our Red Cross kits. Now these same foods were being sold at unbelievable prices: a can of corned beef, $50, gold; a can of Spam, $75; one cigarette, $1.50 . . . and powdered milk, $350.

Heavy trading was going on between these profiteering "dealers" and starving internees who gave up their watches, rings, and fountain pens as collateral with their I.O.U.'s for food. These same dealers were also trading with Jap guards in the night, getting a few kilos of rice, mongo beans or sugar in exchange for American watches, pens, etc., the guards often stealing the rice supplies from their own commissary!

If only I had my tiny Hamilton wristwatch and beautiful diamond ring that had been stolen from our house after internment.

Where were our planes?

Our camp gardens, almost ready to harvest, held out some hope. The greens and vegetables would help so much. But for the second time since the beginning of Los Banos camp, Lt. Konishi, with smirking satisfaction, ordered, "Move over — we take." Not only pushing in our boundaries, but taking away our sorely needed food.

With this twenty-four hours notice, Pat Ryen and his helpers dug up a few plants, picked what greens they could, and said farewell to this beautiful harvest.

We were defenseless. And now a third Christmas was approaching. What could we possibly find for gifts? Stan and Gale had learned how to crochet. With a tiny ball of string, they each made a pair of shoestrings for Daddy and Uncle Jim. I found a handkerchief for Frank Ale. We knit a washcloth for Harold Bayley, our pilot friend, and made a handkerchief for Mrs. Breson . . . enough for a tiny gift at each place.

While the boys were outside, Ralph hoisted down the box of remnants from the previous Christmas and somehow we pieced together a box of crayons and repaired a toy each for Stan and Gale. From a friend I borrowed a pattern for a stuffed toy, a scottie dog, and from a piece of red and white seersucker cloth from an old evening gown I cut out the pattern. With two buttons for eyes and stuffing of dried hemp, we had a fair-looking stuffed toy for Roy.

Despite his depleted strength, Ralph made a few more wire clothespins, straining to twist the wire into shape. These would be welcome gifts for several friends.

Several weeks before, the rumor of more food kits arriving had sent our hopes sky-high, especially when not Lt. Konishi, but the commandant had stated, "You will have a nice Christmas." There were even rumors about the exact content of the kits. Such rumors built up fast, faster than the rumors that followed the sighting of those B-24's. Each day we waited for the food kits to arrive.

Stan was learning to play the Christmas carol, "It Came Upon A Midnight Clear," to accompany the clear soprano voice of another lad. Together they were to perform the carol at different barracks on the day before Christmas and for the children's party on Christmas afternoon. There must be music of some kind for Christmas, I thought, remembering our feeble but heroic performance of the "Messiah" in Santo Tomas Camp. We even had a semblance of an orchestra to accompany the Chorus. But we were strong and more daring then.

THIRD CHRISTMAS, 1944

It was the day before Christmas, our third one spent in camp. Tropical rains beat against the nipa roof of our barracks as I scrubbed the worn clothes in a shallow bucket of soapless water. The three boys were sleeping and Ralph was on camp detail. Suddenly there was a soft knock on the wall behind me. "Grace, are you there?"

I pulled back the door flap. It was Harold Bayley, our bachelor friend, a former test pilot.

"Are you alone?" he asked, shaking off the rain and stepping inside. Then he added in a low whisper, "I have a message for you from a Jap."

"What? What is it?" Harold knew nothing of the "friendly" guard. Earlier in internment, he and his partner had been assigned quarters over on the hillside, beyond the prison barracks, to look after the few pigs which had long since been gone because there was no garbage to feed them. For lack of barrack space, the two men had stayed on in their shack, near the sentry post at the boundary.

"He says for you to come to the water tap on the hillside. Bring Roy. God, what a day!" he continued in a whisper. "One-thirty sharp, the guard said. And when you get there, you're to wash your hands at the faucet. That's it," he finished.

"Do you know what he wants?" I asked quietly.

"Hell, no! But it's his risk, too, you know. Maybe he thinks your baby will be the cover up. I'll be watching from the hole in the east side of my shack. It's 12:30 now." He backed out of the cubicle, closing the door flap.

Ralph was still out on firewood detail when I finished the wash. I awoke Roy and started out. The rains had let up but the soggy clay mud tugged against my wooden *bakyas* with every step. Roy's weight, even though slight, taxed my strength going up the hill.

As I reached the water tap, I caught sight of two guards at their outpost, eyeing me. As I turned on the faucet, there came the sound of boots. Two soldiers stepped up and began washing their rice buckets. I stepped back, recognizing the one. But the other soldier began speaking in clear English.

"I speak for my friend," he said, motioning with his head to the guard I already knew. As he continued speaking, he kept on rinsing his pail, never looking up. "He wish to help you. Not like see boys hungry. But he have no money. He say if you have jewelry, clothes, he sell. Buy food for you. Jewelry, he take first. Tie in small package, front of cubicle tonight. He get in night. Few days he bring back food. Yes?"

"Yes," I answered, trying not to move my lips.

"What food you like?"

We needed protein, but meat and eggs would spoil in this weather. Protein . . . protein . . . "Mongo beans!" I said almost too loud, "Mongo beans." These pellet-sized beans were protein-filled and would not spoil.

The guard I knew glanced behind him, then leaned forward and touched Roy's hand. *"Boisan,"* he mumbled softly. He reached behind a clump of bushes beside the tap and brought out three freshly dug ginger roots washed clean, and laid them by the faucet. "You — Christmas."

The other soldier spoke again. "Tell piano friend. He sell for her, too."

Fumbling for words that he would understand, I finally stammered, *"Dom arigato."* "Thank you" in Japanese.

The two soldiers looked at each other, grinning like children. Fastening their rice buckets to their belts and mumbling excitedly, they shuffled back up the hill to their sentry post.

I quickly stuffed the wet ginger roots inside my blouse and, carrying Roy, started back toward our barracks, stopping off to tell Rosemary. Inside the Parquette's cubicle, we whispered back and forth. Should we take the chance? It could be a ruse, a planned strategy for trapping us. To be caught trading with the guards or with friendly Filipinos on the outside was punishable by death. Death — the ever present threat that was closing in on us anyway. And if we didn't take the chance? Our decision was made.

Rosemary hunted out several pieces of fine Turkish jewelry. "I have no clothes to sell," she said, "but these pieces were gifts to my mother from Turkish ladies in Istanbul. If we survive, Grace, then they have been of some value." She tied them, Oriental fashion, in a small kerchief.

In my cubicle I took down the small native box from the high shelf and looked at my few pieces of costume jewelry. These would bring but little — but the pen! I took out the emerald green Parker fountain pen. I hadn't thought of trading it before, because the barrel was broken and it wouldn't write. Turning it slowly in my hand, my eyes caught the name engraved along the side. "Grace C. Nash." With my name on it, the risk was too great.

I looked over at Stan and Gale lying listlessly on their cots, staring at the rafters. In despair, I stuffed the pen in with the jewelry and tied it all into a small cloth.

On Christmas morning it was just beginning to get light when I pulled back the mosquito net and peered out. The two packages were gone from the step. Inside the cubicle were five small green papayas on the floor. As I reached for them, I saw a card with writing on it. Six points were listed in crude English, assuring me of honesty, best price, no commission, and food as soon as possible. "Burn this," it said.

Before the boys awoke, I quickly kindled a fire and dropped the card into it. The sudden brightness of the flame somehow expressed the hope that rose within me. It was Christmas, after all. The green papayas would be a boon to our diet for several days and we could use them for apple sauce, stewed and seasoned with the ginger root and a piece of cinnamon.

Our guests arrived for Christmas dinner at 4:30, bringing their line chow along. We sat down to an unusual meal — two cans of meat mixed with the mush and greens, and papaya apple sauce for dessert! The three bachelors — Uncle Jim, Harold Bayley, and Frank Ale; then Mrs. Breson and elderly Mrs. McCoy, plus the five in our family. Stan led us in a blessing and we ate long and hearty in contrast to other days.

We had made a policy of inviting guests for each Sunday and for any holiday. Regardless of how little there was to eat, our table and benches were crowded on such special days as July 4th, Thanksgiving, and Christmas. And our guests seemed to be grateful for the touch of family. Roy's sweet ways gave extra joy to us all.

Of all who were with us this day, I think Mrs. McCoy was the most pleased. She was in her seventies, and almost blind, yet she still had the will and courage of a young woman. She depended on her visits with us, she said, to keep her going. She loved the boys and their funny remarks. With her own keen sense of humor, she kept good pace with them. Her late husband, Colonel McCoy, had raised the first American flag in the Philippines in Cebu, 1898! Mrs. McCoy in her younger days had excelled as a pianist. She had organized the first Manila Symphony Orchestra and had kept it going with her financial backing during its first rough years. She had received many young artists and members of the diplomatic corps into their beautiful home on Manila Bay. Her enthusiasm and energy were contagious wherever she went. Now weighing scarcely eighty pounds and barely able to walk, she was determined to live to see the American flag once again fly over the Philippines, her beloved home.

DARING CONTACTS
(December-January, 1945)

Most of us had long since lost our reserve weight. Our memories and vision were becoming dim from gradual starvation. About every third day our legs refused to work, our knees buckling under us. Ralph resembled an adolescent boy who had gained his height but had not filled out. Uncle Jim was hollow-chested and bent as he stumbled along. He was too weak to take Roy for those pleasant walks any more, and some days he couldn't walk to our barracks.

Six days had passed without contact or message from the soldier. I was outside cooking a noon-day broth on the clay pot stove when suddenly the air raid gong sounded over the camp — the signal for everyone to go inside their quarters until the all-clear siren. I couldn't let the fire go out, or leave the promised bit of nourishment for the boys to spoil outside. I fanned the small flame with all my strength, trying to hasten the cooking before Jap guards came through our compound to check.

The sound of thudding boots jerked me upright. Camouflaged in the usual net of green branches over their uniforms, a guard was running toward me. I covered my face against the slapping that was sure to come. I slumped to my knees, ducking my head, when a voice came low and clear. "Have clothes, big bundle ready tonight." Then only the sound of boots thudding on.

When I finally raised my head, the guard was far down the path. What planning this must have taken, plus memorizing those words! I picked up the pan of broth and hurried inside.

Still torn between distrust and hope, I packed together whatever we had left from pre-war days. It was an odd assortment — several pieces of table linen, a black and silver dresser set — wedding gifts from friends in the States, and other things which were inside the chest that had been rescued for us by friends on the outside.

The next morning the bundle was gone from the doorstep. On this same day, the number of guards around the camp was increased and another warning given against prisoner and guard contacts or attempted trading in any form. There was also a new order: "*No* visiting or congregating of prisoners outside their respective barracks!"

Another cut in our food rations. The aching numbness of beri-beri set in. I stopped eating, dividing my portion among the boys. Ralph was smuggling his spoon of mush to Stan and Gale whenever he could. Our nerves were on edge, we could stand no speaking. At the end of the day we sat outside the cubicle, silent in the insect-filled darkness.

The children were too weak to romp or run. Each day they congregated just outside our quarters, leaning against the thin *sawali* walls for support while they talked about food — only food — food they would eat when liberated. There was no conversation about movies, comics or toys; just food — the taste of oatmeal, bacon and eggs, a glass of milk, ice cream and a Hershey bar.

It drove me wild to hear their chatter, hour after hour it seemed. My anger over their hunger as children and ours, as adults, sometimes made me cry out to myself, trying to keep my sanity a little longer.

The only bedtime stories Stan and Gale wanted to hear were stories of imaginary meals, the food they would be eating after liberation. I would begin with breakfast, no ordinary one either, but three courses; then a mid-morning brunch, then lunch that would grow in size to that of a four-course dinner; a four o'clock snack of weighty proportions, and finally a seven-course dinner/banquet.

"But, Mommie," Gale would say, "What will we have at bedtime?"

"I want a big glass of Ovaltine, ten cookies, and a dish of ice cream," Stan would say. "We'll be hungry, you know."

"Me, too," chirped Roy, to remind us that he was "one of the boys."

"Yes, you may have all of that, and an extra glass of Ovaltine," I promised, visualizing my own desires for such wonders. I would tuck them in bed inside the hole-worn mosquito nets where they would spend another restless night bitten by mosquitoes and bedbugs, continually roused from sleep to relieve their weakened kidneys. From lack of protein for so long, the children were all wetting their beds each night. Our diet was 95% water. This meant more washing each day without soap, and more buckets of water to carry from the faucet, a block away.

As our hunger increased, we got less sleep and were faced with more work, yet Ralph and I dared not give up, knowing the frightening condition of our children. In the blackouts we spent wakeful nights staggering back and forth to the outside latrines located between each two barracks. We had been warned against being found outside of our barracks after curfew. We would be shot. No questions asked.

Our cubicle was located at the front of our barracks — the farthest away from the latrine. One night as I was feeling my way back from the latrine, I must have lost my direction. I groped for the wall of our barracks. Moving on, I suddenly realized that I was not in the barracks, but out in the open. I stopped, paralyzed with fear. I tried to figure out from which direction I had come, knowing that I could be shot at any moment.

I heard footsteps on the slag behind me. Quickly I turned around, hoping to get inside or onto the slag patch. In my haste I bumped into the person whose footsteps I had heard. Gasping, I whispered, "I'm lost. Can't find my way."

It was Ralph! He recognized my whisper. "Grace, it's me, Ralph. I'll show you the way." He took my hand and led me back to our cubicle. I sank into bed, exhausted with fright.

Ten days had gone by since the bundle had been taken by the soldier. The boys had been put to bed and we were sitting outside the cubicle in our customary silence, when a broken whisper caught my ear. "Meesus Nash."

Cautiously I answered in a whisper, "Yes?"

"I speak to you, please."

I got up and found my way to the figure flattened against the *sawali* wall of our cubicle. "I come with message," he whispered. He was trying to put something in my hand. I felt the smooth round surface of an egg. "My friend soldier was transferred — last night. He going home, they tell him. He make me promise to keep word with you." A second egg was thrust into my hand. "I will see you get food from money." He drew a third egg from somewhere, whispering on, "He give me paper showing money from clothes and jewelry. I give you," he said, the paper in one outstretched hand, an egg in the other. I was finding it hard to put the eggs into my jacket pockets fast enough. "Very hard to get food," he went on, "each day higher price, but I keep try. Filipino promise me to bring mongo beans, in few days. Maybe fewer beans — price so high." Each hand passed an egg to me. My two pockets were bulging now — three eggs in each, and I knew that four would be their capacity, even with the bantam size of native eggs.

"My friend wish to tell you *he* keep fountain pen — in memoriam. When he look and see your name on it, he think of violin and you. He like so much and thank you for kindness." Two more eggs ended his words. "I send you message when can get food. Your boys velly hungry — I keep promise to friend soldier." Two more eggs were handed to me. "Goodnight."

I whispered a thank you, but he had already disappeared into the night.

I tiptoed carefully into the cubicle to hide our precious

bounty, feeling a surge of joy with eggs for our boys. After whispering the news to Ralph, I went out to the latrine entrance where the only light, a piece of narrow wick, burned. Straining what eyesight I had, I opened the paper close to the tiny flame, and read: "Mrs. Nash 6000 pesos, clothes & jewelry; Pianist 3000 pesos, jewelry; 30 kilos mongo beans. Hope."

Ten eggs! The next day I took Rosemary four eggs and the note. She would accept only three. I gave two eggs to Mrs. Kennedy whose three children were failing in strength too fast. "Never a word," I whispered, "and burn the shells."

With the five remaining eggs, I cracked one each day. Mixing it with water and a few grains of sugar I divided it among the three boys — their first protein since — I couldn't remember.

Chapter Thirteen

SKIPPER WILLIAMS
(January 1, 1945)

 anuary 1st marked the beginning of our fourth year in the hands of our Japanese conquerors, but on this same day came release for our endeared Skipper Williams.

We hadn't seen Skipper for some time but, like Jim Cullens and many of the men in the upper barracks, in their weakened condition the distance was too far. That day Rosemary and I made a feeble attempt to play a few pieces outdoors — a sunset concert for those who could bring their chairs. When Skipper didn't show up, I decided to go to the Infirmary and inquire. As soon as we finished, I closed my violin case and started for the camp hospital.

I was too late. Hugh Williams was gone. "He died of acute colitis," said Dr. Nance. "He'd been eating too much roughage, tree roots that caused an obstruction in his colon. Only an all milk diet might have saved him," he added.

How did we get to know Skipper in the first place? Why was he so dear to us? It wasn't good to like someone so much. Oh, Skipper! I was thinking back to the time when we had first encountered him in 1943 at Santo Tomas Camp, two months after Roy's birth. I was headed for my daily work assignment — cleaning the latrines. Gale and Stan were carrying their pretend mop sticks jauntily, like rifles. Behind us we were pulling Roy in his crude bassinet-on-wheels. Suddenly Stan whispered, "Look at that man, Mommy! He looks like a pirate!"

I turned and saw a gaunt apparition, bony and hollow-cheeked, of sixty-odd years, whose seaman's uniform hung upon him like rags. Yet his burning grey eyes gave him a look of ferocious dignity.

Overhearing Stan's stage whisper, he made a playful lunge at the boys and rasped in a pirate's voice, "And a terrible pirate I once was, buckoes."

I was in no mood for joking. Caged here in Santo Tomas with nearly five thousand, I had work to do. Voluntary assignment, to be sure, but I was a charwoman and Ralph a kitchen lackey. How could we go on telling Stan and Gale that "everything will be all right" when even they were slowly starving before our eyes? And Roy — how much longer could I go on nursing him on this starvation diet?

I glared at this ex-seaman as we hurried on. A few nights later I broadcast a violin program over the camp's loudspeaker system. Afterward I found this seaman waiting for us. He tugged self-consciously at his angular chin and said, "Mrs. Nash, you played 'Danny Boy' tonight — my favorite. I thank you. My name is Williams — Hugh Hosking Williams."

Emboldened, Gale peeped out from behind my skirt. "Were you really a pirate, Mr. Williams?"

"Captain Williams to you, my lad." He winked and waggled a skeletal finger. "You can bet your bones I was, mate."

The next afternoon I was singing softly to Roy in our shack when suddenly the air was rent with nautical cries, "Boom, Boom! Show 'em our colors, mates — run up the Jolly Roger! Give 'em another broadside! Bo—om!"

I looked out. Skipper Williams, his eyes blazing in the sun, was standing on the bridge of an imaginary ship barking orders to a buccaneer crew of two — Stan and Gale. Other children came running to get into the game. I started to protest at the noise, but the objections died in my throat when I saw the boys looking happier than they had in months.

Ralph and I didn't disillusion the boys with what we learned later about their hero. Hugh Williams was actually a retired British ship captain. At the outbreak of the war a small salvage vessel he owned had been bombed from under him in Manila Harbor and, lacking either cash or Filipino friends to slip occasional food to him, he and his Norwegian seamen were even more destitute than we were.

He loved people, especially children, and had a magic power to divert them from the miseries of prison life with his salty stories. He was sorely missed in Santo Tomas Camp when with eight hundred others he was sent to Los Banos. But somehow during the next eleven months of hunger we forgot about him until we, too, became a part of the two thousand now settled into the row-upon-row of barracks at Los Banos.

My next meeting with Skipper was in May, 1944, a month after we arrived. I was standing wearily in the water line, Roy in one arm and clay jug in the other, when Skipper walked up and handed me the can of powdered milk for Roy. And I played "Danny Boy" for him at the first camp show. He celebrated that 4th of July with us as we all raised our tin cups in a toast for our "freedom to come." What a salty sea captain he was, regaling us with his great stories. So knowledgeable, too. They said his evening lectures in Santo Tomas were crowded and people forgot about internment. With children to care for I couldn't attend.

Then, here in Los Banos, a second time I played "Danny Boy" for him — as a special encore at the formal concert Rosemary and I had given. I could see him beaming in his front-row chair Ralph had placed there for him. And when Stan broke his leg, what a morale booster Skipper had been — to all the kids. Even after our rations of rice paste and talinum greens had been cut in half by the sadistic Lt. Konishi, Skipper gathered the kids down under the big acacia tree and told them sea stories to make them forget their hunger. "Ha! you think *this* is bad, mates? You should've been with me the night my ship blew higher'n a kite. There I was, wrestlin' a raft of sharks with m'bare hands!"

I thought about the meal times when he stopped by our cubicle. He would see Stan and Gale looking into their tin plates — scarcely enough mush to cover the bottom — and as their pirate captain he would say, "I never did care much for mush anyway, did you, men?" And they'd manage thin smiles. To be considered "men" by Skipper was their greatest pride.

Once, though, Gale burst into mutinous sobs. "But I'm *not* a man! I'm little and I'm starving!" The captain of the Los Banos Buccaneers put his hand gently on Gale's skinny shoulder. "Lad," he said, "you've been aboard a long time, and to tell you the truth I hadn't noticed." Skipper was closer to tears at that moment than I ever saw him.

And now he was gone. I could only think of the dwindling can of powdered milk on the shelf in our cubicle. "It could have kept you alive, Skipper, and you gave it to Roy," I said aloud as I started back to our quarters, my violin heavy on my arm. "Danny Boy, Oh, Danny Boy . . .!" the Irish air played on in my ears.

MONGO BEANS!
(January 4-6, 1945)

It was January 4th, a bright, hot Sunday morning. We were fanning the smoking green wood into a blaze when a heavy drone drew our attention upward. This was a different sound, a tremendous engine force from far off. Squinting and shielding our eyes from the direct sun, we peered into the sky as the sound became heavier. Suddenly a group of tiny silver-sheened birds came out of the blue cloud overhead. By this time other internees were gazing upwards, spellbound.

"Their altitude must be 30,000 feet," said Ralph. They were directly over the camp now. Suddenly there was a burst of gun fire. Anti-aircraft guns, we thought, yet why would the Japs think they could reach that altitude? It would only give away their gun placements.

The gun fire was repeated, exactly the same as before, then came a third repetition. Ta-ta-ta-tum. Three quick beats and a fourth longer sound. Like a flash I recognized the pattern: the opening phrase of Beethoven's Fifth Symphony! The victory signal! Others had recognized it, too, and a great sigh of exaltation swept over the camp. Our planes *did* know of this camp and they were signaling to us. The Japs had repeatedly warned us that Los Banos camp was unknown to our own forces.

We were beside ourselves with excitement. These must have been land planes; huge land-based planes that were launching their attack in preparation for landings. Our thoughts of hunger were almost secondary to our rising hopes. And we concluded that the September 22nd bombing more than three months before had been done by navy planes from carriers. But now we felt assured of full-scale operations from a land base not too far away. The Japs were decidedly uneasy and before the day was over they had ordered another cut in our rations. It didn't matter, we said silently. Our forces knew where we were and they would soon be coming. Hadn't those victory signals told as much?

January 5th was a stormy, rainy day — one of those ominous, depressing days in the tropics that could easily turn into a typhoon if this were October or November, but *not* in January! What we had been hearing since before dawn was not thunder but heavy guns! Hour after hour those distant roars continued. Maybe coastal shelling had started in preparation for a landing here in the south. After all, we were only thirty-five miles from the Luzon coastline south of Manila.

We stayed inside our quarters most of the day, entertaining visions of incoming American troops and freedom while we talked about food, imaginary meals we would soon be having. It helped to push back some of the gnawing aches of hunger.

The next day, January 6th made me think back to another January 6th — 1936 in Chicago, the day Ralph proposed to me. It was so long ago. A mist blurred my vision. Another January 6th — 1942, the beginning of our imprisonment when we planned for three days instead of three years! And today, 1945 marked the start of a fourth year as prisoners! What else might this day bring? The distant roar of guns had ceased but our excitement was still high. I was returning from the water tap when I saw Harold Bayley hurrying toward me. Remembering the order, "No visiting between prisoners outside of quarters," I simply nodded a greeting.

"Keep walking, Grace," he said softly. "Slowly. I'll follow you. Don't turn around. I have another message from that soldier." Walking closely behind me, I heard his whisper. "He says to tell you the food comes tonight." The earth suddenly seemed to lift under my feet. "I'm to meet him on the hillside, nine o'clock. He'll deliver the stuff to me if . . ."

A low whistle from the left warned us of an approaching guard. It was our camp code, a whistle-warning to each other of "guard approaching." Without finishing his sentence, Harold veered from the path and headed up the hill. I bowed low to the guard as he passed, my spirits soaring with thoughts of food.

* * * * * * * * * *

How much I hoped and prayed for success in Harold's mission — it would be our salvation, and others, too. Ralph and I sat in the ominous darkness to wait, surrounded with the buzzing of mosquitoes.

But what if the food didn't come? I remembered the "if" which Harold had not explained. Not to have the food come would be more than I could bear. It would be like the food kits we had expected for Christmas and they didn't come. I was counting off the minutes now. It was nine o'clock. Harold would be meeting the guard about now. Oh, please make it work, I prayed silently.

About ten o'clock a strange commotion in the high-fenced Japanese barracks directly across the road from ours drew our attention. We had grown accustomed to their nightly grunting and shouting of allegiance to their Imperial Majesty and the Rising Sun, but tonight there was more confusion than usual.

We crept out to the front entrance of our barracks, to the highest ground for vision, and with several other internees who had heard the noise, we stood listening and watching. Something strange was going on. There were little flicks of light shooting through the cracks of the *sawali* fence. "They must have lighted fires in the native stoves to heat their bath water," someone offered.

"Surely they aren't so excited over taking a bath, bad as they need it," came another voice.

"No, no," whispered the serious internee beside me. "Something is really going to happen."

Higher and brighter the flames could be seen through the cracks in the fence. Then they died down — then blazed higher again. All this time soldiers in the adjoining barracks were in a bustle. We could hear their boots in heavy treading. There was mumbling or jumbling of voices going on, and the confusion spread. "I bet they're burning papers," someone suggested. "Maybe they're getting ready to leave camp!"

We had imagined something like that a number of times before, but it had only been troop movements, change of guard, replacements coming in, or truck-loads of troops spending the night en route.

Finally curiosity got the better of several of the men. They pyramided, one on top of the other's shoulders, in an effort to see over the wall. "Yes, they're burning papers all right," came the opinion from the top pair of eyes.

I kept thinking about Harold and his meeting with the guard. Something must have gone wrong. It was past ten o'clock and no sign of him. I moved away from the group at the front of our barracks and sat down on our steps.

* * * * * * * * * *

How long had I been sitting there? Suddenly without warning, a cold bucket knocked against my knees. Someone stumbled over me. "My God, Grace!" he gasped, pushing my hand into the pail.

"Mongo beans!" I almost shouted.

Harold clamped his hand over my mouth and pulled me inside the barracks. "Shut up," he whispered. "Let me tell you what happened." But I was sitting on the floor, running my hands through the rich, life-giving pellets. He woke Ralph, who climbed out of the net to hear his story.

"Listen to me, both of you," he began. "That fool soldier met me on the hillside at nine o'clock sharp — with nothing in his hands. He simply said, 'Follow me,' and lit out across the garden like a beam of light. I started to follow him, crazy-like. Then I came to my senses — I was on forbidden grounds! It was after curfew and I wasn't going to risk my neck now, after staying alive this long. I tried to call to him but it was no use. He was way ahead of me. I went back to my shack and waited.

"Then about fifteen minutes ago I heard something bump against our shack," he said, "and in stumbled this guard, soaked with sweat, and a burlap bag of mongo beans that he dumped at my feet. 'I keep promise to my friend,' he said. He was out of breath but he managed to tell me how he'd run a mile and a half up the mountain to meet a Filipino at the road, then zigzagged his way back to the camp, through his own lines! God, I hate to think if he'd ever been caught with that sack of food — how quick he'd have lost his head."

I let the beans spill from my hands, still dazed.

"Mongo beans! They're stashed all over my shack, Grace. I'll get the rest over to you eventually. I've got to go. It's after eleven o'clock you know."

We thanked Harold in more whispers, and insisted that he

take out two kilos of the beans for his trouble in this long and dangerous transaction. He would agree to only one kilo, he said, and hurried back to his quarters.

Ralph and I lost no time in making a trade, even at this time of night. In fact, most confidential trades were carried out at night throughout imprisonment. I knew of a missionary family who had sugar to trade for much-needed protein beans. In the dark I went to their cubicle and made the deal, sugar for beans. Somehow we measured out can for can in the black of night, and I returned with some sugar, deep brown, sweet — sugar! No questions were asked, no explanations given.

There were more internees clustered around the front of our barracks still curious about what was going on across the road. But by 12:30, too weak and hungry to stay up any longer, we sank down under the mosquito net and fell asleep.

STRANGE INTERLUDE
(January 7-13, 1945)

In spite of the whispering and bumping against our barracks wall, we had fallen into a deep sleep when suddenly we were awakened.

"Grace! Ralph!" Someone was pushing at our elbows and tugging at our mosquito net. "Wake up! Wake up!"

In the pitch black of night, we recognized the voice. It was Frank Ale, from an upper barracks beyond ours. He was standing beside our bed.

"Great news, kids," he said. "The Japs are pulling out of camp! They've turned it over, lock, stock and barrel to our committee."

Was I dreaming? Could this be true? Ralph hugged me. We both hugged Frank. He rushed on to tell the Parquettes and others. It was 3:30 a.m., January 7th. We dressed quickly, whispering fantastic phrases to each other in our jubilance. "That coastal bombardment must have preceded a landing of our forces to the south," Ralph explained. "In that case our troops should be in our camp in a few days!" "A few days!" I repeated.

Within fifteen minutes the entire barracks was stirring and the people were going crazy with the news. As we pushed aside the curtain over our entrance, we heard the last of the Japs driving their trucks out through the front gate. But we were appalled at what else we saw. Our friends and barracks inmates were rushing pell-mell through the *sawali* fence just across the road, into the Japanese barracks. Children and adults alike went milling and yelling into their quarters to loot — each one trying to get ahead of the other!

Soon they streamed back, loaded with furniture, army boots, souvenirs, small sacks of rice or sugar — anything and everything. We stared at them, sickened by their actions.

Stan and Gale had awakened with the noise. Rubbing their eyes as they listened to the news, they were swept away with the same desire.

"No, you will *not* take part in such looting," Ralph said. I repeated, trying to explain the wrong in such an act. "We don't *want* anything of theirs, nor will we *take* anything of theirs," we said firmly. But we had to physically restrain them in the cubicle.

They cried out, "Look, Paul's doing it . . . Jack's got a gold dagger . . . see what Jay has . . ." Stan even argued further. "The Japs have left, besides they hated us and made us starve — why shouldn't we take their things?" Ralph, in his quick firm voice, put a stop to Stan's wishes. We lit a candle to help the boys dress.

Rosemary and Bill came racing in to tell us the news all over again.

"We'll celebrate right now," I said, and told them about the mongo beans and Harold's hair-raising experience, and the sugar we had already traded for.

"I've started some coffee brewing, our last grounds," Bill said. "We'll bring the pot over." He left for his barracks while Rosemary stayed with us, all talking at the same time. Stan and Gale were pacified with a teaspoon of sugar each.

When Bill returned with the steaming coffee soon after four o'clock, we folded our bed against the wall (a contrivance Ralph had invented to make space for our table), and we celebrated. We drank deeply of black coffee with sugar in it — our first in a long, long time.

The monitors in each barracks soon shouted through the corridors that a camp meeting would be held at six o'clock outside the barracks that housed our staff office. "Important announcements. Everyone come." Meanwhile our camp patrol staff had taken positions on each side of the already-looted enemy barracks to prevent any further entrance by internees.

Roy awoke just before six o'clock and the five of us made our way to the camp meeting. The morning sun was just beginning to show a dull pink over the crest of the mountains in the distance. Promptly at six a.m., a recording of the "Star Spangled Banner" was played and a huge American flag was raised over the barracks. A hushed silence swept over the ill-clad, gaunt internees. We wept. Everybody wept in an overwhelming joy. Ralph was holding Roy high on his good shoulder so that he might see the American flag for the first time in his life. Stan and Gale stood in front, on tip-toe. Following our national anthem, the English "God Save the King" was played and their flag, the Union Jack, was raised beside the Stars and Stripes. A prayer was offered. Just as the "Amen" was pronounced, we turned to see a lone plane flying over the mountain against the vivid morning sun! We knew it was an American plane.

The significance of this awe-inspiring service could not be described in any language, but what we felt that morning was fathomless depths of gratitude for our deliverance from further starvation, we thought.

George Gray, our chairman since Mr. Fonger's resignation, spoke to the group about plans for camp order and maintenance. Then came his announcement of "Double portions of mush will be served at eight o'clock, and a noon meal of rice, if possible." Cheers lasted for several minutes before the serious side of our situation could be dealt with.

"It is important for all to know," he stated, "that outside our boundaries are many enemy troops. It is unsafe for anyone to leave camp," he continued. "Each internee must feel his responsibility in keeping order and good behavior in our group."

Our shrunken stomachs were stretched almost to the bursting point that day, and each face, no matter how gaunt, wore a smile a mile wide.

By five o'clock that afternoon, January 7th, 1945, our radio technicians had assembled a radio and loudspeaker for the camp.

We listened to the news from KGEI, USA. More news, and finally Roosevelt's Inaugural Address that marked the beginning of his third term as President! But our weakened minds could not comprehend what we heard, and try as we might, we could not remember at nine o'clock what we had heard at five o'clock other than the fact that American convoys had been sighted near Lingayen Gulf, many miles north of Manila. Nothing had been heard pertaining to any troop landings along the coast near us.

The next six days were exuberant ones, in spite of no sign of American forces near us. The Filipinos sent in a carabao, and we were having meat! Molasses had been procured from somewhere, which added energy and taste to our breakfast mush. Coconuts were delivered in hand carts and we relished the rich delicacy of coconut milk over the mush.

As a special reserve, each internee was given five kilos of raw rice — to save for an emergency. But many internees foolishly traded their portions to Filipinos for bananas and other perishable goods.

From this sudden eating, everyone became ill, of course, yet we couldn't stop. It was like a compulsive addiction — until it was too much and we couldn't finish our portion of rice. Stan and Gale, even Roy, had bulging rice stomachs and they were happy. So were we.

The Japanese headquarters barracks had been cleaned out and scrubbed and made into an office for our gate patrol. Several of the internees who were on guard duty now moved their cots into this barracks to sleep between their patrol hours. Others took posts at the camp boundaries, urging internees not to go out of camp to trade with Filipinos.

We were reminded again that spies were watching our camp closely, and to avoid any serious revolution or possible attack, we must be careful. Yet despite all these warnings, many internees left the camp each day, returning with extra fruit and native vegetables in return for their portions of rice. Everyone joked about the Japs and their hurried exit. But would they return?

How different this January 7th, 1945 was from January 7th, 1942. We had come through a slow but sure hell for three years! But soon we would be welcoming our forces with open arms. No more Lt. Konishi! . . . we thought.

As there were spies outside our camp, the loudspeaker for the camp radio was silenced right after that first broadcast. Instead, news transcripts were read each night by the various monitors in the barracks. From these reports we learned of American landings at Lingayen Gulf, but still no news of any southern coast invasion.

Then, on January 13th, about midnight, we were awakened by our barracks monitor who hurried through the corridor delivering a shattering blow. "The Japs have returned! Everyone stay inside your quarters! Dangerous!"

Soon we heard their boots stomping up the road outside, a string of abusive profanity heralding their arrival. Our hearts sank in despair and fear. We got up quickly and hid our reserve ration of rice. Their angry voices made us wonder just what they might do in such a temper.

Another few minutes and again the monitors conveyed new orders and threats. *"Everything,* including their radio must be returned to Japanese quarters by 7:30 a.m. Failure to do so will result in severe punishment for the entire camp."

The consequences could be terrible for we knew that much of the stolen property had long since been traded to Filipinos for food. But the radio was even more serious. We had taken it for granted that our news sheet and broadcasts had come from the Japs' radio, until rumors circulated that an internee had taken the Japs' radio and traded it to Filipinos outside! Our news reports each night were from another radio! Where had it come from? (Our radio had been hidden by fellow internee Chuck Woodin, inside his mattress!)

Like the sudden appearance of the two flags and the two recordings of the national anthems at sunrise the week before, all must have been hidden in camp from the beginning — awaiting the right moment!

Some of the looted furniture, odds and ends were being taken back to the Japs' barracks as the day went on, but still NO RADIO! Without their loudspeaker, their orders had to be conveyed by our monitors, every few hours — but to no avail.

Finally, after repeated orders continued through the night, on the second day a radio was presented to the Commandant.

"This ees *not our radio!* . . . but WHERE did *thees* one come from?" Their voices got louder and higher, and even more enraged with the sight of another radio, plus their discovery of the depleted rice stocks from the food *bodega*. Our rations were cut to a mere handful of rice.

How thankful we were for our committee's foresight in giving out the emergency five kilos of rice to internees at the outset of the Japanese departure.

Our mongo beans from the enemy soldier had gone fast. After giving Rosemary her portion, there were several families who needed protein badly. Their children were bordering on TB, so we had distributed several pound cans among them.

Our captors had lost face in their sudden exit from camp and their equally sudden return. To lose face was humiliating and maddening to them, and they took out their spite on us. Every hour of the day brought some new threat, and more severe face slappings. But still no radio was produced.

American planes flew high over the camp en route to their objectives, and rumors circulated of our troops advancing slowly towards Manila. Air raids confined us to our quarters so that needed camp work could not be done. Turmoil and disorganization kept everyone in a frenzy.

Although these distant bombings kept our spirits up, it was our emergency rice ration that was our real means of survival. Very carefully we measured a hundred grams (one average serving) from our reserve to add to the lunch soup and scant evening chow. Some of the rice we ground into flour to make unleavened rice patties before bedtime.

Our optimism had been too strong. The little reserve strength we had been able to build during our six days of freedom now dwindled fast under the drastically reduced fare. In an effort to make the mongo beans stretch further, I cut down the daily amount to one tablespoon.

Long after the camp piggery was out of existence, several men who had formerly worked there found a large can of spoiled copra (coconut meal) left from the porkers' fare. Surely if there was food value in it for pigs, there must be some in it for us, Ralph figured. He brought home a can of it to try. We spread it out on a cardboard carton and laboriously picked out the foreign matter — rat manure, spiders, other dead insects, etc. Then Ralph toasted a small portion in our native skillet.

"Doesn't smell too bad," I said, looking into the pan.

"We may be surprised," he answered, pondering over the next step in its preparation.

I became busy with other things, forgetting the rancid coconut. A little while later, he handed me a cup of hot brew. "Have some coffee?" he said.

"Where on earth did you get coffee?" I asked, staring into the cup of brown fluid.

"Ask no questions," he replied, "just enjoy."

Eagerly I drank some. Looking up at him with delight, I heard his answer. ".Copra-coffee. Not bad?"

Amazed, I finished the cup. "It actually tastes almost like coffee. It's great, and the boys can have some, too."

Even Roy enjoyed a cup of "ah-wee," as he called it. And each day we made it steaming hot for lunch. Ralph went further in his research for use of this meal. After the brown liquid had been drained, he dried the grounds in the sun, and bringing out his pipe one night, he filled it and had a smoke! After a few days of copra coffee and "tobacco" we decided to add the dried meal to our broth for lunch — it would add bulk, if our digestive systems could stand it. Roots of trees and dried copra roughage. But our hunger forced us to swallow bulk of any kind, whether it could be digested or not. Roots were our bulk, and rumors our vitamins.

Despite the heavy guard around the camp, several internees were continuing their nightly exits in search of food. Warnings were repeated that any internee caught attempting to escape or found outside camp boundaries would be shot without question. Also, under the close scrutiny of the Jap officers, very little trading of jewelry was possible. Uncle Jim still had his prized pocket watch. Now, although it needed repair, he was determined to trade it for food for us. His own waistline rivaled Scarlet O'Hara's. His chest was so sunken that from a front view all that showed were protruding ribs — no evidence of any stomach. He walked with his knees flexed, and his hands dangled from skeleton-like arms.

Both Ralph and Jim were still doing camp work. They needed

198

more nourishment to keep going, yet I couldn't lessen the boys' portions. The only solution would be to take from my portion. Secretly I began to serve their food before mine so they wouldn't notice my plate. For nearly a week I managed to be busy while they ate, letting on I had already finished my portion. I kept drinking more water, but by the end of the week I knew that another day or two would be all I could last. I had weakened so fast I could hardly stand. What would happen? The boys and Ralph needed my assistance sorely — to prepare what food we had, to tell about the imaginary meals we would some day have, to help with the daily washing. It was useless to go on with my plan. Once more I equalized the portions and tried to keep going.

Stan and Gale often arose at 6:30 to go down to the fence near the Jap garbage cans where many of the children gathered to snatch at the remnants of garbage that sometimes spilled over on our side. If they brought home banana peelings, I diced them fine and cooked them in the skillet until nearly crisp, then added them to the mush. Grubs, or slugs, were a prize catch after hours of searching for them under leaves in the ditches. After the slimy things were scalded, cleaned, and cooked, there were but a few tidbits left, as a special treat.

Uncle Jim was still finagling a trade for his watch through one of the "dealers." It took a week of dickering before the deal was closed. One morning inside our cubicle I found a hand of ripe bananas and five coconuts. Jim was slumped in a camp chair just outside, exhausted from the walk to our barracks.

"Jim," I said, turning to him, "where did these come from?"

"That's the food I got for my watch," he said softly. "Oh, yes, and two packs of cigarettes which I gave to two old men," he added slowly.

I wanted to cry. "Thanks so very much, Jim, but I do feel bad to have you give up your watch."

"The bananas are for the boys," he went on, "and we can make coconut oil from the nuts."

That afternoon, mustering our energy, we started the long process of oil refining. First, opening the coconuts and grating them in the native way which required arm strength and several hours, then pouring boiling water over the meat and squeezing out the sweet milk; we repeated the last process to be sure of all the fluid. Then we boiled the milk, taking turns to stir it continuously until the oil separated from the residue — another two hours. By six o'clock we had nearly a quart of the delicious, sweet coconut oil, a small tin of gray residue, sticky and sweet like candy, and the remaining grated coconut to be toasted for future use.

Jim took a portion of the toasted coconut with him for his morning mush and left the rest of the food for us. I put a teaspoon of oil in our noonday mush, which Jim shared with us. The boys had one banana divided between them each day until they were gone. This nutritious oil was a godsend, and once we even splurged, frying mush cakes in a teaspoon of it!

In their foraging for food over the grounds, Stan and Gale began eating huge black ants. One night when they were getting ready for bed the cubicle reeked of garlic. We had been using our three cloves of garlic most sparingly for seasoning the bitter camote greens. Now I suspected something, but before saying anything to the boys, I first looked on the high shelf where we kept the garlic in a wee native basket. Only one clove was left. I asked them about it.

"Yes, Mommie, we ate it," they said, "but we are SO HUNGRY!"

Chapter Fourteen

BROKEN PROMISE, THE STORY OF PAT RYEN
(1941 - 1945)

veryone in our prison camp knew Pat Ryen*, from the hungry children who tagged behind his two-wheeled cart that was loaded with vegetables for the Mess kitchen to the burly Japanese guards stationed at their outposts just beyond the camp gardens where Pat worked many hours a day under the tropical sun. But few of us knew the whole story about him, or the significance of his actions in those last months of imprisonment.

Gathering fragments from many sources, I have pieced together the story of Pat Ryen, American mining engineer and fellow prisoner.

J. Patrick Ryen came out to the Islands as a mining engineer the year before Pearl Harbor, hoping his bride of four months could join him later.

When he arrived at his location in the Philippines, he found much more to do than superintend the mine. He established a health clinic for the children of his laborers and a recreation center for their use. He improved their living conditions and showed the Filipinos how to make the acid soil yield more crops, and he instructed them in self-government.

Then the Japs came, "like *anay* — white ants that eat from within, leaving an empty shell behind them." Pat hid out in the hills until a messenger came bearing a letter from the Japanese general.

---

*Real names have not been used in this chapter.

201

The letter promised him repatriation within a few months if he would surrender. It would give him a chance to get back to the States, to Opal. Then he could enlist and get in on the battle, he thought. He surrendered.

The repatriation ship, S.S. Gripsholm, left Manila in October, 1943. But Pat was not on the passenger list. He was in the Los Banos Prison Camp.

Among the first eight hundred men who were shipped out in box cars from Santo Tomas camp to start this new camp in the foothills of the Makiling Mountains south of Manila, Pat found life rugged, but there was more land here. The soil could be put to use.

When he suggested planting crops, most of the men laughed. "What the devil, Pat, our troops will be here before any harvest. Why waste your energy?"

He knew it would take time to recapture these islands, but he said nothing. Enlisting the help of several men on two-hour shifts, he went ahead with the planting. This was in May, 1943. By January, 1945, the fourth year of imprisonment begun, these gardens had been harvested and replanted twice. There were over two thousand to be fed, including women and children. Starvation was acute. For many of them this next harvest might mean the difference between life and death. For one person, Elaine Gramercy, it *would* mean the difference. The child she was carrying would never be born unless she could have food.

Then for the second time since the beginning of this camp, the enemy took over the harvest! The anger rose in Pat's throat as he worked against time, loading the cart with greens and what unripe vegetables he could pick before six o'clock, the hour when the Japanese would be claiming it.

As he worked, his iron-black eyes ignited with defiance and hate. What would become of Elaine and the child? In his mind he recounted the times he had asked for extra food for women and children, always refused by the Japs. In desperation he had taken the greens from his own small plot to give Elaine nourishment. She was swollen with Beri-Beri. He had counted on this harvest — and now — He ripped off the young eggplants, too small to give but a taste for two thousand people!

He raised up, wiping the sweat from his ragged sandy beard, as he moved the cart to the end row. A patch of loosened grass caught his eye. He paused a second, then went on loading the cart. But the sight of that loose sod seemed to relieve the twisted anger he had felt. He was remembering the night he had gone out of camp for coconuts and bananas, very successfully, too — even if Elaine hadn't appreciated his efforts. Always her thankless answer was the same: "I don't want this damn baby."

Pat had befriended many so-called eccentrics in camp. But Elaine was different. Her promiscuity and light-fingered touch had caused the entire camp extra hardships. Internees hated her. Even the man involved with her had escaped camp earlier. She had no one to turn to. But an unborn child, starved to death? They could do it to men, but not to an unborn child!

Pat pushed the half-filled cart to the Mess kitchen and dumped the few vegetables into the bin. "I'll be damned if they can do this!" he muttered, going on to his barracks.

He picked the last handful of greens from his own plot and started for Elaine's cubicle. Subconsciously he nodded his head, approving the two decisions he had just made . . . Now, if he could talk to Elaine.

* * * * * * * * * *

After roll call, Pat went to Henk Johnson's quarters. Henk was the only man he confided in. Henk followed Pat outside, where they could talk.

"I'm going out tonight. I wanted you to know, Henk."

Henk grabbed his arm. "No! For God's sake, NO! They've doubled the guard!"

"She has to have some food, and that baby *is going* to be born!"

"You mean Elaine? You'd risk your life for that pregnant prostitute? You can't do it, Pat! I won't let you!"

"No two-bit guards can stop me, Henk. I'm going. Besides, Opal and I are going to adopt that baby, Henk. Elaine has agreed."

Hunger can do strange things to people. It twists one's reasoning, leading to actions that are unbelievable to a normal person. It eats away the soul, while it feeds and enlarges hatreds and emotions to fanatical proportions. A small thing becomes an obsession, and to Pat, who had been steady and level-headed before, this unwanted child had suddenly become a symbol of atonement for an enemy's broken promise. His own hunger made no difference now. There was a child that must be born.

Pat's eyes were half-crazed as he argued with Henk. There was no reasoning with him, his thoughts were warped. He would go, regardless.

"All right, Pat," Henk said in a defeated whisper, "if you're determined to do it, I'll try to help you get back in. Tomorrow afternoon I'll go to the balcony overlooking the ravine — at the Infirmary. That's the only place you can get back in to camp during daylight. If the guards are too thick, I'll warn you with our whistle. You know the signal. But for God's sake, be careful."

Pat crawled under his mosquito net to await the right time for his departure. Getting out of camp wouldn't be too hard. . . No moon until three o'clock. He was exempt from morning roll call because of his garden work. All he had to do was get back before the next night's count as he had done before.

He waited until his twenty-some barracks mates had heaved themselves down for the night, then feigning a trip to the outside latrine, he crept out from his net. With a knapsack folded under his belt, he went from one barracks to another, through the latrines that separated them.

Reaching the last barracks on his route to the garden, he paused, listened for the sound of a guard's boots, then crept stealthily outside.

Feeling his way to the rows of eggplant vines, he crouched, waiting a few seconds to reassure himself, then padded noiselessly in his tough bare feet down between the rows to the spot he knew so well. He pried away the loosened sod and made his way to the outside world.

At 3:30 the next afternoon, Henk started for the Infirmary. He knew that the jungle growth of vines and trees in the ravine where Pat would be coming back to camp offered protection to those who could match their movements with the foliage. But one wrong move and a person might be spotted by the guards in the sentry box on the opposite side of the hill. Now, with the number of guards being doubled, getting back into camp would be close to impossible.

Henk wanted plenty of time to warn Pat in case guards were patroling the area. In order not to call attention to his position on the balcony, he paused a moment, then went inside. He had seen no evidence of a patrol in the ravine.

Just before four o'clock, crouching low, Henk moved out on the balcony to a spot where he could see without being seen. Watching for any sign of movement, he waited. Pat would be coming any time now, he thought, shifting his cramped position. The silence in the ravine grew heavy — the birds weren't singing. Somewhere a twig snapped, then he saw the soldier, camouflaged, moving through the jungle below. Henk gave a low whistle of warning. If Pat heard, he thought, he would lie low until the soldier returned to his sentry box.

Henk was still crouched on the balcony when rifle shots split the air! "God," he whispered, "let him live! Let him!"

Internees quickly gathered in front of the infirmary. Guards were shouting for them to disperse.

Henk was standing beside the doctor when a soldier came up to them. "Follow me," he ordered.

He led them down into the ravine where, face down in the leaves, lay Pat's lifeless body. He had been shot in the back. The knapsack beside him was filled with coconuts and bananas.

As they carried the body into the infirmary, frightened prisoners pressed toward them, tense and waiting. The guard raised his bayonet to clear the path. They backed away, stunned and silent as they saw the body of Pat Ryen, their fellow prisoner.

From the hungry children who had tagged behind his two-wheeled cart to the guards stationed at their outposts just beyond the camp gardens, everyone knew Pat. It was his labor that gave the two thousand prisoners fresh vegetables, a small supplement to the spoonful of rice gruel each day. It was his labor that had nurtured this harvest, the second harvest being taken over by the enemy.

Suddenly there was a stirring among the internees standing there. Someone was pushing through the crowd. Elaine, clumsy and staggering, forced her way up the steps of the Infirmary. "Pat! They killed him!" she cried. "Why did he take such a crazy chance?"

Henk stared at her. "Don't *you* know, Elaine?"

She gasped, then, turning quickly, stalked away.

The Japs changed the hour of Pat's burial three times and ordered that there would be no demonstration. Unannounced, at sunrise the next morning, a few prisoners lowered the crude coffin into the earth. They laid fresh flowers by the grave, flowers they had picked along the way: *red* cannias, *white* phlox, and *blue* cornflowers, a humble tribute to a great American.

Note: Elaine's baby was born after Liberation and adopted by another internee.

Chapter Fifteen

ACUTE STARVATION
(February, 1945)

n our anger and bitterness over the injustice to Pat Ryen, we still couldn't forget our hunger. With plenty of bananas and coconuts outside the fence, either one being an almost complete food, people were bound to attempt escape and return, in desperation.

Some days later, at 7:30 on a hot Sunday morning, again rifle shots pierced the air. Fear stopped my breathing. Who was it this time?

Greater fear seized the camp when the news spread like wildfire from barracks to barracks. They had shot George Lewis — INSIDE the camp boundary! He had managed to get back through the fence before they saw him, but they fired anyway!

The first shots had only wounded him. He could have recovered, some said. But the Commandant refused Dr. Nance's request to treat his wounds. Guards were placed around him to prevent anyone from getting close enough to help him. Exposed to the tropical sun, he lay there until a few hours later when they took him behind the camp to finish the job. He was denied last rites, and his body was thrown into a grave immediately after execution.

We were defenseless but our weakened minds ignited with rebellion. The Japanese laughed in their delight and power to starve, torture and kill us. This sadism was a part of their training and each triumph brought fulfillment of duty, a kind of duty that gave these war lords an added satisfaction.

Slow starvation cannot be described. To be understood it

must be felt. And further torture in this living death came when they denied us salt. The intense heat which had dehydrated our systems now made us suffer even more without any salt.

There had always been a shortage of water, available at only certain hours of the day, but we had filled our jugs and cans when it was available. With so many salt beds in Luzon, we had never imagined that salt would be rationed. But Lt. Konishi had found one more way to make our existence unbearable. He took away salt!

Immediately the trade value of salt soared to that of sugar, so inflated already. Our committee refused to enforce camp work in the gardens, and after several weeks the Japs gave in, allowing a meager portion of salt for each internee.

A mild form of insanity had settled over ninety percent of the camp — the frenzied copying of recipes. I knew that such fanaticism happened to explorers, isolated without sufficient food reserves, but I was determined not to give in to it. Children from ten years old to feeble, aged men who had never cooked in their lives, were now engaged in recipes! Exchanging, copying, talking recipes filled their waking hours — but not their stomachs!

At roll call a picture of chocolate cake or bacon and eggs was passed along the line that each one might feast his eyes upon it while we waited to be counted off by our grunting captors.

Helen Blackledge, one of our friends and mother of two boys, proudly showed me her book of recipes. "And besides this, Grace, I have planned luncheon menus for one whole year without a single duplication!"

Mr. Stahl, an elderly gentleman, brought me two typewritten recipes — salmon casserole and a special salad. "It sounds wonderful, Grace. Thought you might like to try them when we get out."

Recipes, recipes, dreams of food, hallucinations of malted milks, sirloin steaks, Irish potatoes, paraded through my mind. I finally succumbed. Grabbing a pencil stub and Stan's worn notebook, I wrote in feverish speed, gathering recipes from other internees to copy in my book. My mouth watered as I scribbled down the ingredients, imagining the supreme joy of eating the whole recipe, myself!

* * * * * * * * *

Our planes were everywhere now, and on February 18th, five planes skimmed the tops of our barracks as they circled over our camp. The next day, four planes circled in similar style, then three. One internee claimed he saw the pilot and co-pilot as they waved and took pictures just over our heads!

Our nights were horrible as we sat in the mosquito-infested darkness watching the distant glow of fires to the north of us. The whole horizon was a glare of orange and red while heavy artillery boomed. We would watch the streaks of lightning from guns, then count the seconds until the sound from each streak reached our ears. In this way we tried to estimate the number of miles between us and those guns.

Everyone was irrational and short tempered. For some months I had made a habit of going to the latrine at 8:30 each night to join in the give and take of rumors. So many of the women were on the verge of giving up; morose, hungry and exhausted. Somehow I had to think of some joke or rumor to raise their spirits and mine, to provoke a laugh over something that might keep us going one day more.

This nightly association and chance to talk was my only salvation and outlet, for Ralph was too worn to talk at all, yet he disliked having me leave the cubicle. His long silences were nerve-wracking, and yet if I said anything it was the wrong thing. I had learned to remain silent, too. I realized that his great concern over our acute starvation was eating away his normally rational outlook. And now, in the fourth year, he knew that we had but a few days of endurance left. My extrovert-nature compelled me to talk — it was the only means I had of facing any more of this ordeal, and so in those nightly latrine meetings I conjured up whatever crazy remarks, rumors and stories I could imagine.

There was still one can of luncheon meat on our shelf, saved from our food kits of '43, but we dared not touch it until everything else was gone. Each day we stared at the label longingly, yet knowing that this can, when opened, would be our last morsel of food.

On February 21st, the Japs gave each internee one handful of unhusked rice, with the announcement, "No more rations. Thees ees all."

Stan, Gale and Ralph worked tediously over the kernels, pounding the husks loose with a stone, then husking it kernel by kernel. We mustn't lose one single grain.

I sat at the table copying more recipes, working as if there were a deadline, while our planes bombed and strafed within a mile from our barracks! My thoughts turned to the Friday before, February 16th, my last violin playing for the camp. Just at sunset, several of us had volunteered a program out of doors, a short relief, perhaps, from the heavy tension and thoughts of hunger. Rosemary and I had played a few easy, well-known pieces for the hundred or more internees who sat limp in their chairs, listening. My arms were too weak to draw much tone and as I began the strains of Beethoven's Minuet in G, my eye caught sight of four men carrying a crude box across the field beyond. Beethoven's Minuet in G had become a funeral march! How soon would we be taking that path? Three deaths today, the average, and yet our troops were so near . . . or were they? Maybe Los Banos Camp was not important and would be bypassed.

The tenseness of the entire camp was near the breaking point. Something had to happen, and soon. Orders kept coming from the Commandant's office. Unexpected roll calls at any time of day or night. Regular roll call was cancelled. More air raids confined us to our cubicles. Detonations shook the ground as the Japs set fire and dynamited their installations near our camp . . . Their trucks loaded with military supplies and personnel kept coming and going . . . and our planes were in sight each day.

I staggered over to see Rosemary that afternoon during the one hour we were allowed to leave our quarters. Perhaps she and Bill might have something to tell me. Yes, they were still hopeful and their whispered news raised my morale considerably. While Bill rattled some pans to prevent anyone from hearing, Rosemary proceeded, "Do you know what Mr. Ross showed us this morning? Two shiny American dimes! And Bill has seen a fresh American cigarette!" she said.

"How would an internee get those?" I asked.

"Either a guerrilla or an American soldier entered camp last night. And we think he brought some definite information to our camp committee. There was a purpose in his coming. I'm sure! Someone in camp knows — but is probably sworn to secrecy! Did you know that Pete Miles* escaped last night? He said he was going to meet two Filipinos," Bill added.

I returned to our cubicle thinking about what Rosemary and Bill had said. I told Ralph when the opportune time came, and Uncle Jim, who for the first time seemed optimistic! His reaction brought my spirits up higher — maybe he knew something definite that he could not tell. From these whispered hopes, I imagined increased nervousness and anticipation in the faces of many around us. They must have heard something, too, yet each one had to remain silent.

Two American planes flew low over our barracks that afternoon.

The next day, February 22nd, early in the afternoon, only one plane flew over our barracks, circled, and returned, then disappeared over the mountain.

Stan and Gale, Ralph and I worked on the *palay,* husking the rice under the nipa awning over our cubicle. Roy slept on while we continued to count each bomb released from our planes in the distance. So near, and yet, so far.

After two hours of close work on the rice kernels our eyes ached; shooting pains ripped through our heads. Stan and Gale left to go to the latrine and Ralph and I were alone. As we gathered up the grains of rice, the same question was on our lips, "How long could we live?" One week, perhaps, but little longer than that.

Our papaya trees were gone. A few weeds were left in our garden. There was a day's ration of rice under the bed. We all had dry beri-beri which was paralyzing our bones and muscles. Each morning our movements began by inches as we struggled against the aching stiffness in our joints. The dull pain in our emaciated bodies grew deeper each day.

"Ralph, imagine the great joy in Santo Tomas Camp if it's true they are liberated," I said. "I wonder if we'll be alive to feel such joy and taste such food."

Ralph did not reply but sank into a chair. I gathered the two

---

*Pete Miles escaped and made contact with two Filipino guerillas who took him to American forces with his information.

211

cans and started out to stand in line for chow. I would let him rest this time. As I padded down the slag corridor, one of our neighbors called out weakly, "Grace, where are you going with those cans?"

"For chow line," I answered, matter-of-factly, bumping against the *sawali* wall in an effort to keep my balance.

"There *is no* chow! Don't you remember?" she said.

"Oh," was all I could say. I had already forgotten the Japs had done away with camp rations the day before. I turned around and staggered back to the cubicle. Roy was crying. Stan and Gale were bending over him, trying to interest him in a big spider in the corner.

"Ah-wee, wisee," (coffee, rice) Roy kept crying. After dressing him in a wrinkled sun suit, I went outside to start a fire and boil our few grains of rice. While Gale stayed with Roy, Stan helped me fan the smoke into a weak flame. One of us had to fan continuously to keep the green fuel from smoldering out. Choking and coughing from the fumes, we finally had a tasteless gruel to spoon on to the chipped plates.

Our meals were silent ordeals now. Ralph and I were too weak to utter a word. Stan and Gale, realizing that a single word about food would madden everyone, kept quiet. Roy was happy until his plate was emptied and then his cries for more were unbearable. In desperation we took turns giving him some from our plates. We had saved some of what we had cooked, for the next morning and we dared not give him any of that.

Uncle Jim no longer ate with us. He was too weak to walk to our quarters. Roy missed him sorely, and often chirped out his greeting for Jim, hoping it would bring him to our cubicle. This chirp was in imitation of a monkey he and Uncle Jim had visited each day on their walks. Roy had learned to give imitations of the ducks, chickens, and pigs they saw, too.

We knew that Uncle Jim had a shorter time left than we had — his starvation was further advanced than ours because he had given us whatever food he could get.

We went to bed that night, still clinging to the little hope that somehow, somehow . . .

Uncle Jim Cullens, 98 lbs.

Chapter Sixteen

IT'S A GREAT DAY!
(February 23, 1945)

woke up to the smell of smoke. Ralph must have started a fire to warm up our left-over rice. Somehow he always managed to get up first, letting me rest as long as possible. The dawn was just breaking through the haze, so I knew it must be close to seven o'clock roll call time.

Slowly and painfully, I forced myself to a sitting position . . . another day that must be faced, I thought. Each morning it took more effort to get up. I was just reaching for my worn housecoat when the roar of planes flying low over our barracks startled me. The noise was deafening. I stumbled over the chair in my struggle to get into my robe. I could hear people gasping just outside our cubicle. Something unusual, mighty unusual, was happening. I swung back the doorflap to see.

Internees were bumping into each other in their struggles to get outside to see the planes. "It's useless to get in that crowd," I said aloud, and turned to go out the back exit of our quarters.

Ralph met me at the exit way. "Planes, planes — come quick!" he said excitedly, "and I've been hearing ground engines, too."

We both gasped at the sight. Less than a hundred yards from where we stood, the sky was filled with parachutes opening and floating toward earth — each one bearing a soldier! They were like Greek gods coming from heaven! Hundreds of them jumping out of low flying planes that almost touched the tree tops! Our Day of

Liberation . . . !

"Stan and Gale must see this!" I turned to Ralph. His mouth was wide open with wonder and his eyes were smiling as they used to. Pulling Stan and Gale out of their beds, I took them outside in time to see the last plane unload our uniformed gods!

Our own American paratroopers! We watched in breathless awe while they slowly floated to earth just beyond the Japanese headquarters across the road from us. Many were still in mid-air when gun fire began, but the sound came from behind our barracks, not in the direction of the paratroopers.

We pulled the boys into our cubicle. "Get into our air raid ditch," said Ralph, and while he helped Stan and Gale into the open pit that he and Uncle Jim had dug months before, I lifted Roy out of bed and quickly shoved our last spoonful of sugar into his mouth. Our sugar had been carefully rationed only for him these last weeks, and he licked his lips in delight over the sweet, tasty treat.

The shooting was heavier now as I carried Roy into the soggy hole filled with spiders and muck. Ralph was tugging at the boys' frame slat beds to put a covering over our heads. Then he shoved a mattress on top of the slats for protection. I became frantic as the firing grew steadily closer and louder.

"Get in, Ralph, hurry, quick!" I said. He pushed the mattress in place and climbed inside — none too soon, for bullets began spitting and hissing all around us.

Stan and Gale, still in their pajamas, were squatting down in the mud and gazing out through the opening of our shelter to view the planes that were flying back and forth over the camp. They shouted their reports every second.

"Another plane, Mommie, Dad, here they come again — they're circling round and round!"

The bullets flew faster and thicker, fairly spitting across our heads while Roy kept chirping, "Bull, bull, Mommie, bull-bull," his term for bullets.

Suddenly Gale turned around and, looking so serious, said, "Mommie, do you suppose we could open that can of meat today? The Americans are here!"

"Yes, Gale-Boy, we'll have it for breakfast," I answered.

That was enough. Both Stan and Gale fairly jumped up and down on their knees in the sticky mud. Roy clapped his hands. "Me, too! Me, too!"

All this was going on inside our foxhole against the din of rifle fire. I shuddered to think of our troops in the thick of the give and take.

In the midst of all this noise of planes and gun fire, we heard shrieks of, "Help, help, first aid, quick!" from the barracks just below ours. We feared that the family across the way had been hit and I prayed for them — and at the same time silently gave thanks for our dugout. (No one was seriously wounded, just a skin grazing from a passing bullet.) Gale had made it possible when he had brought home that rusty shovel, uncovered in a ditch in the camp. Our prize scavenger, he never returned empty-handed — firewood, precious rusty nails, grubs . . . and once a tiny bouquet of wild flowers which he had stuck into our one jelly glass for a centerpiece as a surprise.

The distant engines Ralph had heard now sounded heavier and closer. We heard loud cheers coming from internees in the lower barracks. "Tanks must be entering the camp," Ralph said. And Stan and Gale imagined tanks they had seen so often on the streets in Manila — parades in which the same tanks circled again and again to give the impression of greater numbers of them.

Gun fire seemed to have stopped and we raised the frame covering. The sound of Oriental voices made us quickly duck down again. As I peeked out of the side opening in our trench, my exuberance stopped suddenly. I saw a large group of short brown-skinned men talking loudly as they came running in our direction. My heart pounded in terror. I looked once more. They were *not* Japanese! Each one wore a battered helmet, unlike Jap gear, and had a "G" string around his waist, and was carrying a shining new rifle! "They're Filipino guerrillas, Ralph!" I said in great relief.

We climbed out of the hole just as some paratroopers stormed through the *sawali* fence across the road from us. They were huge! The one in the lead wore a strange apparatus. He walked up our path. Stan and Gale looked up at him, speechless. An aerial of some sort extended above his head. He stopped a few feet from us and we heard him speak softly into a strange looking mouthpiece.

"How is it back there, Jerry? Have you got 'em all cleaned out?"

In a second's pause, we heard the quick reply in telephone voice. "Got 'em all but one — can't seem to dig him out!"

"Well, get in there and finish him, Jerry," spoke the leader.

"A walking telephone, it must be," I said in amazement. The paratrooper was covered with grime. Perspiration dripped off his uniform. I poured water from our native jug and handed it to him. "This is all I can offer you," I said. He took it in a gulp.

"Are you going to take us out of here in a few weeks," I asked, breathless with excitement.

"No," he answered, looking at me strangely.

"In a few days?" I asked.

"No, in a few minutes!" he replied.

"In a few minutes," I repeated, dazed and unable to comprehend.

"You bet," he said, striding on through the barracks.

I picked up Roy, and my paratrooper was gone. "Stan and Gale," I called, "get dressed quickly. Ralph, we're going!" All thumbs, I struggled to dress Roy and change to my slacks. Ralph was already gathering things to put in his bag.

Someone called through the barracks. "Head for the tanks, everyone who can walk, out on the road! Take what you can carry! Five minutes to get out!"

I grabbed my one dress, a handful of Roy's clothes, a handful of my music, and stuffed it all into a suitcase, then Stan's tiny case with violin and bow, and my violin, yes, my violin. "Must have," I said aloud.

"Boys," I called, "take some of your clothes, whatever you can carry." Stan was out of sight, but Gale broke into sobs.

"Mommie, Daddy, hurry! Come or we won't be saved! The people are all going!"

I looked out to see the road lined with internees. I tied other things in a *tampipi* and turned to pick up my suitcase. Gale's cries kept increasing as he paced in and out of the cubicle.

"The fires are burning," he said. "Come, please, Mommy, Daddy!"

I gave him the *tampipi* to carry. "Go on, Gale. We're coming now." He started out, looking back every few steps and still pleading between sobs. Ralph was systematically packing things into his bag, as if for a business trip.

"Ralph, come on, we can't wait any longer," I cried as I gathered up the two violins and my suitcase. "Me, too! Me, too!" was all Roy said as he clutched my trouser leg with his two hands.

I could feel the heat of the flames from the Japanese barracks, soaring and crackling a few yards away. Ralph went doggedly on, packing things into his one suitcase. Gale was lost in the milling mob ahead.

Just as I reached the roadway, Roy's stifled cry made me drop my luggage. Someone had knocked him down in the crowd. He was sprawling in the dirt at my feet. I grabbed him up, just as dozens more feet seemed to tread past the same spot. Jean Aaron stopped and picked up one of my pieces of luggage while I brushed the dirt off Roy, trying to comfort him.

I hoisted him with one arm and was trying to manage the other two pieces of luggage when a voice said, "Here, let me help you." I looked up, way up, to see a giant paratrooper swing my luggage up effortlessly. I held Roy and tried to keep pace.

The flames were hot. I turned around to look back for Ralph. The rear of our barracks was now ablaze, too, and there he was, outside our cubicle, still collecting things. Another figure was there helping him — it was Uncle Jim. In despair, I shrieked, "Ralph, Jim, COME!" My voice was lost in the roar of fires. I stumbled on, thinking that I might never see my husband again.

The sight of fellow prisoners plodding down that road towards the tanks ahead is one I shall never be able to erase from memory. Some were staggering a few steps at a time under the load of knapsacks, heavy bags, native *tampipis,* while others carried only a few papers or a weather-beaten briefcase. Some had nothing in their hands but a tin of corned beef, ripped open, and they were stuffing the precious morsels into their mouths. Others were scooping out handfuls of cooked rice, eating it as they walked. It was hideous, and pathetic.

To avoid bumping crowds of people, I edged over on the road. I stumbled. Trying to get my balance, I looked down. There beside the roadway lay a Jap soldier, dead at my feet. I gasped and looked away. But it might be the friend of the soldier, the one who got us food. I must see. But the crowd was forcing me on, unyielding to any attempt to turn back.

"Isn't it wonderful, Grace! A day we'll never forget," someone shouted.

"Never forget," I repeated mechanically. I mustn't look back, I mustn't think about what I had just seen.

I finally caught up with Stan and Gale as we reached the appointed spot, exhausted. "Where's Daddy, why doesn't he come? He'll be too late!" they repeated over and over. I felt the same frantic hysteria over his deliberate packing. Life was much more precious than any material things we had.

Huge tractor tanks backed up toward the waiting crowd. One by one, the tanks were loaded with these human skeletons, pulling away to make passage for the next tank. Hundreds of people were ahead of us, some pushing through the lines to be sure of getting on — before their turn. We sat on our luggage hoping that somehow Ralph would get to us in time. Several internees offered a handful of rice to the boys, who shyly at first, then eagerly, stuffed it into their mouths.

"Here are Daddy and Uncle Jim," shouted Stan. They had suddenly appeared beside us. We'll be together, I thought, and hopefully there are enough tanks to hold the rest of the people.

Uncle Jim looked different to me. Then I realized it was because a white shirt covered his shrunken body and stooped shoulders. "You know, Grace, last night I laid out my one shirt and this pair of shoes," he said. Sure enough, his bare feet were encased in a fine pair of shoes! "I wanted to be ready," he continued, "and I felt something might happen, any hour!"

At last our turn came. The strange, huge tank let down its rear gate and we climbed inside, twenty or more people. Several priests, nuns, and ourselves. As I sank down on a piece of luggage, I offered a "Thank God" for this miracle! It was the most beautiful limousine I shall ever see, I thought. The rear end was closed now and we were deep inside, in the bottom of this giant vehicle.

As it pulled away, the soldiers climbed to the top, on the rim, and started to get their machine guns, which flanked the sides, into position. We were following the line of tanks ahead; soldiers on top, their guns in readiness.

Soldiers on our tank tossed over a package of their rations to us. We tore open the boxes, and soon Roy, Gale and Stan were munching on *American crackers!* Every now and then I saw the soldiers looking down at us with tears in their eyes.

"Where are you taking us?" I asked.

"Across Laguna de Bay," came the answer. And no sooner had we hit the water than Jap guns on the shores to our left opened fire.

I wanted to shout to the soldiers to get down in the tank, but they were firing their guns faster than we could count. The hot empty shells came pinging into our laps, now and then singing our flesh. Our planes were flying over us, back and forth as the battle raged two-thirds of the way across the large lake.

Stan and Gale were high with excitement. As soon as the firing ceased they climbed up beside the gunners. Roy was content with his cracker, ready to sleep on my lap. We were saved, just in time, and then I thought of Skipper Williams — if only he could have been alive for this day! Burt Fonger, Bill Waldo, Helen Toyne, Pat Ryen . . . and so many others.

When we reached the opposite shore, we were in American lines. Officers were there to meet us. Strangely enough the first one we saw was Captain McMicking of Manila, whom we had known before the war. He grabbed our hands in happy welcome! But sadly, a few days later we learned he had gone into Manila to find most of his family massacred by the Japs!

On the beach we were still exposed to the tropical sun for three more hours until Army trucks arrived for the last part of our rescue. Our destination was to be "Muntinglupa," the new Bilibid Prison Farm which our forces had taken from the Japs only twenty-four hours before.

The long trip over hot, dusty roads through small Filipino *barrios* proved taxing to our weakened systems. Our skin, because of malnutrition, was burned deep by the sun and wind. I had covered Roy's face and shoulders with my jacket, but Stan, Gale and Ralph were completely exposed from the waist up. But in the great thrill and excitement of our rescue we did not realize our serious hurts and burns. Filipinos lined the roads en route, shouting *"Mabuhay,"* and waving their "V's" for victory.

At five o'clock that afternoon we looked up to see a huge American flag flying over the top of the Administration Building of New Bilibid Prison Farm, our quarters for the next six weeks.

We climbed out of the trucks, stiff and sore, and rejoicing! We were told to form a line to receive mail at the Red Cross desk, also a bar of chocolate and a package of cigarettes. Ralph and I wept each time our eyes met, so great was our happiness.

We received a stack of Red Cross messages from our families and friends, but we had to find shelter and relief for our boys. We glanced hastily through the mail as we walked to the prison barracks, happy, hungry and exhausted. Finally we were given floor space in one of the dormitory-like rooms, and we got in line, a mile in length, to receive some food.

It was seven o'clock when we reached the food buckets. Stan and Gale had fallen down on the grass, but when food appeared they got up and stared at the army plate and cup containing two tablespoons of thick corned beef and vegetable stew and a third of a cup of tomato juice. The first taste, and their eyes gleamed — yet they held the food in their mouths, unwilling to swallow it. It was too good, they said. We were forty-five minutes eating that first meal!

Openly, I cried. Around us, all were weeping, some holding each taste in their mouths lest they lose the beautiful sensation. Others gulped their food down in three swallows, then screamed for more! Stan and Gale were over six and seven years old now, but they weighed less than they had at three and four when we were first interned!

After the boys went to sleep on army blankets which we had spread on the stone floor, Ralph and I walked outside, anxious to ponder over our mail and talk with our troops. We wanted to hear about all that had happened while we had been isolated.

The first one we spoke to was an officer from the Intelligence Corps. What he told us gave me insomnia for the next forty-eight hours. He related quietly how important our rescue had been, rushed ahead of their planned mission when news reached MacArthur's headquarters that our camp was to be annihilated on February 23rd! "We still don't know," he went on, "whether it was scheduled for your seven o'clock roll call this morning or in the afternoon when thousands of retreating Jap troops would have reached your camp — to massacre all of you."

This officer went on to say that the troops who had rescued us had been volunteers from different units and had not worked together before, except for the entire 672nd Amphibian Tractor Battalion to every man. Guerrillas had volunteered, too, going through the rice paddies and enemy lines during the night to occupy positions around the camp at each guard outpost in readiness to open fire as the paratroopers dropped. The Amphibious tanks had crossed the lake during the night, timing their entrance into Los Banos Camp immediately after the firing of guns around the outposts. Everything had had to be planned to the minute in order to avoid great loss of life. And it had worked; the paratroopers dropping at three minutes before seven o'clock roll call, when the Jap soldiers in the barracks were outside doing their calisthenics, unarmed.

We learned about the siege of Manila still going on, and 152,000 civilians killed in the liberation of this one city. Out of these rubbled ruins and broken lives, could a people ever rise again? What great strength it would take just to clear the harbor of sunken ships, to carry away the smoldering ruins where the stench of burned human flesh repelled and sickened even the strongest! But hardest of all, I thought, would be to clear away the memories, the hatred.

For us it would be different. We could go home to a new life — on lease, a lease that had been extended by the sacrifice of others, and justified only if we could make each day count to the utmost.

Coming home would be so wonderful, I thought. There would be no problems. Our boys would have security and a fine education. How exciting it would be to start all over again.

In the immediate days following our rescue we lived in a state of high tension, experiencing great surges of energy from even small portions of food. We could eat only two servings for the five of us — then sudden waves of nausea that sent us moaning to our cots. Unused to such nourishment, our stomachs rebelled. Stan and Gale managed better and were gloriously happy, spending their days with G.I.'s, riding on their shoulders or in Army jeeps, their pockets bulging with chewing gum and chocolate bars. Roy, too, climbed into the front seat pretending to drive, then shrieked with delight when the Captain took him for a ride.

One night at bedtime Stan did not appear. We started out to find him. Edging off the path as a big army truck rounded the corner, we heard Stan's voice. "Hi, Mom and Dad." The truck pulled up, headlights glaring as Stan climbed out. "Gee, it's fun to drive a truck," he said, waving goodbye to his pals.

War was still raging in the Philippines and one battlefront was near our location, Muntinglupa. Heavy artillery shook the ground intermittently while loudspeakers gave out announcements and trucks brought in supplies, mail, and more news from Manila. Any news from Santo Tomas was passed around quickly. We learned that our Pan American friends, the Fennels were safe, and soon to be flown back to the States on a Pan-Am plane . . . that my pregnant island-cohorts were pregnant again! Phyllis, about to have her second; Mary's second, already born; and poor Mona, expecting, was very weak and being taken home on a hospital ship. Strange memories flashed through my mind.

We had surprise visitors, too. Ah Kwai San, our Chinese amah, appeared, her face black and blue, badly swollen, and her hair singed. She hugged Stan and Gale over and over, and wept openly. "You must hurt awful, Ah Kwai," said Stan, looking into her swollen eyes. "I missed you," said Gale. Her story was one we'd hear repeated many times in the next weeks — that of hiding under bushes, crawling from ditch to ditch, under buildings during the shelling and burning of the city. "And Ah Kew?" I asked. Kwai San's voice lowered. "She was killed with a bullet," she whispered.

Kwai San had brought her night clothes. "I sleep nearby," she said, patting Roy's cheek. "I take care Roy few days, okay?" "We would love that, Ah Kwai." And I meant every word.

A messenger came, asking for Ralph. "Mr. Navarro wishes to see you." Navarro, boyish-looking and efficient, had been Ralph's secretary. We hurried to the Main Building but we hardly recognized the elderly couple standing there, the woman's shoulder covered in thick bandages. They grabbed Ralph's hands. "Mr. Nash, you are alive! Our prayers have been answered," said Mr.

Navarro. They too had fled with their children to escape the holocaust. "Bullet wounds, but they're healing," explained his wife.

"Mr. and Mrs. Nash, we have come to offer you our house, north of Manila. It is still standing," said Mr. Navarro, "and we can stay in a schoolhouse nearby with thirty other families." Their generosity brought more tears as we thanked them. "We must remain here until ships are ready to take us to the States," explained Ralph.

Everyone wanted to go to Manila but sniper fire and transportation delayed permissions. Meanwhile we wrote letters home. I joined a combo and played in the hospital ward tents each afternoon. Rosemary and I assisted in an evening floorshow and gave a concert of "old favorites" in the Mess Kitchen, joined by a redheaded paratrooper who sang. A member of our rescue mission, he was a graduate of Eastman School of Music. His voice thrilled us and we hoped for more concerts, but he left the next day on another mission. "There were seventy-five in our unit when we started," he had told us. "Only ten guys now."

Finally our turn came to go into Manila. As we neared the city there were no landmarks. "Where are we?" I asked Ralph. Tears came to his eyes. Our city, our home, gone! No branches, no leaves, and the giant Acacia trees that lined the boulevard — their trunks were shredded! The Manila Hotel was a shambles; our Post Office, a hollow shell. The Metropolitan Theatre where I had played with the symphony, demolished! Only rubble and the stench of burned human flesh remained. On to Santo Tomas where we recognized only a few people among the hundreds of new faces. Everyone was hurrying hither and yon. Jean Salet, still young and beautiful, waved to us as we left. We must find the Zippers and Brimos. My address book had contained memos of our debts but it had burned in Los Banos. The driver of a pony caratela took us through the shell-torn streets to a lean-to garage amid the rubble. Here we found Dr. Zipper. "I'm reorganizing the symphony," he said, hugging us. "This is my office. We're going to start concerts soon." Sketchily he told us of their miraculous escape after a shell had hit their apartment. We asked him for a statement of our debts. He looked at us through tears. "We have our lives, what more do we want? The slate is wiped clean and we start from here on!"

We went on to the Brimos. Their answer was the same. "You

owe us nothing. We are alive. You are alive. Say nothing more." They too had narrowly missed massacre by hiding in a field trench for days without water. Their home and possessions were gone but they had found shelter with a dozen other families in a large structure north of the city . . . Ralph somehow located Mr. Fabian, his accountant, who had gotten food, mattresses, other things into Santo Tomas for us. Yes, they had survived and their home, also north of the city was intact. He loaded Ralph with food, toys for our boys, and best of all, shoes that his own boys had outgrown.

Back in Muntinglupa that night, I dreamed of the city we had known and loved being swept away into ashes and rubble. I awoke to find it was not a dream!

Each letter from home made us more anxious to be on our way, and finally, after six weeks, our orders came. We were to be ready at 4 a.m. the next morning. Loaded into U.S. Army trucks, we started before dawn amid the din of G.I. voices. "Get a malted for me, you lucky devils!" they shouted. "See you after Tokyo!"

We boarded the S.S. Eberle, once a Coast Guard ship, now a troop ship carrying five thousand — 2500 troops and 2500 ex-war prisoners. Artillery guns were stationed around the deck. Instead of freight in the holds, there were five tiers of hammocks where Ralph, Stan, and Gale would bunk. Roy and I shared a cabin with sixteen other women and their babies, thirty-five in all. Two destroyers escorted us out of the harbor into enemy-infested waters at full speed ahead. The next day, waylaid in Leyte Harbor, we heard the shattering news of President Roosevelt's death.

This was a sweltering, body-to-body filled ship that proved to be so top-heavy in the raging typhoon that soon hit us, that we rolled from side to side, nearly capsizing for two days. We all nearly died — but we were thankful for that storm when the Captain told us that two Japanese submarines pursuing us, had had to turn back, saving us from being torpedoed!

COMING HOME
(April-May, 1945)

After twenty-two days in this steaming, sealed, blacked-out ship we docked at San Pedro, California on May 2nd. Reveille had sounded at 4 a.m., breakfast was at 5, and then hours of waiting; endless waiting. Exhausted and hungry, we struggled down the gangplank at 4:30 p.m. Anticipation of this long awaited moment had drained our emotional stamina. With my violin and few pieces of frayed luggage cleared, we were given sandwiches and milk at the Red Cross booth, then our mail. Two large brown envelopes were handed to Ralph. A bus was waiting at the curb, they said. As we started to climb in, the violin was grabbed from under my arm — the instrument I had fought both soldiers and gunfire to keep. "No luggage inside the bus," the man said. Ralph quickly retrieved the case. "The violin stays with us. It won't stand the crushing with other luggage," he explained. The driver leered at the flimsy shrapnel-torn case but no argument would alter his decision. We stood on the sidewalk while the bus was loaded with others. Finally we were given transportation in a station wagon to Los Angeles. We settled ourselves and tore open the containers of mail.

From that moment on I saw nothing of the landscape; the shocking news in the first letter I opened was a final blow. My father was dying of cancer! Could we get a plane for Cleveland immediately? Nothing of this had come in letters we had received after liberation, yet here were copies of cables they had sent to us and to the Red Cross, asking for priority for plane travel!

As we climbed out of the station wagon in front of the Elks Club, a member of the welcoming committee pressed two wilted sweet peas into my hand. Two wilted sweet peas . . . and I couldn't even cry! We walked into the building where the revolving doors held on to the boys. When we finally pulled them out they stood at a distance and stared at the magic. Roy cried, "Me, too, me, too!" but Ralph dared not release him.

"I must get to a telephone," I repeated to the elderly lady escorting us to the first table. "Fill these out, please, then on to the next table," she said. "But a telephone, just a telephone," I asked again. "After you finish registering," came her reply as she pushed ten cards and a pen toward me.

I was desperate. Ralph quickly set Roy down, took the violin from me and grabbed the pen. I turned away, searching through the mob for an exit, forgetting our three sons now lost somewhere in the milling crowds.

"Grace Nash! Grace!" the voice startled me. Irene Barnett

stood at my side. She had been interned at the Assumption Convent and had given me that drink of whiskey after my fall. "What can I do for you?" was her question.

"Just get me to a telephone, Irene, quick." Without further talk she raced me through the halls to a booth and within three minutes I heard my sister's voice from Cleveland. "Grace, how are you? Where are you?" "Father, is he still alive?" I asked. "He's waiting for you," she said. "We sent cables and have tried to get priority for you. No luck. See what you can do. Are you all together?"

I managed to assure her that we were all right before my voice choked. "Goodbye, Mabel, I'll let you know as soon as we get tickets." I stood there rubbing my eyes. My forehead felt lumpy and hot. Those damned hives again. Will they never leave me? I had had them since February 23rd, the day we were rescued, with only spasmodic relief since then. Irene, waiting for me, took me back to Ralph who was still filling out cards. I finished signing mine just as a tear dropped on my signature, making it into a splotch.

Where are the boys, we wondered, staring into the large reception room, now a mass of humanity. Suddenly I saw a rolling movement among the feet. There was Roy, rolling on the thick carpet, between, through, and over feet. Ralph stooped to pick him up. "No, Daddy, no!" He took Ralph's hand in his and pressed it into the carpet. "Feel! Feel!" he said, his eyes beaming.

We found Stan and Gale on the elevator. They had been going up and down for twenty minutes. We held their hands in ours while we finished the routine of lines for ration cards and relatives. We had no relatives there. After two more hours of cross examining there was food for the boys and an American toy for each. Roy hugged his stuffed dog and begged for one more roll on the carpet before we could leave for the hotel nearby.

We carried our bags to the hotel desk, Stan and Gale ahead of us. We registered and started for our room. The boys had disappeared again! We called their names. Where could they be? Searching frantically upstairs, back to the lobby, then back to the room. The sound of heavy water pressure coming from the bathroom made us rush to the door. Ralph turned the knob and there in the tub, nearly running over, were Stan and Gale splashing in glee.

"It's a bathtub, isn't it?" shouted Stan. "And there's warm water, too," added Gale, kicking up his feet. They slid on their stomachs as Roy looked on, amazed. He had never seen the like!

There were other surprises too. The doors were opened and shut a thousand times. The light switches, a magic miracle. The glass windows, a moving picture of real life outside — streetcars, autos, and myriads of people. Their beds were cushions of comfort, and pillows could be thrown across the room! It was all too wonderful!

Ralph and I could not relax. We called his family in Seattle, Buffalo and Sacramento that night, but we could not sleep. How many nights had we gone without it? And now, either our beds were too soft or our minds too muddled. I must get a plane to Cleveland!

The next morning the boys made more discoveries — a vacuum cleaner, orange juice, and more doors that would open and shut! We had much to do — plane tickets, shopping for clothes from skin out. While I shopped, Ralph negotiated for reservations. Self-conscious and nervous, I chose my first piece, a bright red spring coat. With the clerks' patience and forbearance, we managed from underwear to shoes for all. Ralph's size was well under what he had worn in 1941.

Back at the hotel there was a message from a Mrs. Bennett. "You're all invited for dinner tonight. We'll call for you at 6 o'clock." I was puzzled. "Who is this person?" Ralph thought for a minute. "Ah, Mr. Bennett was the new Branch Manager at Los Angeles, but I have never met him."

This would not be easy, I thought; an unlikely experience for everyone. How would the boys react to a nicely laid table, silver, napkins and goblets? Hurriedly I explained how to use a knife and fork, a glass instead of a tin cup. They were bewildered. I tried to feel elegant but our new clothes didn't seem to belong to us. We stared at each other, at ourselves in the mirror, uttering compliments. "I must remember to put on my hat, wear my gloves and carry my purse," I said aloud. It was all too difficult and complicated.

As soon as we arrived, Roy was content to roll on the carpet. Stan and Gale tried each door and light switch until they spied the radio. At the table they insisted on a spoon, stared at the French china and refused to drink out of the top-heavy goblets. All in all, it was an evening I wanted to forget.

After exhausting all resources for air reservations to Cleveland, we had one plane ticket, so Roy would go with me while Ralph, Stan and Gale would take a train to Seattle, to his sister's home. I had been warned that with this 'no priority' ticket I might be taken off at any stop. "I'll get there," I said, "once I get on the plane." Roy and I *were* taken off at each stop, four in all, but we got back on again through the insistence of two G.I.'s and one sailor who gave up their tickets, and the undercover work of the pilot and stewardesses.

Our plane touched down at the Cleveland airport on May 7th where Mabel and her small daughter were waiting. After a huge hug for each of us, she took our luggage and we raced toward home, an hour's drive away. I was completely numb. The once familiar landmarks were meaningless and cold. As we rounded the drive, a large American flag waved gently from the front yard.

Three figures came on to the porch, Father, Mother, and my older sister. I hurried out of the car with Roy. Surely I was glad to see them. As I reached the steps, I heard my Father's voice, only a rasp: "Jason! My Jason! You're home!" Tears came to his eyes as he patted Roy and put his hand on my shoulder. He could not bend. His side was partially paralyzed from pain. We were hugged and kissed and I returned the affection — without feeling or emotion. WHAT was the matter with me? I had survived for this moment; longed for and dreamed of it hundreds of times. It was here, wasn't it!

We went inside. Father choked when he tried to speak and his voice sounded far away. Radium and x-rays had burned away most of his vocal chords. His face, still familiar, now wore deep lines of suffering. He had been a handsome man and I could remember saying a prayer every now and then asking God to make my father President, please! I followed him into the livingroom where he painstakingly sat down and beckoned me to put Roy on his lap. Roy was content and unafraid. Like every other child before him, he liked Father instantly. "Dink of watah," was all he asked and Mother brought a cup of water to him.

I tried to feel and to talk but my words came out meaningless, as if I were listening to a stranger. I felt nothing. "Damn you! Damn you! Why don't you cry? You're home! Home! HOME!" I shouted silently.

"I can't feel," came the answer. I fought back the cold fear that was taking hold. "It's true, I've lost — I've lost my emotions. I'm nothing but an empty shell! No soul! God, help me!" I stared aimlessly at the furniture, "Was that a new chair? curtains?" trying to cover a growing histeria. Nothing was real. I looked again at Father, tried to talk with him but each attempt caused more choking. Roy was asleep on his lap.

"Grace, come and see the delicious things the neighbors have sent for you. You must be hungry," said Mother, leading me to the pantry where plates of cake, meat loaf, fresh eggs and homemade butter covered the shelves. "Mrs. Nichols baked the angel food, her specialty, you know. She's anxious to see you, Grace. Her son is in Leyte now."

"Harry, a soldier? He was only in grammar school when I left!" "And Mr. Loomis brought over the eggs — from his own few chickens. He said you'd need some eggs for those three boys. Even though he's stone deaf he's been such a help to your father." Mother continued.

"Mother, I must be dreaming. I'm not really home, am I? I'm sure I'll wake up in Los Banos, starving!" I pinched my stomach hard, the hundreth time perhaps since the ship had docked five days ago.

Mother spoke softly. "It's hard for us too, to realize that you're home and safe after all these years of heartbreak and worry. Many times I sat down at our bountiful table and couldn't eat a bite, knowing that you and your family might be starving. Your father would scold me and say, 'Queenie, Grace wouldn't want you to do that. Ralph will see that they're all right. Now eat your dinner,' but I couldn't." Mother hugged me and wiped her eyes.

My thoughts were back in Manila again, the battles raging, soldiers loading into trucks, the surgical ward, amputees and faces with only noses showing. "You lucky devils, going home!" their voices rang in my ears.

"Mother, for thirty-eight months I dreamed of the future, of coming home, eating food, seeing all of you — and now that I'm here, I'm *not* here! I'm still in prison! I can't get away from the past!"

"It will take time, Grace, and we'll understand. We'll help you."

* * * * * * * * *

Father's strength seemed to rally with our return. His love for Roy was returned and their bond of affection grew with each day. When Ralph and the boys arrived from Seattle, Mabel and Jack took us into their spacious home near Cleveland. We had plenty of food, shelter, bedrooms and bathrooms, but we couldn't adjust to this civilization, forgetting to close doors and flush toilets! I came down to breakfast barefooted. Habits are so hard to break. We still preferred eating with a large spoon. The boys rushed in to the refrigerator ten times a day. "Not hungry, Mom. Just wanted to see if there's food for supper." Gale dreaded bedtime. Sleep meant nightmares of Japanese men chasing him with bayonets. And Roy's question whenever meat was served, "Bow-wow, Mommie?" had to have a 'Yes' answer so he could eat with delight. And after each meal routinely, the three of them went under the table to salvage the crumbs.

With so much happening, our concern over Father, the boys' medical and dental checkups, family members coming and going, press interviews, et al that we didn't hear the many complaints about rationing, cigarettes, etc. that the G.I.'s had warned us about. We simply avoided crowds, standing in lines, cocktail parties and movies. Whenever a stranger was introduced, instinctively I looked at the person as a fellow prisoner and saw what (s)he would be like.

Father had become noticeably weaker, unable to speak or eat. Yet he wanted so much to live, to have his grandsons near him . . . there was so much he wanted to tell us. My heart ached, and alone, I cried and cried.

* * * * * * * * *

The sadness of breaking up our family home after three generations made our grief more acute. In each room we heard again Father's voice, his apt humorous remarks as we sorted and packed our childhood belongings, read old diaries, looked at photographs, and then burned boxes full of memories. Mother would be going to California with my sister Margaret, and we were staying temporarily with Mabel and Jack.

In September the boys entered public school — Stan in third grade according to the note from his Los Banos teacher, Mrs. Harrah, and Gale in first grade. They said very little about their classes but before school started Stan had made sure that we wouldn't tell anyone about prison camp. With Gale's flushed cheeks and his continuing nightmares, I took all three again to the pediatrician. "Gale may be contracting Rheumatic Fever," said the doctor. "Keep him in bed until noon each day. School in the afternoon only."

It was a frightening blow! And suddenly school became so unimportant! Stan's condition was improved. A month before, x-rays had shown that cartilages above both knees had stopped growing from lack of calcium and malnutrition and he had been ordered to sit on the davenport, walk slowly and never run! Heavy doses of calcium were correcting the problem, and although Roy still gave the appearance of being chubby, his distended stomach from malnutrition was gradually receding.

Their first snow time was wonderful, but the need to put on snowtogs, mittens and boots would take much reminding and practice. Special days, other than birthdays and Christmas, were not understood or enjoyed. The Fourth of July was a horrendous experience when the sound of fireworks sent them trembling, running for cover. Halloween turned out to be both frightening and foolish. "Why would anyone want to be hideous and scary like that?"

Slowly and steadily their health and ours improved. The boys were eating and sleeping better. Gale was still limited to half days in school as a precaution. Ralph was deep into bus prefabrication designs, and I was playing violin and speaking to clubs and colleges.

Mabel and Jack had put up with us so graciously — our strange habits and recovery, with its ups and downs. It was time they had relief. Although houses were still scarce, we finally found one and bought it. It had a curious history, and after being unoccupied for more than a year, there was a variety of non-paying occupants from basement to attic but it was ours and we loved it — creaky floors, squirrels, mice and all. We filled it with "early farm" furniture and on December 15th moved in and set about making it livable. The next week we sent out our Christmas greetings. The verse had practically written itself, in our fivefold joys and gratitude!

* * * * * * * * *

1945 CHRISTMAS CARD

'Tis the night before Christmas
   in the year '45
After three years internment,
   we've come back alive!

Our stockings we'll hang
   by the chimney with care,
And know in our hearts
   St. Nick will be there.

The children we'll tuck
   all snug in their beds,
After three years without them,
   Our home torn in shreds.

And I in my nightie
   and Ralph in pajama,
We'll just settle down
   with no fear of old "Homma."

When out on the lawn
   there arises a clatter,
We'll know it's not Japs,
   this year, no matter!

It used to be bombs,
   ugly soldiers galore,
But thanks to MacArthur,
   we have them no more.

And now, once again
   to our eyes may appear,
A sleigh full of toys
   for our three boys dear.

Whose courage and faith
   in USAFFE's return,

Kept us going through internment,
   a living hell you may learn.

But five strong we are now,
   and if you must know —
Nash production ne'er ceased
   because of war in the East!

The Japs did their best
   to make life the worst;
They put us in prison
   for this third babe at first!

We know a great deal
   of the sorrows of war,
But this Christmas to us
   means rebirth to us all.

We're thankful for life,
   food and fam'ly and friends,
In a land so secure,
   that we're fast on the mend.

We'll feast on a turkey
   instead of carabao (ow)
Have Irish potatoes,
   not tasteless lugao (ow)

A hot bath in a bathtub,
   a clean towel, and soap,
In privacy we dreamed of,
   and no Japs to provoke.

No chow lines to stand in,
   no camp work to do;
A table to sit at —
   our pleasures not few.

We're hungry no more,
   we have shoes on our feet;
We can say what we wish
   to our friends when we meet.

Real coffee for breakfast,
   cereal and cream;

After years of sad mush
   until we could scream.

We're thankful indeed
   to get back after this,
And be here to give you
   our best Christmas wish:

For YOU:
No enemy planes loaded with bombs;
No enemy guards sealing your homes;
No sordid atrocities committed on end
By a merciless enemy, again and again.

No hunger that weakens your mind to a blank,
Paralyzing bones, from your head to your shank.
No roll call to stand for, no fires to fan;
Dishes to eat from, instead of tin cans.

With peace and security, a place you can rest,
To appreciate life in our land that is best;
A merry Christmas for you,
   A happy New Year, all through.

— The Ralph Nashes

* * * * * * * * * *

Epilogue

SINCE THEN
(1946 - 1984)

orty years have gone by since our imprisonment and heroic rescue, yet wherever we go we find reminders of those grim years: people, incidents and events; a phone call, a knock at the door or a letter in our post box. Meeting people who had a part in our survival will always bring a quickening heart throb — like meeting Charlie Spray of the 672nd Amphibian Tractor Battalion who knocked at our door one Saturday, and later invited me to speak at their 30th Reunion in Rockford, Illinois. Imagine coming face to face with all those guys and knowing that every single one of them had helped to rescue us that morning of February 23rd, 1945!

Two years ago in a midwest airport between planes, I met Corporal Jasper Bryan Smith, Ret., also of the 672nd Battalion. He was their signal man who, escorted by two Filipinos, came across the lake in a sanpan during the night and crept through the jungle to Los Banos Gate, ready to wave in the paratroopers with his semaphore penants, showing them where to drop, while Jap guards unarmed and unknowing, were doing their calisthenics a few yards away!

We continue to meet members of the 11th Airborne, those *Angels of Mercy** who made that dangerous low jump inside the prison boundary or were in the line of fire at other points during that mission.

We had always wondered where that American flag came from, the flag that was raised in Los Banos on January 7th, 1945,

237

when the Japs left the camp for six days. Last week when a surprise visitor from Oklahoma City, Patty Gene Croft Kelly came, we found out. "It was my mother's flag, Selma Croft," she said. "It was presented to my father in 1919, by General Leonard Wood in Manila. Mother kept it with her all through internment — but showing it that morning could have cost us our lives!" she continued. "Because, when the Japs returned on January 13th, they had heard about the American flag being raised inside our prison and seemed to know it had come from *our* barracks. We were surrounded by guards for two days and they searched every cubicle several times! Fortunately, the man who had hoisted the flag for Mother that morning had not yet returned it to her," she finished. Patty Gene was seventeen years old, a member of my Junior Orchestra when war began. "I still have that flag at home in Oklahoma!" she said.

Sometimes, in the most unlikely places there are sharp reminders. A few days before last Christmas, 1983, when I was shopping in Scottsdale, something on a gift counter caught my eye — some bright-colored wire clothespins in a miniature basket. I looked again. They were Ralph's clothespins, exactly! — only made of plastic and dipped in paint. "Made in Taiwan," his design is now in production by someone else!

Sitting here on our patio in Scottsdale, there are moments when it still seems like yesterday; even the memory of that day in Mr. Rellini's Violin Shop in Akron, Ohio — fifty years ago when I got the violin — it's as clear as the Arizona sky! I wish Mr. Rellini could know that I have kept those two promises: first, to "guard it always," and second, never to tell what I paid for it. I do understand his answer to my unspoken question that day, that someday I would understand . . . It proved to be "Four Strings to Our Survival"!

I'm no longer playing. The violin needs a new owner, but with our grandchildren already teenagers, we may have to await a great

---

*Bob Fletcher, Skeeter Young, the Marshall brothers, Chuck McCreary, Al Banidetti, Sgt. Roseberry, Capt. Ringler, Pilot Don Anderson, Col. Burgess and Maj. Anderson, Henry Sioux Johnson, Harold Greer, George Doherty, and so many others who were involved . . .

grandchild! It's simply that after two separate incidents that occurred in the same year, 1960, my life has taken a new direction. When my hands became swollen with arthritis I had to give up playing professionally; second, as assistant director of the Music Center of the North Shore (Chicago), I attended a Music Conference in Toronto, Canada where I heard children making music *their* way — in rhythmic speech, singing and playing specially designed *Orff* instruments (xylophones, glockenspiels, drums and other percussion) in ensembles so breathtakingly beautiful it was a long awaited answer to music in the classroom as it should and could be. I returned to Toronto in successive summers to study, while starting such classes in the Music Center under Dr. Zipper and at a nearby public school. Once again I was teaching general music classes, but in such a different way and with resounding results!

When Ralph retired from engineering and we moved to Arizona, he joined forces with me, transcribing my manuscripts of songs and verses into published books. Our work is still in performance, only with a different focus — teaching teachers, writing, and traveling. In fact, we have recently returned from the Orient — Japan, China, and the Philippines — our first visit since World War II. My travel diary is still open on the desk.

(Japan) My summaries read: "Japan's progress since 1945 in industry, education, and culture has surely evolved out of the change-over from their military dictatorship of more than two decades to a civilian government with complete disarmament and purging of all military influences! (a deserved tribute to General MacArthur) Japan today is indeed an example to the world, a peace-loving anti-war nation and a leader in new ideas, products, education, and the Arts. What stronger message is there for peace and disarmament?"

(China) "Eighteen exciting days of travel in this vast land of an industrious people who honor honesty! We never locked our doors, day or night. China has no beggars today; the people have food and shelter, and they smile; the children are irresistible to teach, eager fast learners.

(Manila) "When our plane touched down at Manila Airport and the soft tropical air touched my face, I felt we had come home. It was a good feeling to see this once beautiful city, so ravaged by war, now rebuilt and whole — a teeming city of high rises and resort hotels, a cultural arts center . . . and the people very much the same — gracious, witty, and soft-spoken. Manila, with its wonderful pre-war memories.

During our stay in Manila we found several familiar buildings that had been restored as landmarks: the Metropolitan Theater where I had first played; the Ellinwood Church where we were married. The American School is now International School of wide acreage and buildings, and the Manila Hotel, rebuilt and much enlarged, is regarded as one of the great hotels of the world!

Beyond the iron gates of Santo Tomas lies the largest university in the Far East! We drove to the site of Los Banos Prison Camp, now a large pasture land for carabao. Two wartime buildings remain. One contains a bronze plaque about our incarceration and the 'cruel mistreatment of civilians by our Japanese captors.' (See replica of plaque on back cover.)

Muntinglupa (New Bilibid Prison) where we were taken after our rescue in February, 1945, is again the Federal Prison of the Philippines for life-time criminals. We saw Filipino guards patrolling from their rooftop sentry boxes. Behind the prison is a green meadow with one large mango tree in the center, from which General Yamashita was hanged February 23, 1946, convicted in war crimes trials on documented proof of his planned starvation-death of 2200 civilians in Los Banos camp, and the massacre (by beheading and burning) of a like number of Filipino men, women and children in a nearby barrio — in retaliation for *our* rescue. I turned away, trying to stifle my bitter thoughts.

In our visit to Fort Santiago in Manila we saw this infamous prison of Spanish origin in the Walled City of Manila. It was equally infamous under the Japanese, and few, if any, prisoners ever survived their inhuman tortures. In my mind were faces, remembered.

We had heard about Forbes Park, Memorial Cemetery for more than 67,000 Americans and Filipinos who lost their lives in the Pacific Theater of World War II, but to behold those acres and acres of white marble crosses set in velvet green lawns stretching as far as I could see, was almost more than I could bear.

These three things I cannot forget: the mango tree behind Muntinglupa Prison compound, Fort Santiago prison in the

Walled City, and Forbes Park Memorial cemetery. Each one brings memories that tear at my heart.

But there are other feelings; good feelings about our sons and their families for whom this book is written: Ralph S. (Stan), professor of English and principal violist in a symphony in Norway; Gale B., Math professor in Western Colorado University, and a skilled stone mason; Roy L. who wears a beard and has changed his profession from hospital administrator to custom builder of fine houses and cabinets — a creative craftsman in wood and masonry in Denver. Our best investment would always be in our children, and theirs!

Boys have a way of growing up, whatever their environment. Over the years we've had many changes in location and unexpected ups and downs, crises and celebrations (a sequel to this saga?) but somehow they made it — through college and beyond. Their children will, too; and be honest and forthright like their fathers and grandfathers because that's the way they are!

Our flexibility in meeting different circumstances and situations is hard for some to understand. "But isn't everything gravy from here on?" we have to say. Each day holds challenge or promise in some form.

Outwardly none of us shows signs of war imprisonment, but inwardly not a day goes by that our thoughts and actions are not in some way affected by what we have lived through, and for each of us our need to live — to LIVE TO THE FULLEST — NEVER STOPS!